Imagining
AUTISM

Imagining
AUTISM

Fiction and Stereotypes on the SPECTRUM

SONYA FREEMAN LOFTIS

INDIANA UNIVERSITY PRESS
Bloomington & Indianapolis

This book is a publication of

Indiana University Press
Office of Scholarly Publishing
Herman B Wells Library 350
1320 East 10th Street
Bloomington, Indiana 47405 USA

iupress.indiana.edu

The paper used in this publication meets the minimum requirements of the American National Standard for Information Sciences—Permanence of Paper for Printed Library Materials, ANSI Z39.48–1992.

Chapter 2 first appeared as "The Superman on the Spectrum: Shaw's Autistic Characters and the Neurodiversity Movement" in "Dilemmas and Delusions: Bernard Shaw and Health," ed. Christopher Wixson, special issue, *SHAW: The Annual of Bernard Shaw Studies* 34 (2014): 59–74. Copyright © 2014 The Pennsylvania State University. This article is used by permission of The Pennsylvania State University Press.

Manufactured in the United States of America

Library of Congress Cataloging-in-Publication Data

Loftis, Sonya Freeman, [date]
    Imagining autism : fiction and stereotypes on the spectrum / Sonya Freeman Loftis.
    pages cm
    Includes bibliographical references and index.
    ISBN 978-0-253-01800-7 (hardback : alk. paper) — ISBN 978-0-253-01813-7 (ebook)
1. Autistic people in literature. 2. Identity (Psychology) in literature. 3. English fiction—History and criticism. 4. American fiction—History and criticism. 5. American drama—20th century—History and criticism. 6. English drama—20th century—History and criticism. 7. Stereotypes (Social psychology) I. Title.
    PN3426.A87L64 2015
    820.9'3561—dc23
    2015011624

1 2 3 4 5   20 19 18 17 16 15

For Matt Loftis

My life started the day that I met you.

CONTENTS

ACKNOWLEDGMENTS

Thanks to those who commented on chapters in progress, including Bruce Henderson, Christopher Wixson, Linda Zatlin, Lisa Ulevich, Allison Lenhardt, and Stephanie Frankum. Special thanks to my mentor at Morehouse College, Linda Zatlin, who encouraged me to pursue disability studies in the first place. In addition to social coaching me all over campus, Linda uplifted my heart during one of the most challenging years of my life. Lisa Ulevich, wonderful friend, occasional coauthor, and brilliant thinker, has influenced my interpretation of the texts examined here more than she could possibly know. Thank you to those who provided the world's most loving childcare while I was writing, including my wonderful in-laws, Jan Loftis and April Ledford, my sister Kristen "Dill" Fish, and, of course, my parents. Special thanks to Yolanda Gilmore Bivins of the Atlanta University Center Library: you go above and beyond the call of librarianly duty! Finally, thanks to my wonderful students at Morehouse College: you inspire and challenge me on a daily basis.

Imagining
AUTISM

Introduction

(Behavior is communication.)
(Not being able to talk is not the same as not having anything to say.)
—Julia Bascom, *Loud Hands: Autistic People, Speaking*

Even though the stereotype of autistics is that we lack empathy, I could not sleep after I heard about the shooting at Sandy Hook Elementary School in the winter of 2012. I read headlines online each morning, and, like many other people across the nation, I prayed for the families involved. Three days after the tragedy, I saw a headline connecting the killer at Sandy Hook with Asperger's syndrome. After carefully insuring that the volume was turned down low (loud noises terrify me, even when they are coming from my own computer), I clicked on the video. I covered my mouth with my hand and rocked back and forth slowly while the news clip, now turned down to a "safe" level, blared bad news. The media said that the Autism Research Institute had released an official statement: "Our thoughts and prayers are with the community of Newtown, Connecticut. . . . The eyes of the world are on this wrenching tragedy. . . . [M]isinformation could easily trigger increased prejudice and misunderstanding. Let us all come together and mourn for the families." Because the college where I work as an assistant professor was out for the holiday, I had all day to work on a new article. Instead, I opted for the uneasy comfort of pacing around my living room. Mingled with my sorrow for the tragedy was a new fear of how the actions of one individual might influence the public perception of people on the autism spectrum.

Later, people asked me about the tragedy at Sandy Hook. If someone who uses a wheelchair committed a crime, would you ask your neighbor who also happens to use a wheelchair for insight into the psychology of the killer? Such questions oversimplistically reduce neurological difference into a universal way of thinking, as though all people on the spectrum think alike, our thoughts and personalities reduced to a mythological, biological destiny. While autistics may think differently from neurotypicals (people who do not have autism) by definition, this does not mean that people with autism are a homogeneous group with a universal psychology—far from it. Autistics display a fantastic variety of personality types, skill sets, and interests. Furthermore, the media coverage following the tragedy forwarded a stereotype of people on the spectrum as violent. There is no scientific evidence linking autism with violent crime. In fact, studies have shown that people with autism are far more likely to be the victims of violence than the perpetrators: social naïveté and physical signs of difference can make autistics the target of abuse and victimization.[1] The media frenzy in the winter of 2012 was a disturbing example of the dangers of stereotyping, and it had the potential to do real damage to the (already marginalized) autistic community. The media hype was only one more example of our culture's simultaneous obsession with and yet prejudice against autism spectrum disorder.

This book examines the interrelationship of literary representations of autism, cultural stereotypes, autistic culture, and disability identity politics. Deconstructing cultural stereotypes of people on the spectrum and exploring autism's incredibly flexible alterity as a signifier of social and cognitive difference, this book focuses on some of our culture's most canonical responses to autism, examining the role of autism and autistic characters in modern literature. Beginning "before the diagnosis" in the works of Arthur Conan Doyle and Bernard Shaw and extending all the way to contemporary fiction by Mark Haddon and Stieg Larsson, this book examines literary characters clearly presented as being on the autism spectrum, as well as those widely suspected by readers to be autistic. From the standard classroom staples to the best sellers of the past decade, the surprisingly frequent presence of autistic characters in popular literary works testifies to our culture's interest in cognitive difference and to the disruptive power of disabled figures in normative discourse. In a culture that has traditionally prioritized the written word, the place of literature in the cultural stories we tell about ourselves holds incredible myth-making power. And cultural stories—whether told by the news media, the literature taught in classrooms, or a television sitcom—matter. They influence the way we think about people with autism, the way we think about disabled people as a cultural minority group, and the way our society regards, values, or disvalues anyone who is different. Left critically unexamined, previously ignored from both a disability studies standpoint and in terms of autistic culture, these literary depictions of life on the spectrum are left to stand as representative of what autism is—such depictions remain unquestioned, unexplained, and unexplored. Illuminating the space between the stereotypes and the search for autistic identity (or perhaps sometimes the overlap between and the disturbing interdependence of the two), the chapters that follow examine the assumptions that underpin common literary stereotypes of people on the spectrum and explore the implications that these fictional depictions have on public perceptions of the condition. I hope that this book, as the first book on autism and literature, will contribute to increased attention to our society's many fictional depictions of mental disorders, encourage an increased understanding and acceptance of neurological difference, and help to bring mental disorders into the field of disability studies.[2]

Disorder versus Diversity: Autism and Autistic Culture

Since the passage of the Americans with Disabilities Act in 1990, the disability rights movement and disability studies have had a growing presence in both popular culture and academia; however, people with autism have been largely excluded from that movement.[3] Although mental disability is increasingly taking a place in the field of disability studies at large, it has frequently been excluded from disability scholarship. As David Mitchell and Sharon Snyder explain, "From the segregation of special education classrooms to the systematic murder of people with cognitive disabilities in Nazi Germany, the fate of people with physical disabilities has often depended upon their ability to distance themselves from their cognitively disabled peers. This internalized oppression has resulted from institutionally enforced hierarchies of disability."[4] Only recently have those with autism and other neurologically based mental disorders begun to take a larger role in disability activism. As pervasive developmental disorders, autism and Asperger's syndrome (AS) are part of a wider condition known as autism spectrum disorder (ASD), a diagnosis that has as core characteristics difficulty with social skills and communication (communication skills range from nonverbal to garrulous but awkward), a limited range of interests (the "special interests" associated with the autism spectrum can range from train schedules to molecular structure), and sensory integration problems (hypersensitivity to light, sound, and touch).[5] People on the spectrum often have poor physical coordination and demonstrate self-stimulating behaviors (such as rocking, pacing, or hand flapping). At least, these are the official diagnostic terms forwarded by the *DSM* (the *Diagnostic and Statistical Manual of Mental Disorders*), which is used by psychiatric professionals in diagnosing autism. While some autistic qualities can be disabling in everyday life, some autistic characteristics can confer strengths as well. Some people on the spectrum have unusual memory skills and heightened powers of concentration. While people with autism may inadvertently come across as cold or aloof in social situations, we are often praised for unusual honesty and directness, detail-oriented thinking, and a passionate dedication to our chosen careers. Some people on the spectrum have high IQs and are very gifted in their areas of special interest.[6] As "a physical condition with profound effects on consciousness and social life manifested at markedly different levels of severity, 'autism' is an extraordinarily unstable category."[7] Indeed, it is this very instability, the tension between ability and disability, that has brought ASD into the realm of popular culture.

In the past twenty years, ASD has become a source of public fascination.[8] Recent *New York Times* articles describe AS as "one of the most intriguing labels in psychiatry" and autism as "the most puzzling of childhood disorders."[9] Indeed, the media often present ASD as enigmatic: the association is common enough that a jigsaw piece is the international autism awareness symbol. Autism lies on the outskirts of scientific inquiry and medical data: the cause is unknown, there is no known cure, and there are no approved medications or treatments. In fact, this lack of medical consensus may contribute to public interest in the condition: "Because it is seemingly beyond current scientific knowledge, and because it evades a popular idea of the rational, autism appears to be otherness in the extreme and, as a consequence, the source of endless fascination."[10] Disability studies scholar Stuart Murray argues that the danger of such fascination, of regarding autism as exotic or spectacular, lies in popular representations of those on the spectrum as figures of "difference and otherness" who represent "the alien within the human, the mystical within the rational, the ultimate enigma."[11] Unfortunately, this can lead to an autistic being treated as "more a puzzle than a person."[12] There are other reasons ASD has become the medical "condition of fascination" for our particular historical moment.[13] Diagnosis of ASD is on the rise: "Between 1994 and 2004, the percentage of students in K–12 schools labeled as having autism rose 525 percent."[14] Amid concern about a so-called autism epidemic, stereotypes abound. People on the spectrum are metaphorically represented as machines, aliens, or computers, and pop culture has perpetuated the erroneous stereotype that all people with autism are savants.[15]

Yet as people on the spectrum have begun to take a larger role in disability activism, an autistic community and subculture have emerged, and that community has begun to redefine the terms used to describe autism and to challenge and change public perceptions of what it means to be "autistic." Traditionally, autism has been defined under a "pathology paradigm": it is most commonly understood as a mental disorder requiring treatment or cure.[16] Autistic self-advocates, however, point out that cognitive differences are not always deficits and argue that differences in neurology need not be pathologized. In opposition to the pathology paradigm (the language of the medical establishment, which perceives autism as a mental disorder), they advocate the neurodiversity paradigm, arguing that variety in neurology is a normal part of human diversity.[17] Thus, autistic self-advocates maintain that autism is not a mental disorder but a different way of being. Perhaps the most extreme version of this argument is represented by groups in the UK arguing that people with AS should be protected not under disability laws but under laws that protect other minority groups (such as ethnic, cultural, and sexual minorities) from discrimination in the workplace. Proponents of neurodiversity align themselves with the larger trend in disability studies that regards disability as a social construct. Although disability has been traditionally thought of as an individual medical problem in need of a cure, disability studies scholars oppose this dominant discourse by pointing out that disability is one form of human diversity and that disability is only problematic in the context of a society that is not designed to accommodate difference.[18]

Clearly, a pathological approach to autism and a neurodiversity approach to autism each present a different set of philosophical and ethical problems. These very different approaches affect public perceptions and, ultimately, the way our society treats people on the spectrum. On the one hand, regarding autism as a form of diversity could minimize the disabling aspects of autism and turn attention away from the need for support (and consequently reduce research funding and public support for accommodations and treatment). Murray cautions that people should not "seek to unambiguously 'rescue' an idea of autism that is uniformly positive, as that runs the risk of replacing one scheme of misrepresentation with another."[19] On the other hand, regarding autism as a mental disorder rather than as a form of diversity could minimize the ways in which this condition is socially constructed. It could also overlook the fact that autistic traits can confer strengths along with impairments. The field of disability studies at large argues that all disabilities are socially constructed: distinguishing between "impairments" (the fact of physical difference) and "disability" (society's lack of accommodation for difference or impairment), disability studies scholars argue that a person who uses a wheelchair is impaired in his or her inability to walk but will only find this mobility impairment disabling when faced with an environment that uses stairs instead of ramps.[20] In the case of ASD, the socially constructed nature of "social impairments" is perhaps even more readily apparent. If an autistic person and a neurotypical person have a conversation in which a misunderstanding occurs, who has caused the miscommunication? While some might blame the autistic person's impaired communication skills, it is also possible that the neurotypical person, by listening more patiently or speaking more clearly, might help to alleviate the miscommunication. But while the autistic person may not understand what the neurotypical person is thinking, the neurotypical person may not understand what the autistic person is thinking either. Autistic people and neurotypical people sometimes think differently on very fundamental levels. The misunderstanding works in both directions and could be understood as being caused by differences in communication styles. Of course, it is possible to find some middle ground between the neurodiversity and pathology paradigms. As Mark Osteen argues, "Disabilities are not either physical facts or discursive constructs, but both."[21] One can recognize autism as simultaneously both a disability and a valuable form of human diversity.

As the autistic community struggles between these paradigms, the terminology surrounding ASD has become increasingly complex and politically charged (and to many people, simply confusing). Indeed, the politics of autism are so heated and complex that it may seem impossible to say anything about the subject without offending someone. First, there is general disagreement in the autism community regarding the question of person-first language.[22] Generally, the parents of children with autism (particularly those who are labeled "low functioning") have argued that the preferred terminology should be "person with autism" in keeping with the larger trend in the disability rights movement to put people first and to emphasize that autism is a medical condition and not who the person is. Proponents of the neurodiversity paradigm, however, argue that "having autism" implies that autism is a disease or defect; they promote the term "autistic," which suggests autism as an essential part of personal identity. In this book, I have chosen to use the terms "person with autism" and "autistic" interchangeably. While some might associate terms such as "mental illness" and "mental disorder" with autism, these terms present their own issues. Technically, autism spectrum disorder is not a form of "mental illness." "Illness" implies the corruption of originally "healthy" function, and many believe that people are born autistic.[23] "Mental disorder" is accurate from the perspective of the psychiatric community but is generally rejected by proponents of neurodiversity. The question becomes "disordered compared to what standard?" and one could argue that the term "disorder" prioritizes the neurotypical way of thinking as normal, natural, and neutral. I sometimes use the terms "mental disability" and "cognitive difference" to refer to autism. Although disabled people often find the term "differently abled" patronizing (it minimizes the challenges of navigating

Imagining Autism

a world designed for the able-bodied), "cognitive difference" recognizes the concerns of the neurodiversity movement. Although some people use the terms "intellectual disability" and "cognitive disability" interchangeably, these two terms denote very different conditions. While "cognitive disability" can indicate a wide range of conditions, the term "intellectual disability" generally refers to people with IQs that are measured to be below average. However, IQ is a particularly problematic way of measuring the intelligence of autistic people who are nonverbal. What is true for the general public is especially true for those who do not communicate in traditional ways: in defining intellectual disability, "the proviso, of course, is that intelligence has no clear definition, nor is there any way to measure it."[24] Finally, people with autism are sometimes described as being "on the spectrum," because medical discourse refers to autism as a spectrum disorder. This term is also somewhat ambiguous, since autism is not the only spectrum disorder in psychology (for example, schizophrenia is also considered to be a spectrum), but in popular culture the term is generally used to refer to autism only. Some autistic self-advocates reject the idea of autism as a spectrum, arguing that the concept of a spectrum serves to separate autistic people into "high-functioning" and "low-functioning" groups.

Second, the "difference" between AS and autism has long been unclear in the mind of the general public. Originally identified as two separate conditions, they have often been considered related in the medical community, with autism being diagnosed when an individual has autistic traits and language delay in childhood and Asperger's being diagnosed when an individual has autistic traits without language delay.[25] The artificial distinction between the two conditions (in adulthood, those diagnosed with AS and classic autism may be much alike) has long been recognized, and in the *DSM-5,* the diagnosis of Asperger's was eliminated, and those with AS are now generally placed (along with those with "classic autism") under the larger diagnostic heading of ASD. Even before this official diagnostic change, many people with an AS diagnosis self-identified as "autistic." Because people who once received an Asperger's syndrome diagnosis are now described as having autism spectrum disorder, I frequently use the terms "Asperger's" and "autism" interchangeably and do not always distinguish between individuals who received one diagnosis or the other. Some would argue that it is important to use these terms interchangeably, because the division between those with AS and those with classic autism divides the autistic community, obscuring the connections between autistic people with divisive terminology that prioritizes some autistic people over others.

Generally, the autism community has objected both to terminology that divides autistics from each other and to terminology that suggests that autism is a deviation from an imagined "normal" person. The rise of online communities for autistics has led to the creation of a language of our own. "Aspie" is slang for Asperger's, and "Autie" is slang for classic autism. Perhaps the most powerful term invented and embraced by the autistic community is the term "neurotypical" (NT). The term gives autistics a way to describe people who are not on the spectrum—a rhetorical position essential in the ongoing rewriting of the pathology paradigm. As autistic self-advocate Nick Walker points out, "The most insidious sort of social inequality, the most difficult sort of privilege to challenge, occurs when a dominant group is so deeply established as the 'normal' or 'default' group that it has no specific name, no label."[26] The very existence of the term opens opportunities for individuals on the spectrum to discuss, examine, and challenge "neurotypical privilege."[27] Disability studies scholar PhebeAnn M. Wolframe lists some of the privileges that people in our society who have never been diagnosed with a mental disorder can probably count on: "I can criticize the mental health system . . . without being called a conspiracy theorist, or having my opinions dismissed as a sign of illness. . . . I am unlikely to be incarcerated without being charged with a crime, given a chance to defend myself, or being allowed to speak with a lawyer or other advocate. . . . I am unlikely to be forcibly subjected to treatment which, though carried out in the name of my health and well-being, might be considered torture in other contexts [restraint, unwanted medication, electroconvulsive therapy]."[28] But most neurotypical privilege is more subtle than this: how autistics walk and speak, how we choose to dress, and even the foods we choose to eat can all be construed by psychiatrists as signs of mental disorder.[29] For example, interview practices that favor neurotypical body language and communication styles, as well as work environments that create sensory issues or encourage the social exclusion of autistics can make it more difficult for people on the spectrum to find and maintain jobs. Certainly, the community's use of the word "neurotypical" is a part of what Snyder and Mitchell have termed the disability rights movement's "political act of renaming that designates disability as a site of resistance and a source of cultural agency previously suppressed—at least to the extent that groups can successfully rewrite their own definition in view of a damaging material and linguistic heritage."[30] Overall, a term such as "neurotypical" destabilizes common conceptions of what is considered "normal."

Another set of divisive (and controversial) labels in the autism community are functioning labels, with those who can speak and/or live independently generally labeled as "high functioning" and those who need support in daily living and/or are nonverbal generally labeled as "low functioning." Functioning labels can serve a practical purpose in helping to determine accommodations and therapies. However, functioning labels also present problems on multiple levels because the division between the groups is unclear: a "high-functioning" verbal autistic might live independently but be unable to cross the street by herself, while a "low-functioning" autistic who does not speak might have a high IQ and communicate brilliantly by writing. In any case, these ambiguous terms are clearly implicated in the pathology paradigm, since in many ways "'high-functioning' means 'closer to passing for neurotypical.'"[31] Indeed, the very question of "passing" for neurotypical is controversial in the autistic community for many of the same reasons that passing for straight is controversial in the LGBTQ community. Passing may help one to avoid social stigma, but it perpetuates the belief that the autistic individual is a deviation from an imaginary "normal" person.[32]

While the various debates surrounding the terminology of autism might seem superficial to some, the language we use may shape public attitudes, legal policy making, and even future directions for research about the condition—and some of the terminology currently in use by the medical profession can be objectifying and dehumanizing. Disability studies points out that labels are "a matter of discursive production and policy rationale rather than empirical accuracy."[33] In *Mad at School: Rhetorics of Mental Disability and Academic Life,* Margaret Price notes that "the problem of naming has always preoccupied DS [disability studies] scholars, but acquires a particular urgency when considered in the context of disabilities of the mind, for often the very terms used to name persons with mental disabilities have explicitly foreclosed our status as persons. Aristotle's famous declaration that man is a rational animal gave rise to centuries of insistence that to be named mad was to lose one's personhood."[34] Specifically, ideas about theory of mind (ToM) can be especially dehumanizing for people on the spectrum, since such ideas propose that people with autism do not understand that other people have minds, thoughts, and feelings and that we are frequently unaware that those minds, thoughts, and feelings may work differently from our own.[35] In other words, the medical community has often suggested that people on the autism spectrum lack empathy or have deficits in empathy in various ways. This supposed lack of empathy (or problems with empathy) is intimately tied to larger questions of what it means to be human. According to disability studies scholar Melanie Yergeau, "Theories about ToM not only deny autistic people agency; they call into question their very humanity."[36] For example, it might be assumed that someone who lacks ToM is unable to understand his own condition or to tell stories about his experiences of what it means to be autistic. Ideas about ToM have led to common depictions of people on the spectrum as narcissistic. Problems with empathy have sometimes been incorrectly interpreted by the media to mean that people with autism cannot feel love or form emotional bonds with other people. Such misinterpretations have also led to assumptions about false connections between people with autism and violent behavior. Many autistics have argued that they do feel empathy, and they dismiss medical constructions of ToM that they feel dehumanize autistics. Indeed, Simon Baron-Cohen's theories about ToM are the latest in a series of potential explanations for autism (in the 1950s, Bruno Bettelheim's notion of "refrigerator mothers" told an earlier generation of autistics that their parents had caused their autism with a cold parenting style).[37] Ian Hacking has responded to Baron-Cohen's theories by proposing that autistic people are not "mindblind" (lacking in the ToM that allows neurotypical people to apprehend each other's intentions) but rather have a "form of life" that does not easily translate into neurotypical language (bodily or linguistic).[38] As Hacking points out, "There is a partial symmetry between the autistic and the non-autistic. Neither can see what the other is doing. The symmetry is only partial because we have an age-old language for describing what the non-autistic are feeling, thinking and so on, but are only creating one for the autistic."[39] If autistics truly have a deficit in ToM, then why is it that neurotypicals find it so difficult to intuit the intentions of autistic people (assuming that neurotypical ToM is intact)? Thus, Hacking argues that the autistic "form of life" is so radically different from the neurotypical mindset that there is little shared referent between the two (and thus many opportunities for misunderstanding).[40]

The medical discourse about autism can also be objectifying in more subtle ways. Disability studies at large has long called into question the "objective" nature of medical discourse.[41] Medical discourse constructs a definition of autism using the language of "deficit" and "loss" ("a deficit in social skills"), and the sheer volume of negative stereotyping that bombards the newly diagnosed (or the families of the newly diagnosed) can be overwhelming—unfortunately, some of that stereotyping comes from presumably "factual" medical and educational literature.[42] When the outside observer is placed in the position of authority and considered the expert, it can reduce the perception of authority held by those who have experienced autism firsthand. Medical discourse can displace the experiences of people with autism, giving the impression that autistic people are not trustworthy narrators and that we do not have an understanding of our own life experiences. As disability studies scholar Bill Rocque notes, "In the representations of autism produced within medico-therapeutic fields, the person labeled autistic rarely has a voice. Instead, it is the expert who speaks from a position of authority in academic journals and other organizational literature."[43] The idea of what kind of therapy or cure might be appropriate for autism is also a controversial subject. While some desire a cure, others who feel that autism is central to their personal identity are offended by the very idea of it. Therapies such as Applied Behavior Analysis (ABA) are also controversial within the autism community, and some autistics have written about experiences with therapists and educators that could be classified as child abuse.[44] Therapy for people on the spectrum often focuses on teaching autistics how to pass for neurotypical, and some autistic self-advocates have argued that children on the spectrum are frequently taught to ignore or deny essential parts of self-identity in the name of therapy. Proponents of ABA point out that reducing autistic traits makes it possible for autistics to function in neurotypical society, that ABA can help to minimize the disabling aspects of the condition, and that it can greatly increase quality of life for people on the spectrum. Although some of the language and practices of the medical community can be seen as objectifying or dehumanizing, many people with autism have benefited from such therapies and treatments. Ironically, the very list of characteristics that define how autism is diagnosed originates from within the medical community, thus making it seemingly impossible to completely extricate autism from medical definitions. While some autistic self-advocates find themselves at odds with elements of the medical establishment, many of these same individuals say that they are glad to have a diagnosis.

Postmodern Pleasures and Misleading Metaphors

The past decade's explosion of fictional representations of autism brings together multiple topics of particular interest to our historical moment: autism can be seen as part of modernism's interest in consciousness and fragmentation and postmodernism's destabilizing repetitive aesthetics.[45] Indeed, one notices that the list of characters examined in this book begins with Sherlock Holmes (1887): Conan Doyle was writing in a time frame that coincides with the advent of modern psychology and the beginnings of literary modernism. Concerned with the fragmentation of modern consciousness and experience, modernism was eager to take the new discoveries of psychology to the minds of literary characters (see the examination of autism and interiority in chapter 4's discussion of *The Sound and the Fury*). Autism is disruptive to notions of consciousness and perception, destabilizing the very idea of a shared reality. Sensory sensitivities (e.g., intense reactions to bright lights, loud noises, or crowded places) can mean that two people (one autistic and one neurotypical) can stand in the same space but have completely different perceptions regarding the activity in that space. Neither person is delusional. Neither person has a sensory impairment. Yet the radical difference in what they perceive calls into question the very nature of a shared reality. While it seems clear why modernism provided a unique niche for autism, literary works of postmodernism have had symbolic uses for the condition as well. Interrogating the boundaries of the human with cyborgs, moving art from fragmentation to pastiche, focusing on the beauty of recycling and repetition, postmodernism has clear analogues with the public perceptions of autism. In fact, there is something peculiarly postmodern about autism itself, a condition that Murray defines as being about "pleasure": "the pleasure of the straight line of toys, of the endlessly repeated video, of that bit of wallpaper."[46] I would argue that if autism is about pleasure, then it is the pleasure of repetition. Although special interests are sometimes viewed as unhealthy obsessions, the pursuit of a deep interest is often about the pleasure of repetition (the same topic, the same approaches, time and again). Many of the repetitive rituals and routines associated with autism (the same route to school every day, the same meal for lunch, the same seat in the classroom) are often depicted as limiting, but when viewed through the lens of repetitive pleasure, they could be seen as liberating: the autistic enjoys what she enjoys for its own sake.[47] There is something aesthetically postmodern about this pleasure of repetition, especially in cases of echolalia, which is sometimes more than the simple repetition of sounds, words, and phrases heard elsewhere—it can also be communication through pastiche. In the age of the cyborg, autism (at least for many people) has become a symbol that destabilizes the boundaries of the human: mental disabilities are a "disruptive force, challenging our conceptions of intelligence, agency, and what it means to be human."[48] As a social disability (the impairment of social skills is central to the diagnosis), autism is particularly disruptive to social norms. Some literary critics have suggested that autism evokes metaphors representing the isolation of postmodern societies in which individuals are separated from each other by technology and ideology: "We have come to understand our state of affairs as autistic, a metaphor for the lack of communication among states and individuals in the late capitalist reality of the postmodern world."[49] The modern (and postmodern) era has certainly created the ideal historical moment for exploring ASD.

Indeed, the contemporary moment does seem to be "the age of autism": while other conditions received public attention in earlier decades of the twentieth century (e.g., schizophrenia and multiple personality disorder), public interest in autism suggests that the fascination with autism is a specifically modern/postmodern phenomenon that reflects contemporary cultural concerns and values. In fact, ASD has gained so much public attention in recent years that philosopher Ian Hacking has used the condition as an example of "making up people." By this, Hacking is not suggesting that autism is not a real medical condition or that autistic people do not exist. Rather, he argues that the act of diagnosis and labeling is a "moving target."[50] As Hacking explains, "I have long been interested in classifications of people, in how they affect the people classified, and how the affects on the people in turn change the classifications. . . . Sometimes, our sciences create kinds of people that in a certain sense did not exist before. I call this 'making up people.'"[51] In other words, the ways that we think about, describe, and write about autism affect people labeled as "autistic," and this in turn affects the way that autistic people understand themselves, the way that their identity as autistics is enacted, and the way that people perceive and interpret the behavior of autistics. This creates a "looping effect" in which the thing defined (autistic people) is potentially susceptible to shifting cultural definitions and labels (the cultural conception of what it means to be autistic).[52] In "Making Up People," Hacking describes "transient mental illness": "'transient' not in the sense of affecting a single person for a while and then going away, but in the sense of existing only at a certain time and place. Transient mental illnesses can best be looked at in terms of the ecological niches in which they can appear and thrive."[53] At a biological level, autism is probably not "transient" in the sense that Hacking describes (his most famous example of "transient mental illness" is the phenomenon of "mad travelers," a mental illness that appeared in the 1800s only to later disappear from psychiatric practice), but there is no doubt that concepts of what it means to be "autistic" are extremely fluid.[54] Hacking describes "highfunctioning autism": "In 1950 this was not a way to be a person, people did not experience themselves in this way, they did not interact with their friends, their families, their employers, their counselors, in this way; but in 2000 this was a way to be a person, to experience oneself, to live in society."[55] Changing diagnostic regulations and cultural perceptions mean that there are many people who are now considered "autistic" who would not have been considered "autistic" in 1950. Autistic people (like gay people or communist people) may be "made up" in Hacking's sense of the term, but this does not mean that the biological and psychological traits of autism did not exist before the modern era. Of course, philosophizing about the nature of disability identity as a cultural construct or regarding autism as a metaphor for the postmodern world does nothing to mitigate the real-world effects of actual impairment. It does not change the reality of those in need of care or the daily lives of those who serve as caregivers.

Even as autism has become a modern symbol representing the fragmentation of consciousness and a postmodern symbol aligned with the aesthetics of repetition, it is also increasingly becoming a part of the series of civil rights movements that have preoccupied the better part of the twentieth century. Ableism (discrimination against people with disabilities) damages everyone in our society. As Price argues, "Ableism impairs all of us" because it "contributes to the construction of a rigid, elitist, hierarchical, and inhuman" environment.[56] Rocque argues that by presenting autism as neurodiversity, autistic self-advocates "open up spaces for valued social identities and alternative embodiments" that have been previously excluded from society.[57] This alignment of the struggle for autistic rights with the struggles of other minority groups has meant that stories of autistic lives are reaching ever-larger audiences who feel that they can relate to these struggles. Certainly, depictions of autism are appearing more and more frequently in contemporary literature—and many of them have never before been examined from a disability studies perspective.

Although a disability studies approach to literature has become increasingly common in recent years, studies of cognitive difference have been largely omitted from the growing body of disability studies scholarship. The overlap between autism and literature has been particularly overlooked—perhaps because the psychiatric community has frequently described people on the spectrum as disliking fictional literature. (As a professor of literature, I like literature very much—and I know many other people on the spectrum who also enjoy fictional literature.) Although other cultural representations of autism (the media, television, film) hold their own power, the canonical works that are taught in the classroom (the works I will examine in this book's first four chapters) hold a special cultural capital and authority. While autistic characters like Harper Lee's "Boo" Radley and Arthur Conan Doyle's Sherlock Holmes have long been classroom favorites, these characters have not received serious consideration from a disability studies perspective; indeed, their status as autistic characters is all but ignored. Meanwhile, new classics of children's literature, such as *The Curious Incident of the Dog in the Night-Time,* are bringing new stereotypes and misconceptions about autism into the public-school classroom. Even best sellers that would not be considered classroom-worthy (such as *Extremely Loud and Incredibly Close* and *The Girl with the Dragon Tattoo*) are shaping cultural perceptions of people on the spectrum. As Rosemarie Garland-Thomson explains, "It is literature . . . [that] uncovers the richest tradition of disability. . . . [D]isability as both image and concept pervades language and literature."[58] Even with the incredible rise in autism spectrum diagnoses in the past twenty years, people with autism still represent less than 1 percent of the general population: thus, the nondisabled audience must "primarily come to know disabled people . . . through representations of their lives, experiences, and bodies that have been manufactured by those outside of the immediate disability experience."[59] Many people who do not personally know anyone with autism have read the best-selling *The Curious Incident of the Dog in the Night-Time*—and that novel's vision of autism is both creating and perpetuating stereotypes about people on the spectrum. While some fictional depictions of autism may forward negative stereotypes, it is also possible for them to work subversively against such stereotypes: "Fictions representing autism can be correctives to . . . 'deterministic' accounts . . . and release the condition from its often pejorative subject positions in, say, the case studies of medical research or the sentimentalizing narratives of mainstream news media."[60] As autistic self-advocate Meg Evans argues, "As we work to create more opportunities in society for ourselves and our children, we are storytellers above all else."[61] Although this project focuses primarily on literary representations of autism, I will sometimes discuss pop culture representations (television shows or films) that have been influenced by literary representations of those on the spectrum (e.g., later adaptations of the Sherlock Holmes stories in chapter 1).

One of the most prominent features of narratives about autistic characters is the common use of metaphor to describe the condition. Scholars have frequently noted this alignment of disability and metaphor. As Susan Sontag says of AIDS, "Any important disease whose causality is murky, and for which treatment is ineffectual, tends to be awash in significance. First, the subjects of the deepest dread . . . are identified with the disease. The disease itself becomes a metaphor."[62] Mitchell and Snyder describe this common connection between disability and metaphor as "the *hypersymbolic* nature of disability" in literary works.[63] Indeed, the feeling of unease that surrounds any unexplainable condition contributes to the phenomenon of describing that condition through metaphor, to "giving the thing a name that belongs to something else."[64] Autism is often described using military metaphors ("we are battling autism"), kidnapping metaphors ("our child was stolen by autism"), and barrier metaphors ("she is trapped behind the wall of autism").[65] All of these metaphors imagine autism as a condition that is separable from the autistic person, and they are frequently employed in ways that render the person with autism passive.[66] As Zoe Gross points out, "Many of the metaphors which surround autism foster the exclusion of autistic people by portraying us as non-entities—corpses, empty shells—or as beings without agency, awaiting rescue."[67]

Yet autism is not just described through metaphors—it has itself become a metaphor for otherness that is not specifically autistic. Rosemarie Garland-Thomson describes disabled figures "as magnets to which culture secures its anxieties, questions, and needs at any given moment. . . . [T]he disabled figure . . . exists in society to be exploited for someone else's purposes."[68] Our society's current fascination with autism—increased diagnosis, increased public awareness, and increased attention to research and therapies—has only continued to feed the popularity of autism as a public trope, increasing the "exotic" appeal that the spectrum has for majority nondisabled audiences. The seemingly inexplicable or ineffable nature of the condition has made its metaphorical uses in our society particularly charged. Murray describes autism as "an almost ubiquitous frame of reference for recent notions of difference" and "a floating term working through loose generic associations" that can stand in for "odd, strange, difficult and even dangerous."[69] Overall, literary works frequently use autism as a fluid signifier to represent various aspects of the neurotypical world that are considered outcast or alien.

Savants, Supercrips, and Other Stereotypes

While such metaphors can be damaging to the public perception of autistic people, other kinds of stereotypes haunt literary representations of those on the spectrum. One of the most common is the stereotype of autistic people as silent, cut off from the rest of the world by an inability to communicate. Although autistics are often imagined as people who do not speak or communicate in any way, the vast majority of adults on the spectrum communicate by speaking, and many people on the spectrum who do not speak communicate by signing or typing. If behavior is a way of communicating, then even autistics who do not use conventional methods (speaking, typing, or signing) are not without any form of communication. Yet the stereotype of the incommunicative autistic has contributed to larger perceptions about those with mental disabilities as being unable to communicate with others or represent ourselves. As Price notes, "To lack rhetoricity is to lack all basic freedoms and rights, including the freedom to express ourselves and the right to be listened to. . . . [S]ome rhetors—including the 'severely mentally retarded and mentally ill'—are denied these basic freedoms and rights even by the most liberal measures."[70] Since our society commonly imagines the mind as the symbol of what separates us from animals and depicts cognitive function as the very thing that makes us human, those with cognitive disabilities and differences are frequently depicted as less than human. This has led to the popularity of tropes that associate autistics with aliens and robots—both figures that are represented as lacking qualities (emotion, feeling) that make for a complete human. The autistic mind is commonly compared to a machine or computer, metaphors that again suggest a less-than-human quality to those with cognitive differences.[71] Of course, the real-world results of imagining those with autism as less than human—derision, discrimination, and even abuse—can be devastating.

A plethora of other stereotypes appear in literary depictions of people on the spectrum. Autism is often represented as a personal tragedy: along with this notion comes the stereotypical depiction of autism as a threat to families and children. (Indeed, the insistence in the popular imagination that only children have autism is both pervasive and curious. Since autism is a lifelong condition, it is clear that autistic children grow up to be autistic adults.)[72] Autism continues to be popularly figured as a mystery or puzzle and is even sometimes depicted as mystical: autism often creates "an amazed, fearful or bewildered attention" and causes people to imagine "mythical or archetypal figures—the alien, the changeling, the child bewitched."[73] The popular link between mental disability and art (and mental disability and genius) frequently appears in literary works about people on the spectrum, and the media present the figure of the eccentric genius as the hallmark of the Asperger's stereotype.

Indeed, the figure of the autistic savant is one of autism's most popular stereotypes. Elevated skills in various areas (memory, math, language acquisition) evoke a wonder and shock that could only be described as a kind of "freakshow response."[74] While the special skills of savantism create an "exotic" display, they also serve to reassure majority audiences about the nature of autism itself: savantism provides what Murray describes as the "compensation cure," leading society to imagine that "these skills act to compensate for the disability with which they are associated."[75] Thus, savants are imagined as "overcoming" social disability through amazing mental achievements, as though a disability in one area is erased or canceled out by achievements in another area. The image of the savant, who overcompensates for disability through genius in a narrow field, has his or her parallel in the "Supercrip" stereotype (the physically disabled individual who overcomes tragedy) of disability studies at large.[76] According to Murray, "savantism . . . allow[s] for the difference of autism to be dissolved in the realm of the unknown in a manner that generates no fear or unease."[77] While the fantasy of savantism as a compensation cure may make autism "safe" or appealing for the majority nondisabled audience, it forwards largely negative stereotypes for individuals on the spectrum. Both the Supercrip and savant figures suggest that people with disabilities are only "worthy" if they overcome or overcompensate for characteristics that may form an integral part of personal identity.[78] Further, the myth that everyone with autism is a savant creates unrealistic expectations for people on the spectrum, the majority of whom do not have savant-level skills.[79] Unfortunately, as disability studies scholar Mark Osteen points out, the messages sent by media representations of autism often tell viewers and readers that "autistic people can be either geniuses or freaks; what they are not is regular people."[80] It is not surprising that people on the spectrum have banded together to oppose and rewrite negative stereotypes perpetuated by the majority culture. As I discuss in chapter 2, the self-advocacy of autistic adults has been surprisingly ambiguous, and it is not always clear if self-construction within the autism community is dismissing the savant stereotype or attempting to embrace it.

Literary Alterity

The following chapters are grouped thematically but move in roughly chronological order, with each chapter focusing on literary characters who express a common stereotype about the autism spectrum. Each chapter deconstructs a different cultural stereotype (e.g., the silent figure trapped by his imprisoning interiority, the genius savant made famous by his incredible intellect, the brilliant detective linked to the criminal mastermind by their common neurology). Although the works of literature examined here represent a wide variety of genres, I have limited myself to characters who are popularly imagined to be on the spectrum. For example, chapter 2 examines the recent (and surprising) emergence of Bernard Shaw as one of the historical figureheads for the neurodiversity movement. While Shaw may or may not have had autism spectrum disorder, this chapter explores the reasons for (and the implications of) the movement's claiming of the playwright. While some of the literary characters I examine are identified as autistic by authors or publishers (such as Christopher Boone of *The Curious Incident of the Dog in the Night-Time*), others live in fictional worlds in which the characters surrounding them guess or believe that they may be on the spectrum (such as Lisbeth Salander of *The Girl with the Dragon Tattoo*). Others are presented as having an unidentified mental disability that clearly aligns with autistic characteristics (such as "Boo" Radley of *To Kill a Mockingbird* and Laura Wingfield of *The Glass Menagerie*).

Figured as alien, represented as mystery, cast as outsider, characters on the spectrum become a protean symbol of difference in literary works, standing in for a variety of chaotic forces (creativity, disease, disorder). This ever-moving signifier plays a paradoxical role in the construction of autistic identity, as many fictional depictions of life on the spectrum simultaneously forward both negative and positive images: these tropes are frequently adopted into the autism community at the same time that they may undermine self-advocacy and disability activism. Simultaneously limiting and liberating, such fictional figurations often oscillate between binary opposites, replacing one fictional extreme with another. Overall, there is a sense of historical connection among these representations, even when authors do not recognize their own creations as possessing autistic traits. Through these works, one can trace evolving cultural attitudes toward autistic characteristics. A cluster of major themes group these characters together: these figures all struggle with social alienation and explore the limits of verbal communication. Many of them also suffer under neurotypical systems of judgment and even face the denial of autistic subjectivity (see chapter 3). Examining these works as a group highlights the shifting cultural stereotypes grafted onto representations of cognitive disability throughout the twentieth century.

The first chapter begins with Sherlock Holmes, arguing that Conan Doyle's famous sleuth initiates a long-standing tradition of detective figures with autistic traits. This chapter examines the ways in which such detective heroes perpetuate potentially dehumanizing stereotypes about autistic people. Although Watson recognizes Holmes as a genius, he still objectifies his friend, frequently thinking of Holmes as an unfeeling machine. In his struggle to understand the "mystery" that is Sherlock Holmes's mind, Watson casts the detective figure as a "puzzle" in need of a neurotypical solution. Later popular culture adaptations of Conan Doyle's Sherlock Holmes stories also employ autistic detectives—and like the original Holmes, these figures may perpetuate some of the same dangerous stereotypes.

The second chapter explores the popular stereotype connecting creativity with mental disorders, focusing on the figure of Bernard Shaw, a playwright whom some proponents of neurodiversity have claimed as autistic. Although it seems unlikely that Shaw had ASD, his unconventional and iconoclastic plays present heroes with a variety of autistic traits. Shavian heroes such as Saint Joan and Henry Higgins are social outcasts whose stories prioritize and celebrate eccentric individuality. Yet the character traits that have encouraged the autism community to embrace such figures may also forward stereotypes about people on the spectrum, encouraging readers and audiences to believe that all autistic people are geniuses and savants.

The third chapter examines representations of victimization, violence, and sexuality as they relate to the depiction of autistic characters. This chapter explores the fluid boundary between fiction and reality in literature about autistic figures, contemplating the various ways in which reality influences fiction (and fiction influences reality) in cultural discourses about characters (and people) with autistic characteristics. Autistic people are particularly likely to be the victims of filicide: media coverage that is sympathetic to autistic filicide, presenting parents as overwhelmed by their children's care or depicting murder as an act of mercy (highlighting the pain the disabled child was believed to be suffering), suggests a lack of cultural value placed on autistic personhood. Assumptions that devalue autistic identity and stereotypes that create fear and discrimination may be in dialogue between media interpretations of actual events and depictions of characters in fictional works. Fictional depictions found in literary texts and the public interpretation of actual events become mutually sustaining social artifacts that forge a cultural connection between autism and death. Examining *Of Mice and Men* and *Flowers for Algernon,* this chapter argues that the interconnection of the "cure or kill" trope of disability studies and real-life events tragically reinforces cultural attitudes that regard neurotypical subjectivity as the only subjectivity.

The fourth chapter addresses literary works in which characters with autism appear to be locked within themselves, confined by a tragic interiority, unable to communicate. The ghostly figure of Arthur "Boo" Radley from *To Kill a Mockingbird,* the painfully awkward Laura of *The Glass Menagerie,* and the silent, childlike Benjy of *The Sound and the Fury* are all outsiders who prove central. Indeed, these works present autistic characters as empty reflections, able only to point outward to the needs of nondisabled characters. The strong network of associations in these works connecting race, disability, and socioeconomic class shows that these characters' superficially central place in the narrative is the ultimate marginalization. As the monolithic nature of the narrative replaces one group with another, what appears on the surface to be empathy and tolerance suggests further stereotyping and discrimination. These "monstrous" figures either unite the family unit or destroy it, either strengthen the community with their outcast status or symbolize the community's ultimate decay by remaining within it. In the end, the Gothic mode proves to be the ideal genre for symbolically representing cultural anxieties and fears that interweave autism, family, and tragedy.

In chapter 5 I explore the increase in fictional depictions of autism in recent years. *Extremely Loud and Incredibly Close* and *The Curious Incident of the Dog in the Night-Time* are both best sellers narrated by autistic child detectives. In spite of the sharp difference in tone between the two novels, both characters come from families that are torn apart by tragedy and strife. Both child narrators also function in their fictional worlds as symbols for larger social concerns: Oskar's unspoken disability and struggle to communicate symbolize the larger cultural trauma surrounding 9/11, while Christopher's autistic characteristics are stereotypically represented as the cause of his family's drama. Ultimately, both characters become symbols that reflect outward—these autistic children stand in for larger cultural anxieties regarding the instability of the postmodern family and the struggle to establish emotional connections in a postmodern world.

The final chapter focuses on the power of diagnostic labels, examining the role of autism (simultaneously both implied and denied) in *The Girl with the Dragon Tattoo*. Lisbeth Salander's "outsider" status may make her a sensational and appealing heroine, but her depiction as a potentially autistic hero may be less liberating than it originally appears. Although the other characters conjecture about her place on the autism spectrum, the Millennium Trilogy ends by affirming Lisbeth's neurotypicality. Indeed, it seems that she can only be presented as a heroine if she is *not* autistic. While Larsson's trilogy capitalizes on the aura of mystery that surrounds its detective figure, the novels are only able to redeem Lisbeth and offer her triumph by denying, erasing, and silencing the narrative about mental disorders and social injustice that they initially espouse.

Although the works of literature examined here are diverse, ranging from play to novel, from the Victorian to the postmodern, from Pulitzer Prize–winning novel to popular best-selling crime fiction, these works are tied together by two important factors. First, all of these works employ or rewrite common autism stereotypes. Second, all demonstrate autism's place in our culture as a shifting symbol of difference. Both stereotypes and metaphors, whether optimistic or pessimistic, encouraging or discouraging, activist oriented or commercially motivated, have a profound effect on public perceptions of autism and especially on questions of identity and self-construction within the autism community itself. Such fictional figurations of life on the spectrum stand in uneasy balance between the negative stereotypes propagated by medical discourse and the heroic Supercrips praised by the news media. As these literary works tell their own stories about mental disability, they open up fictional spaces that move between and against more established texts: "Imaginative literature takes up its narrative project as a counter to scientific or truth-telling discourses. It is productively parasitic upon other disciplinary systems that define disability in more deterministic ways."[81] Like any minority group subject to stereotyping, adults with autism have internalized some of the cultural stereotypes that surround them.[82] Autistic culture is still under construction. The rethinking and rewriting of the medical and popular discourses that currently define autism are an ongoing project, and autistic identity itself could be seen as a moving signifier. Maybe the first line of this book, which suggests that I might have some kind of limited capacity for empathy, is merely a sign of my own internalized oppression, of listening to stereotypes, of letting popular representations and constructions tell me how "autistics" should be.

ONE

The Autistic Detective: Sherlock Holmes and His Legacy

"I am a brain, Watson. The rest of me is a mere appendix."
—Sherlock Holmes in Arthur Conan Doyle,
"The Adventure of the Mazarin Stone"

Sherlock Holmes has long been rumored to be on the autism spectrum. From chat on fan sites to direct diagnoses in the *New York Times* and *Psychology Today,* he is the literary character most commonly associated with autism in the popular imagination.[1] Yet despite the ongoing scholarly conversation regarding Arthur Conan Doyle's work, the significance of the great detective's autism "diagnosis" has been largely overlooked. While it would be impossible to diagnose a fictional character with a neurological difference, it says something about the way that the public imagines autism that Holmes is consistently imagined and described as a person on the spectrum. Indeed, Conan Doyle's famous character popularized the stereotype of the detective with autistic traits, thus perpetuating several common tropes about autism.[2] While the cultural fantasy of the autistic detective may seem to dispel the darker fantasy of those with cognitive disabilities as dangerous criminals and social problems, such detective figures may actually work to reinforce these stereotypes. Furthermore, the presumably redemptive fiction of the autistic hero often proves oddly dehumanizing: even as his incredible feats of deduction are praised as the work of a genius, Holmes is objectified by his beloved Watson, who constantly compares the brilliant sleuth to machines and repeatedly describes him as "inhuman." Indeed, Watson customarily imagines the famous detective as distant, callous, unknowable, and inexplicable. As Watson (representing the neurologically typical reader) struggles to solve the enigma that is Holmes, he establishes a legacy of mystery and mysticism surrounding the autistic detective that carries over into the famous figure's many pop culture analogs.

Emulating Conan Doyle's famous tales, contemporary crime fiction frequently creates detective characters with autistic characteristics. For example, popular television shows such as *Criminal Minds* and *Bones* present detectives with autistic traits who are clearly constructed to remind audiences of Holmes. While figures such as Spencer Reid and Temperance Brennan (and other crime fighters following in Holmes's shadow) may seem to counteract fears of people with cognitive disabilities as deviant, criminal, or dangerous, they may actually reinforce those stereotypes. Dwelling on the mystery and exoticism of alterity, such figurations also cast the character with autism as a puzzle in need of an outside solution.

Diagnosis and Deduction

The claim that Conan Doyle's famous detective has Asperger's syndrome (AS) is ubiquitous enough to appear in a variety of popular venues, and his diagnosis has been pursued by both fans and professionals; unfortunately, most of the discussions of Holmes's autistic traits present negative stereotypes as a part of their analysis, offering an extremely superficial and one-sided view of autism. A 2009 article in the *New York Times* describes Holmes as "mind-blind," "cold-blooded," and "rude," using these demeaning descriptors as diagnostic criteria for the popular sleuth.[3] Autistic people generally consider the term "mind-blind" to be derogatory, and the idea that all people with autism are cold-blooded and rude is obviously a damaging stereotype.[4] Another article, published in 2010, describes Holmes as a character with Asperger's who can solve crimes because he thinks outside of "normal, balanced cognition."[5] Such readings set neurotypical thinking up as the natural norm and suggest that other ways of thinking must be inherently inferior. A 2011 article in *Psychology Today* explains that Holmes must be autistic because "his obsessive interest in the craft of crime-solving crowded out almost everything else from his life, including the possibility of warm and reciprocal relationships."[6] Clearly, people on the spectrum are incapable of warm and reciprocal relationships (our ability to use sarcasm is also often falsely maligned). In *Autism: Explaining the Enigma* (2003), Uta Frith presents Holmes as a "creature of cold reason who is incapable of warm-hearted relationships" and explains that he is juxtaposed with Watson, a character who is able to have "warm feelings."[7]

Certainly, the suggestion that Holmes (and the autistic population he is imagined to represent) is completely incapable of emotional connections is a disturbing one. In sum, such readings frequently present autism as "abnormal" in relation to an imaginary neurotypical norm and encourage false stereotypes of autistics as emotionless, lacking in empathy, and incapable of love. Perhaps even more problematic is the potential interpretative looping that can result when the psychiatric community itself identifies a literary character as having a specific cognitive disability. Holmes's supposed diagnosis was the subject of a letter to the editor in a 2013 issue of the *Journal of Autism and Developmental Disorders*: Eric Altschuler suggests that studying figures like Holmes might help to determine how prevalent autism was in previous generations.[8] Such arguments demonstrate how a fictional character can be labeled based on stereotypes and then used as an exemplar for actual autistic people. Suddenly, it is not autistic people who are the interpretative template for the literary character; instead, the public perception of the literary character may reshape and inform how autism is defined as a social construct.

However, the ongoing conversation about Holmes and autism rarely addresses the difficulties inherent in "diagnosing" a literary character or the narrow view of people on the spectrum that the resulting analysis often offers. Amateur diagnoses based on popular stereotypes foster a one-dimensional way of thinking about people on the spectrum. In addition, such informal diagnosis may lead people to think that the experience of being autistic can be reduced to a list of criteria in the *Diagnostic and Statistical Manual of Mental Disorders*. For those who self-identify as autistic, being on the spectrum is not just a list of traits but an entire person, an entire life experience. That experience is always much more than (and sometimes simply *other* than) the diagnostic criteria. The diagnosis of a literary character may be misleading in that even the best-drawn character can never have the full roundness of a real person. One may wonder on what level Holmes's autism is merely Conan Doyle's "narrative prosthesis."[9] Because Holmes is a literary construct, it is also important to note that his autism diagnosis is partially a function of Watson's neurotypical narrative. Almost all of the reader's perceptions of Holmes are filtered through Watson's narrative voice: it might be more accurate *not* to say that Holmes is autistic but rather that Watson perceives him as autistic. Thus, the adventures of the autistic detective, as narrated by his neurotypical sidekick, are presented with an extra layer of interpretative data—as readers, we perceive both Holmes's autistic traits and Watson's neurotypical reactions to those traits. In fact, Watson's invisible, default position as neurotypical narrator mirrors the assumed norm of the majority perspective in our society at large. The neurotypical narrative perspective Watson offers elides the issue of autism as a subjective social construct: because Watson's voice narrates Holmes's story, the reader is placed in a default neurotypical position and is encouraged to perceive Holmes's actions and words through the interpretative lens of Watson's "normative" social expectations.

The dangers of diagnosing a literary character with autism spectrum disorder (ASD) are manifold, and the very question of Holmes's status on the spectrum raises larger questions about disability representation and the definition of autism itself. The question of who "controls" the autism diagnosis or "defines" what it means to be autistic is already a fraught one within the autism community.[10] One potential answer is that the psychiatric community (via the *DSM*) defines autism. But a growing body of collective literature written by autistic people, the reported individual experiences of people on the spectrum, and popular culture representations of autism all add different angles to that definition (or, in the case of some narratives written by autistic people, completely rewrite it).[11] Autobiographies written by people on the spectrum present an increasingly common way of "talking back" against the definition of autism presented in the *DSM*.[12] Of course, one potential definition of autism is that it is not neurotypical—autism is a social construct that exists solely in opposition to what is considered normative and could be described as whatever a particular society perceives as falling outside of that norm.[13] Ultimately, autism is a fluid signifier that works through multiple meanings in our culture.[14] All of the possible sources of definition for the condition are subjective—and despite the vaunted objectivity of the medical profession, the criteria provided by the *DSM* are as subjective as any others.[15] In any case, the popular culture conception of what it means to be autistic may have little to do with the diagnostic criteria provided by psychiatrists. When it comes to "diagnosing" a character like Holmes, social norms and popular stereotypes may play more of a role in constructing and defining autism than the reported life experiences of actual autistic people or the diagnostic criteria given in the *DSM*. Ultimately, no one representation can ever encapsulate the incredible diversity of the spectrum—and while Holmes is probably an autistic character by most definitions, he is not an autistic person.

In many ways, the popular association of Holmes with the autism spectrum is unsurprising, as Conan Doyle's character adheres to a plethora of autism stereotypes: Watson perceives Holmes as having intense interests, struggling in the social sphere, and displaying unusual body language.[16] Certainly, Holmes approaches his work with an intense single-mindedness (both crime solving and his chemical experiments). As Watson explains, "His zeal for certain studies was remarkable, and within eccentric limits his knowledge was so extraordinarily ample and minute that his observations have fairly astounded me."[17] Watson understands Holmes's knowledge to be deep rather than broad—but, more importantly, the depth of that knowledge "astounds" him, and he finds it "extraordinary." Watson, representing the neurotypical reader, is unable to understand or appreciate Holmes's deep interests and perceives them as mysterious. This lack of understanding contributes to the stereotype of autism as a "puzzling" and mysterious phenomenon. Watson describes Holmes as choosing his work over human companionship: "So engrossed was he with his occupation that he seemed to have forgotten our presence" (*Study*, 32). The emphasis here should be on the word "seemed"—as is so often the case, Watson cannot really tell the reader what Holmes is thinking, again contributing to the stereotype of the autistic mind as mystery. Certainly, Holmes's fields of interest often seem too narrow to interest a wider audience: "I have been guilty of several monographs. They are all upon technical subjects. Here, for example, is one 'Upon the distinction between the Ashes of the Various Tobaccos'. In it I enumerate a hundred and forty forms of cigar, cigarette, and pipe tobacco, with coloured plates illustrating the difference in the ash."[18] The unusual depth of Holmes's interests may make them seem eccentric and exotic to some readers.

In addition, the other characters frequently perceive Holmes as socially awkward. However, what the other characters interpret as bluntness or rudeness could also be construed as a misunderstanding caused by fundamentally different ways of thinking. In *The Hound of the Baskervilles*, Mrs. Lyons seems quite shocked by the detective's behavior, as "Holmes opened his interview with a frankness and directness which considerably amazed her."[19] Given the context of his interview with Mrs. Lyons (Holmes is trying to apprehend a murderer before he kills again), Holmes's haste and directness are quite appropriate. It is true, however, that Holmes often forgets social niceties, even going so far as to slight royalty in "A Scandal in Bohemia": "He bowed, and, turning away without observing the hand which the king stretched out to him, he set off in my company for his chambers."[20] His responses also sometimes show a lack of understanding of Watson's feelings. After giving a rather unkind account of Watson's alcoholic brother in *The Sign of the Four*, he apologizes by explaining, "Viewing the matter as an abstract problem, I had forgotten how personal and painful a thing it might be to you" (*Sign*, 9). Later, Holmes actually groans at the announcement of Watson's engagement—hardly the kind of response his friend could have been hoping to elicit. Holmes often oscillates between silence and long monologues, speaking with "the air of a clinical professor expounding to his class" and avoiding small talk (even with Watson and his fiancée): "Miss Morstan and I chatted in an undertone about our present expedition and its possible outcome, but our companion maintained his impenetrable reserve until the end of our journey" (Sign, 39, 19). The "impenetrable" nature of Holmes's silence suggests the common stereotype of those with autism as trapped by an imprisoning interiority, separated from the rest of the world by a chasm of silence.[21] Watson perceives Holmes's communication style as alienating the police and making it difficult for Holmes to work with a team to solve cases: "One of Sherlock Holmes's defects—if indeed, one may call it a defect—was that he was exceedingly loth to communicate his full plans to any other person until the instant of their fulfillment" (Hound, 146). Even as Watson contemplates Holmes's communication style, he questions whether or not this difference should be regarded as a "defect." Overall, the other characters perceive Holmes as noncommunicative and disengaged. As a result, Holmes spends a great deal of time in solitude: "while Holmes, who loathed every form of society with his whole Bohemian soul, remained in our lodgings in Baker Street, buried among his old books" (Adventures, 5–6). Overall, Holmes's general isolation and lack of social skills align neatly with autism stereotypes.

In addition, Holmes frequently engages in self-stimulating (stimming) behaviors and displays atypical body language: through the reactions of the neurotypical characters, the reader is encouraged to interpret these autistic traits as signs of illness and symbols of Holmes's ineffable mystery. Holmes's habit of repetitive pacing is a source of concern for both Watson and the landlady. Mrs. Hudson expresses her worries to Watson: "I am afraid for his health . . . he's that strange, sir. After you was gone he walked and he walked, up and down, and up and down, until I was weary of the sound of his footstep. Then I heard him talking to himself and muttering . . . and now he has slammed off to his room, but I can hear him walking same as ever. I hope he's not going to be ill, sir. I ventured to say something to him about cooling medicine" (Sign, 71). Although Watson knows that Holmes has a habit of pacing when he is thinking, even Watson worries when the detective continues to pace all night: "I was myself somewhat uneasy when through the long night I still from time to time heard the dull sound of his tread" (Sign, 72). The neurotypical characters perceive Holmes's stimming as "strange" and "ill," and it makes them "uneasy." Mrs. Hudson also indicates that Holmes's stimming makes her "weary": in the formation of negative stereotypes, not only is neurotypical taken as the default normal, but autistic differences that are viewed as annoying are also those most frequently pathologized. In addition to this stimming behavior, Holmes exhibits atypical body language that Watson finds difficult to interpret: because of his inability to decode his friend's expressions, Watson often imagines Holmes as cold and emotionless. According to Watson, Holmes rarely seems focused on the person he is conversing with and is often looking elsewhere. Indeed, it is remarkable how often Holmes either sits with his back to Watson or converses with clients with his eyes shut. At the beginning of *The Adventures of Sherlock Holmes,* when Holmes has been separated from his dearest friend for a very long time, his greeting strikes Watson as cold and aloof: "His manner was not effusive. It seldom was; but he was glad, I think, to see me. With hardly a word spoken, but with a kindly eye, he waved me to an armchair" (*Adventures,* 6). As well as Watson knows Holmes, he still cannot truly read him. Because the stories are narrated from Watson's perspective, Holmes's body language is judged against a neurotypical standard. Thus, Holmes's natural body language is interpreted by the other characters as mysterious and unreadable, and his stimming behaviors are presented as a sign of eccentricity and ill health.

Indeed, the reading of Holmes as autistic has become popular enough that recent adaptations of the Sherlock Holmes stories, such as the 2009 and 2011 *Sherlock Holmes* films directed by Guy Ritchie, suggest the possibility of an Asperger's diagnosis for Holmes. Both films hint that Holmes is autistic through scenes that simulate sensory overload. In the first film, Holmes seems overwhelmed as he waits for Watson and Mary in a crowded restaurant.[22] The camera zooms in on various details of the Victorian dining room, moving quickly from shots of clattering forks and knifes, to dessert plates, to ticking pocket watches. As the sound track increases the background minutia into a crescendo of sound, the camera focuses back on Holmes, showing him sweating. He seems startled and distracted when Watson and Mary make their entrance. The 2011 film uses a similar tactic to suggest overload in a crowded party scene. As he moves around the dance floor looking for clues, his waltzing partner asks him, "What do you see?" "I see everything," Holmes responds, "but not what I am looking for. That is my curse."[23] Even as Holmes complains about "seeing too much," the camera mimics his inability to focus in the crowded room, closing in on first one minor detail of the dance floor and then another, presenting a confusing series of fast-paced but disconnected images in rapid succession. But even as these films hint that Holmes's detail-oriented vision could be impairing, they simultaneously suggest that his sensory integration dysfunction is a savant skill. Holmes perfectly fits the stereotype of the autistic savant so pervasive in popular culture, as he has an incredibly detail-oriented mind combined with phenomenal memory skills. The awe and wonder customarily evoked by the autistic savant clearly contribute to Holmes's popularity, as his method of deduction inspires a sense of wonder both in the other characters and in audiences.[24] Indeed, the myth of the autistic detective is largely based on the premise that sensory integration dysfunction makes one unusually observant—and that this heightened awareness and observational ability allow the detective to solve the mystery. These films simultaneously present sensory integration issues as a source of both possible impairment and otherworldly power: not only is the heightened visual input the camera suggests aligned with Holmes's ability to solve crimes, but he proves to be a superior fighter in scenes that slow down the action of the film to show him using that same sensory perception to anticipate his opponents' every move. The films also hint that Holmes may be impaired in some aspects of daily living. Watson worries about leaving Holmes to live on his own—even with Mrs. Hudson there to keep an eye on the detective. When Watson checks in, the concerned landlady insists that Holmes is not eating or sleeping and that he should be placed in a sanatorium. Indeed, it is not perfectly clear whether or not the Sherlock Holmes of Guy Ritchie's films is capable of living on his own.

While the BBC's *Sherlock* makes no references to sensory problems or executive dysfunction, the series is more overt in stating that Holmes may be on the spectrum. The police are in the habit of referring to Sherlock as "the freak." He finally makes his preferences clear: "I'm a high-functioning sociopath. Get your terminology right."[25] Unfortunately, the show may lead viewers to falsely conflate the terms "autistic" and "sociopath," since *Sherlock*'s protagonist has many autistic traits.[26] While exploring the mystery at Baskerville, Watson and Lestrade find themselves wondering if Holmes is on the spectrum. Watson confides in Lestrade about how Holmes really feels: "You know, he's secretly pleased to see you here."[27] Lestrade agrees, "Yeah, he likes to see familiar faces together. It appeals to his . . ." While Lestrade hesitates in obvious confusion, Watson finishes the sentence, "Asperger's?" The series, however, never pursues this hint any further, and it is clear that whatever impairments this particular Holmes character may have are largely social. Ultimately, whether Holmes meets the modern diagnostic criteria for autism is irrelevant: as a literary character frequently connected with autism in the popular imagination, this figure has the power to perpetuate stereotypes about autism. Overall, Holmes's informal diagnosis may actually help to spread misinformation about people on the spectrum.

Cognitive Difference and Dangerous Stereotypes

In the original Conan Doyle stories (and in many later adaptations and retellings of the Sherlock Holmes myth), the autistic detective is frequently compared to criminals—an association that subtly links cognitive difference with criminality.[28] Although research in multiple fields has repeatedly disproven the myth that connects cognitive disabilities with violent behavior, this stereotype persists.[29] According to Peter Beresford:

> A powerful medical psychiatric tradition has for more than a century now shaped attitudes, responses and understandings towards mental health service users. It has framed us as pathological, as defective, as problems, as unpredictable. . . . Psychiatry has helped us become confused about what bad and mad mean. Increasingly when some terrible crime is committed . . . then we are encouraged to feel the person must be mad to do such a thing. . . . [T]hey are included as mentally ill and increasingly shape public and personal understandings of madness and distress and couple it more and more closely with crime, violence and threat.[30]

Of course, what is at stake in such figurations of mental disability is a threat to the definition of "normalcy" itself: society neutralizes this threat by attempting to cast criminals as fundamentally Other.[31] As Margaret Price has argued, representations of mental disability as the cause of violence "locate madness within the individual killers, marking the 'crazy,' 'troubled' aspects of their personalities, and hence reify 'our' (the putatively normal readers and creators of such representations) status as normates."[32] In other words, we want to believe that terrible crimes must be committed by someone "unlike us." Of course, one does not have to be "different" or set apart to be a criminal. Unfortunately, cognitive disability is often falsely offered as an explanation for criminal behavior (especially in the media).[33] Although cognitive difference might be "assumed to be the cause" of criminal actions, such representation of disability "operates . . . as a mechanism through which [criminals] are placed in a space of unrecoverable deviance."[34] Whether in fiction or in life, the idea that mental difference causes violence may actually encourage violence and discrimination against people with mental differences.[35] Clearly, using autistic traits as markers of criminal deviance for fictional characters has serious consequences.

On the surface, it seems that the cultural fantasy of the autistic crime fighter serves to dispel the false stereotype of people with cognitive disabilities as criminals—but in the Sherlock Holmes stories, cognitive difference is equated with deviant criminality, and Conan Doyle depicts Holmes as a hero who triumphs over the hereditary brain difference that links him to the criminal underworld.

While Holmes ultimately becomes a symbol of justice and the law, the implied connection between autistic traits and criminal behavior continues to haunt the original Sherlock Holmes stories and later popular culture adaptations of these tales, perpetuating false and damaging stereotypes in surprisingly subtle ways. In fact, Holmes often seems a little too interested in crime—his intense interest in illegal activity and those who engage in it often makes other characters uneasy. In fact, crime is his special interest. The detective brags of his "knowledge of the history of crime"; Watson notes that Holmes's "knowledge of sensational literature" is "immense," for "he appears to know every detail of every horror perpetrated in the century"; the police describe the consulting detective as "a connoisseur of crime" (*Study*, 20, 16, 118). Indeed, Holmes knows more about organized crime than the very criminals themselves, for he claims that "there is no one who knows the higher criminal world of London so well as I do" (*Memoirs*, 250). Holmes is filled with energy and purpose when a crime is committed, since it gives him a project to work on, and he laments any pause in the flow of challenging cases: "'There are no crimes and no criminals these days,' he said, querulously. 'What is the use of having brains in our profession?'" (*Study*, 21). The stories are haunted by the idea that Holmes's intense interest in crime might actually make him into a criminal. Watson observes Holmes at work and wonders if his eccentric roommate could prove dangerous: "So swift, silent, and furtive were his movements, like those of a trained bloodhound picking out a scent, that I could not but think what a terrible criminal he would have made had he turned his energy and sagacity against the law, instead of exerting them in its defense" (*Sign*, 43). Watson believes that the very characteristics that make Holmes a successful crime fighter might also make him a successful criminal. In "The Final Problem," Holmes brags to Watson that "in over a thousand cases I am not aware that I have ever used my powers upon the wrong side" (*Memoirs*, 263). Yet the very statement suggests that there is a danger of Holmes using his immense intellect in favor of the criminal element rather than against it. Again and again, the implication is that Holmes's unusual mind, his cognitive difference, is a sign of criminal deviance.

In a further connection between cognitive difference and illegal activity, the heroic detective seems to be linked to his archnemesis by common neurology. Holmes and Moriarty are inextricably connected—specifically through their unusual minds and ways of thinking. The detective and the criminal mastermind admire each other's work as equal "connoisseurs of crime." Holmes uses words such as "genius" and "wonder" to describe Moriarty's work, confessing that "my horror at his crimes was lost in my admiration at his skill" (*Memoirs*, 251, 253). Moriarty, too, admires the work of Holmes: "It has been an intellectual treat to me to see the way in which you have grappled with this affair" (*Memoirs*, 255). Specifically, it is the mind that connects detective and criminal as they admire one another's intellect. Sometimes the two men seem to think not just with equal minds but with one mind. "I know every move of your game," Moriarty warns Holmes (*Memoirs*, 255). When Watson asks, "What will he do?" Holmes responds simply, "What I should do" (*Memoirs*, 260). "All that I have to say has already crossed your mind," Moriarty says. "Then perhaps my answer has crossed yours," Holmes responds (*Memoirs*, 254). Although thinking like a criminal is an implied part of the detective's job description, Holmes is a little too good at it. Moriarty is Holmes's equal in many ways; indeed, if Holmes has autism, then so does Moriarty: Holmes suggests that Moriarty's unusual mind is the product of heredity, and the parallels between the two characters suggest an inherited cognitive difference in both detective and criminal. Holmes describes Professor Moriarty as "endowed by Nature with a phenomenal mathematical faculty . . . but the man had hereditary tendencies of the most diabolical kind. A criminal strain ran in his blood, which, instead of being modified, was increased and rendered infinitely more dangerous by his extraordinary mental powers" (*Memoirs*, 252). Moriarty's extraordinary math skills, given to him at birth (by "Nature"), are linked to his criminal tendencies, which are also described as hereditary. According to Holmes, Moriarty was born a criminal, doomed by biology and, apparently, by an extraordinary mind that only makes him all the more dangerous. Of course, Holmes's extraordinary mind also has a hereditary basis—one need look no further than his brother, Mycroft, to see that being an eccentric genius runs in the family.[36] If Moriarty is destined by heredity to become a criminal, Holmes seems destined by heredity to think like one. In short, Holmes and Moriarty are closely linked by their unusual minds, and both characters display traits associated with the stereotype of the autistic savant. Conan Doyle's depiction of Holmes as being connected to Moriarty through common neurology establishes a false equation between cognitive difference and criminal deviance.

Again and again, the connection between criminal and detective is a link forged by unusual minds: the multiple doppelgängers in *The Hound of the Baskervilles* all adhere to a variety of autism stereotypes. The novel's plurality of eccentric scientists and doctors, all of them loners, all of them socially awkward, all of them intensely interested in esoteric subjects, reminds readers that Holmes is inextricably joined with the criminals he pursues. Dr. James Mortimer, a scientist with an intense interest in phrenology, talks about nothing but the shape of people's skulls. Holmes immediately observes the characteristics that he and Mortimer share: "You are an enthusiast in your line of thought, I perceive, sir, as I am in mine" (*Hound*, 8). Early in the novel, Mortimer and Holmes compare their "special hobbies." Mortimer explains that he knows everything about different skulls "because that is my special hobby. The differences are obvious. The supra-orbital crest, the facial angle, the maxillary curve, the—" Holmes interrupts the long-winded scientist to explain his knowledge of crime: "This is my special hobby, and the differences are equally obvious" (*Hound*, 32). Watson is also quick to recognize the similarities between Holmes and Mortimer, "for when Mortimer pressed his questions to an inconvenient extent I asked him casually to what type Frankland's skull belonged, and so heard nothing but craniology for the rest of our drive. I have not lived for years with Sherlock Holmes for nothing" (*Hound*, 107). Yet the murderer in *The Hound of the Baskervilles* also proves to be an eccentric scientist, one with a special interest in entomology. Specifically, Stapleton's intense interest in collecting and cataloging insects serves as a symbol of his deviant criminal behavior, as though an unusual interest were in itself a sign of criminality. Watson describes the killer: "In that impassive, colourless man, with his straw hat and his butterfly net, I seemed to see something terrible—a creature of infinite patience and craft, with a smiling face and a murderous heart" (*Hound*, 126). Here, Stapleton's "straw hat" and "butterfly net," the symbols of his intense scientific interest, figure into the description of him as a sinister killer. His "impassive," seemingly stoic, and aloof exterior is equally implicated as a sign of his criminal tendencies. Watson describes the interior of Stapleton's house: "The room had been fashioned into a small museum, and the walls were lined by a number of glass-topped cases full of that collection of butterflies and moths the formation of which had been the relaxation of this complex and dangerous man" (*Hound*, 153). Like Moriarty, Stapleton is dangerous because "complex" (or perhaps complex because dangerous?). The naturalist's special interest in bugs is presented as disturbing, as his hobby of trapping, killing, and labeling insects under glass is placed parallel to his endeavor to kill the heirs to the Baskerville estate. Throughout the novel, the intensity of his interest in insects is a sign of his criminal mind. The multiple scientist figures of *The Hound of the Baskervilles* clearly align Holmes with the criminal Stapleton.

It is remarkable how often Holmes is mistaken for a criminal, a rule that applies both to Conan Doyle's stories and to later adaptations of Holmes's character. Always found in possession of information he could not possibly have and often in the wrong place at the wrong time, he is constantly asserting his innocence. As Watson remarks in "The Final Problem," "One would think that we were the criminals" (*Hound*, 260). In *A Study in Scarlet*, Holmes objects, "Don't go arresting me for the murder. . . . I am one of the hounds and not the wolf" (*Study*, 39). Indeed, the doppelgängers in *The Hound of the Baskervilles* ensure that Holmes is indistinguishable from the villain he pursues—even to Watson. "So you actually thought that I was the criminal?" Holmes asks his friend with surprise (*Hound*, 123). The escaped convict whom Holmes is mistaken for in *The Hound of the Baskervilles* is a man of bestial intentions, driven to murder by "his brutal and violent nature"—an impulse to criminal activity that is apparently inborn (*Hound*, 94). Watson believes so firmly in a hereditary basis for the criminal's deviant behavior that he is shocked to learn that the convict is related to the servant at Baskerville Hall: "Sir Henry and I both stared at the woman in amazement. Was it possible that this stolidly respectable person was of the same blood as one of the most notorious criminals in the country?" (*Hound*, 93). Watson describes the convict as a "fiendish man, hiding in a burrow like a wild beast, with his heart full of malignancy against the whole race which had cast him out" (*Hound*, 36, 98). At the time, he does not realize that the outcast figure he is describing is actually Sherlock Holmes.

Various modern retellings of the Sherlock Holmes myth return to the idea of an unusual mind as the characteristic that links Holmes with the criminals he pursues. In the 2009 *Sherlock Holmes* film, Lestrade bails Holmes out of jail with the comment "You would have made a good criminal in a previous life." The police of BBC's *Sherlock* are determined to believe that the eccentric detective is doomed to become a criminal. "One day we'll be standing around a body and it will be Sherlock Holmes that put it there," Sergeant Donovan says as she warns Watson to stay away from Holmes. When Watson responds with surprise, wondering why the detective would commit a murder, she explains that he will no doubt "get bored."[37] Certainly, Holmes frequently behaves destructively out of intellectual boredom (his spells of cognitive ennui result in cocaine abuse and firing bullets randomly at the walls of his apartment). The BBC website describes Sherlock as "brilliant, aloof and almost entirely lacking in social graces. Sherlock is a unique young man with a mind like a 'racing engine'. Without problems to solve, that mind will tear itself to pieces."[38] Like the original Conan Doyle stories, the BBC's *Sherlock* emphasizes the destructive potential of the detective's mind. If pointed in the wrong direction, Holmes's mind has the power to destroy. The show also depicts Sherlock as cold and emotionless. "They care so much,"

Sherlock says wistfully as he watches a group of mourners. "Do you think there's something wrong with us?," he asks. "Caring is not always an advantage," Mycroft responds.[39] The detective's indifference to death and mourning may be yet another hint at a potentially criminal mind, building on the misconception that people who act based on logic (rather than emotion) may be dangerous. While stories about Holmes evoke wonder with his savant skills, they also evoke fear at the idea of his unusual mind, as cognitive difference is equated with danger and destruction.

While Conan Doyle's stories suggest a link between autistic behavior and criminal activity, there are other ways in which Watson's attitude toward Holmes perpetuates negative stereotypes about cognitive difference: Watson constantly compares Holmes to machines and imagines him as being incapable of emotion. As Watson complains to his friend, "You really are an automaton—a calculating machine. . . . [T]here is something positively inhuman in you at times" (*Sign*, 15). In "A Scandal in Bohemia," Holmes's relationship with Irene Adler causes Watson to reflect on his friend's apparent inability to love: "It was not that he felt any emotion akin to love for Irene Adler. All emotions, and that one particularly, were abhorrent to his cold, precise, but admirably balanced mind. He was, I take it, the most perfect reasoning and observing machine that the world has seen; but, as a lover, he would have placed himself in a false position" (*Adventures*, 5). Again, Holmes is presented as a machine rather than as a person. His intense reliance on logic is interpreted as a sign that he could never love. Asexuality and objectivity are frequently linked in fictional depictions of autism, a connection that is especially clear in the detective's relationship with Irene Adler. Watson imagines love (and, by extension, sex) as being opposed to the objectivity and reason that he imagines Holmes as representing. Although Watson is determined to believe that Holmes is incapable of love and uninterested in sex, Conan Doyle's text hints at other possibilities. Holmes describes Adler as "a lovely woman, with a face that a man might die for" (*Adventures*, 7). Indeed, he agrees to be paid for a job with a photograph of Adler in evening dress. Watson goes so far as to admit that for Holmes "she eclipses and predominates the whole of her sex" (*Adventures*, 5). Although Watson seems to perceive Holmes as asexual, Conan Doyle leaves the sexual ambiguity that surrounds Holmes open to interpretation. In any case, Watson's depiction of Holmes leaves room for yet another autism stereotype, as people on the spectrum are often imagined or depicted as asexual.[40] It is significant that the clues that lead Watson to interpret Holmes as asexual are linked to Holmes's strong connection with logic and objectivity. Clearly, being logical does not preclude sexual desires or relationships. Watson, however, imagines love as being diametrically opposed to "reason" and "observation"—two areas in which Holmes excels. Because Watson imagines Holmes as a machine, Watson creates a false binary in which someone who solves problems with reason or strives to think with objectivity must be diametrically opposed to sexual feeling. Watson's interpretation of events ignores the intensity of Holmes's interest in (and potential attraction to?) Adler. Ultimately, the encounter with Adler is yet another example of Watson shaping the reader's perception of Holmes, as Watson links sex and objectivity, implying that the two cannot possibly coexist. According to Watson, love would pose a problem to Holmes as a crime-solving machine: "But for the trained reasoner to admit such intrusions into his own delicate and finely adjusted temperament was to introduce a distracting factor which might throw a doubt upon all his mental results. Grit in a sensitive instrument, or a crack in one of his own high-power lenses, would not be more disturbing than a strong emotion in a nature such as his" (*Adventures*, 6). Holmes is described as a machine that is not designed to handle strong emotion: the crack in the high-powered lens, like the grit in the sensitive instrument, like love in the heart of the character with autistic traits, is presented as out of place.

The false stereotype that people with autism are emotionless is equally damaging—and this is yet another stereotype that Holmes helps to perpetuate through his intense focus on logic. Holmes constantly dismisses emotions for the sake of logic: "Detection is, or ought to be, an exact science, and should be treated in the same cold and unemotional manner" (*Sign*, 5). He feels that too much emotion would get in the way of his job: "A client is to me a mere unit, a factor in a problem. The emotional problems are antagonistic to clear reasoning" (*Sign*, 15). He explains his choice of logic over emotion to Watson: "Whatever is emotional is opposed to the true cold reason which I place above all things" (*Sign*, 119). Furthermore, readers' attention to Holmes's intellectual prowess (he is a character defined by his cognitive ability) combined with the reading of him as autistic (he is a character defined by his cognitive disability) has led to a myopic focus on Holmes's mind—thus perpetuating yet another autism stereotype. As Holmes says in "The Adventure of the Mazarin Stone," "I am a brain, Watson. The rest of me is a mere appendix."[41] Many critics have been quick to accept Holmes's claim that he is "a brain," while the other aspects of his character are cast aside as less worthy of discussion. Yet this perception of autistics as disembodied or only mind is an incredibly painful reduction that ignores the humanity of autistic people.[42] Perhaps one of the most disturbing aspects of these tales is that Holmes generally agrees with the negative ways in which Watson interprets his autistic traits. He encourages other characters (and, by implication, readers) to imagine him as all brain, to fixate on cognitive difference as a source of inhumanity. As Holmes is reduced to a disembodied mind, only the signifier of difference remains. Unfortunately, interpretations of Holmes's character that take the great detective at his word and focus exclusively on his mind may help to perpetuate this stereotype.

Watson not only imagines Holmes as a cold, mechanized container for facts but also describes him as a constant source of mystery, a puzzle for Watson (and, by implication, for the neurotypical reader) to solve. Another common stereotype of people on the spectrum is to represent them as problems, mysteries, or puzzles. The other characters dwell on Holmes's autistic traits as symbols of mystery and exoticism, thus casting the character with autism as a puzzle in need of a neurotypical solution. When he first introduces Holmes and Watson, Watson's friend Stamford goes so far as to describe Holmes as "inexpressible," claiming that many people have tried to unravel his secret, always without success (*Study*, 8). Watson responds with pleasure, "Oh! A mystery is it? . . . I am much obliged to you for bringing us together." In this case, the detective proves to be the true mystery of the mystery novel. Stamford warns, "You must study him then. . . . [Y]ou'll find him a knotty problem, though" (*Study*, 12). Holmes will become Watson's object of study, a problem that can hardly be untangled. Watson later explains "how much this man stimulated my curiosity, and how often I endeavored to break through the reticence which he showed on all that concerned himself" and says that he "eagerly hailed the little mystery which hung around my companion, and spent much of my time in endeavoring to unravel it" (*Study*, 14). Although Watson approaches Holmes's mystery from a humanistic perspective, Mortimer is certain that Victorian science can explain Holmes's mysterious mind: "You interest me very much, Mr. Holmes. . . . [A] cast of your skull, sir, until the original is available, would be an ornament to any anthropological museum. It is not my intention to be fulsome, but I confess that I covet your skull" (*Hound*, 8). Overall, Holmes is regarded as a mystery by Conan Doyle's other characters: this construction of Holmes as a human puzzle reflects one of the media's most common tropes in depictions of autistic people.

Holmes's Autistic Legacy

As the single most famous detective in the history of the mystery genre, Conan Doyle's character has influenced a wide variety of detectives, many of them with autistic traits. The figure of the autistic detective has enjoyed a recent comeback in television shows that feature detective heroes with autistic characteristics: Spencer Reid of *Criminal Minds,* Temperance Brennan of *Bones,* Charlie Eppes of *Numb3rs,* Gregory House of *House,* and Adrian Monk of *Monk* all have character traits that could be traced back to Holmes's autistic tendencies.[43] While these crime fighters and mystery solvers may reassure majority audiences that the stereotypical autistic savant works for law and order rather than against it, many of these television shows maintain an ambiguous liminality between criminal and crime solver and develop an aura of mystery around characters with autistic traits. These shows frequently present the autistic detective as an enigmatic and exotic source of alterity, drawing the neurotypical audience in with the wonder of his or her savant skills and fixating on the dangerous potential of his unusual mind. Two examples of this popular trope are the autistic detective of the aptly named *Criminal Minds* and the female Holmes of the police procedural *Bones.*

Dr. Spencer Reid, of CBS's popular *Criminal Minds,* is clearly imagined by the show's writers as a latter-day Sherlock Holmes: the show also hints repeatedly that the young detective has autism yet never overtly acknowledges it. Depicted as a socially awkward genius, Reid has multiple PhDs, a photographic memory, and a detail-oriented vision of the world. His savant-level skills amaze the members of the FBI squad with which he works, and he communicates with his team members primarily through monologues. Early on, the show establishes a connection between Reid and autism when a criminal claims that everyone ignores "the autistic leanings of the very insecure Dr. Reid."[44] As the camera pans in on Reid's face, his expression remains perfectly blank: he has nothing to say in response to such a claim. In a later episode, the victim of a crime has AS, and Reid rattles out a detailed definition of the disorder for the other members of the team. Alex Blake, the squad's new recruit, asks innocently, "Well how about you?" He responds with confusion, apparently not understanding: "What's that?" Behind his back, his coworkers smile and nod knowingly at Alex. Later, she apologizes for bringing it up: "By the way, no offense earlier when I suggested you had Asperger's." Clearly oblivious to the implications of their earlier conversation, he responds: "None taken. When did you do that?" "That's what I love about you," she says with a laugh. "You're not sensitive like some people. Think about how much time we would save if everyone got straight to the point." So intent on looking for clues that he speaks with his back turned toward his new colleague, he agrees: "Yeah, cut out all the handshakes and 'how do you dos.'"[45] Reid routinely struggles with intense light sensitivity, a problem that he frequently hides from his coworkers. When he finally goes to a doctor for testing, he is referred to a psychologist. Clearly angry, he tells the physician: "I know very well what mental illness looks like. . . . It's not that! It's not!"[46] As the camera shoots from Reid's perspective at the beginning of the episode, the hospital corridor of fluorescent lights is blindingly bright. His coworkers, especially Derek Morgan, keep a close watch on him, always on the lookout for signs of disorientation. Yet the repeated hints never yield to any public diagnosis for Reid. While the show capitalizes on the awe and wonder evoked by its savant figure, it avoids confirming that Reid is on the spectrum. Perhaps an admission of diagnosis would damage the popularity of the character or ostracize those audiences that might view the depiction as politically incorrect. But while episodes avoid revealing Reid's diagnosis, screenwriter Sharon Watson has stated in an interview, "I think he has Asperger's."[47] In any case, Reid's implicit disclosure (we know he has autism, but we do not know he has autism) contributes to the show's connections with Conan Doyle's tales of Sherlock Holmes and ultimately, to implied comparisons between Reid and the very criminals he pursues.

Multiple allusions to Conan Doyle's work demonstrate the show's awareness of participating in the autistic detective tradition. Reid has phone conversations with his girlfriend that center on detective fiction, especially *The Sign of the Four*. The detective also conducts a passionate epistolary affair with the young woman under the pseudonym Joseph Bell (one of the proposed real-life models for Sherlock Holmes). When Reid's girlfriend is abducted, the kidnapper refers to herself as Adam Worth (one of the proposed real-life models for Professor Moriarty). However, the kidnapper proves to fall far short in this regard: although she tries to set herself up as a nemesis worthy of Reid, her clues are childishly simple compared to the kinds of clues Reid is used to unraveling. In the final standoff, Reid is able to manipulate this "Moriarty" by hailing her scientific work as genius and by claiming that he understands how she feels: "You have a brain that doesn't play by normal societal rules," he tells the criminal.[48] One can only assume that Reid thinks of this ploy because his own mind doesn't play by normal societal rules. Clearly, the show imagines Reid as its Sherlock Holmes character.

In depicting Reid as autistic, the show makes use of multiple autism stereotypes. First, the brilliant Reid is frequently portrayed as being unable to take care of himself and in need of help from his neurotypical friends. The other characters worry about Reid and clearly believe that he struggles with some aspects of self-care ("Are you eating? Are you sleeping?"). He is also the object of constant social coaching, particularly in the area of girls and dating. When Alex asks why Reid thinks that a girl would not like him, he responds helplessly: "I'm weird." Derek spends an entire episode trying to build Reid's social confidence and teaching him how to pick up a girl in a bar. Furthermore, the show fosters the common stereotype that aligns "genius" with mental disorders. Although a mental disorder runs in Reid's family, it is not autism: his mother has schizophrenia, and numerous episodes show him visiting her at an institution. Although there is no link between autism and schizophrenia, the association between "genius" and "mental disorder" remains clear, and the connection between Reid and his mother highlights this stereotype for viewers who may not identify his behavior as autistic.[49] In fact, the actor's depiction may conflate the two conditions: Matthew Gray Gubler, who plays Reid, describes the character as "an eccentric genius, with hints of schizophrenia and minor autism, Asperger's Syndrome."[50] Finally, Reid is disembodied and imagined as all mind in much the same way that Holmes is. Reid does not have his first girlfriend until he is in his early thirties, and he is only able to attract the young geneticist (Maeve Donovan) because she is fascinated by his unusual mind. Although she has seen a scan of his brain, she has never seen a picture of him. Their brief affair, conducted completely by phone and letter, depicts a romance based purely on intellectual attraction: they admire each other's scholarly publications but never touch. Of course, Reid's asexual approach to his relationship with Maeve suggests yet another autism stereotype. Overall, *Criminal Minds* characterizes Reid as autistic partially through a series of easily recognizable stereotypes, using these traits as shorthand for an implicit autism diagnosis.

Like the original Holmes stories, the show aligns the autistic detective's amazing mind with the minds of dangerous criminals. If it is the FBI profilers' job to think like criminals, Reid is clearly the best at the job. Out of all the characters on the crime-fighting team, Reid is indispensable, for he is the detective who most often cracks the case. Many episodes end with a revelation coming from Reid, as his savant skills allow him to perceive or remember details forgotten by others. The very title of the show, however, points to Reid's liminal status between crime fighter and criminal. In many episodes, the climax shows the FBI team presenting a criminal profile that could be used to describe Reid: the criminal often proves to be intelligent, to be socially isolated, and to have poor social skills. In fact, the other characters are sometimes disturbed by how easily Reid perceives what a criminal might be thinking or planning. In an early episode, Reid expresses sympathy for an intelligent young man about his age, a socially awkward nerd doomed by an uncontrollable desire to stab women. When Derek expresses concern over the young detective's sympathy for a killer, Reid explains, "I know what it's like to be afraid of your own mind."[51] Not only does this description imply that the autistic mind is frightening, but it also clearly links the autistic detective with the criminal—Reid can understand the killer because they both have minds that inspire fear. This episode suggests that Reid's sympathy for the murderer is not just sympathy: it is a connection between two minds, a shared neurological makeup. Even more overtly than the Sherlock Holmes stories on which it draws for inspiration, *Criminal Minds* suggests that autistic traits create an unusual link between criminal and crime fighter, forwarding a false stereotype that links cognitive disability with criminal behavior.

Dr. Temperance "Bones" Brennan, the scientist turned detective (like Reid, she has three PhDs) of the Fox series *Bones,* has many autistic traits that are reminiscent of Sherlock Holmes: like the original autistic detective figure, Brennan has intense interests and struggles socially.[52] Certainly, Brennan is passionately in love with her work as a forensic anthropologist. Many episodes feature long montages that show her assembling skeletons alone in her lab, suggesting both her devotion to the job and the many hours that she spends in solitude. Soundtrack choices emphasize her emotional connection to her work and her social isolation: songs that would traditionally be considered romantic play in the background as she stays overnight at her lab, staring all night at skeletons.[53] Indeed, she spends her vacation days from the Jeffersonian Institute in Washington, D.C., working to piece together corpses at other locations, a habit her lab assistant describes as her "vacation work."[54] In addition to her unusually intense interests, Brennan frequently struggles socially. "I apparently don't read people very well," she admits in one episode.[55] As she struggles to make small talk, she exclaims with frustration, "I thought it was good to start with 'good morning.'"[56] Brennan is the object of constant social coaching from the other characters—particularly from her supervisor at the Jeffersonian; her FBI partner (and later romantic interest), Seeley Booth; and her friend Angela Montenegro. "You have many skills, Temperance," her supervisor laments, "but not one of them includes communicating with the average person on the street."[57] When a local sheriff observes Brennan at a crime scene she remarks, "Not big on small talk, is she?" "Dr. Brennan's very focused," Booth explains with embarrassment (he has just been giving Brennan a lecture on how important it is to establish a good relationship with "the locals").[58] "What if I'm only good with bones and lousy with people?" she laments to Angela, confessing, "My most meaningful relationships are with dead people." Trying to help Brennan connect with her coworkers, Angela advises: "You want some advice? Offer up a little bit of yourself every once in a while." Her colleagues clearly regard her as distant and disengaged, because Booth offers the same advice: "Getting information out of live people is a lot different from getting information out of a pile of bones. You have to offer up something of yourself first."[59] The depiction of Brennan as socially awkward is unsurprising: the show's creator, Hart Hanson, stated in an interview that he based Brennan's character on a friend with Asperger's. However, Brennan's diagnosis is never revealed in the show because of "the needs of a broadcast network like Fox to get as large an audience as possible."[60] Hanson said that "if we were on cable, we would have said from the beginning that Brennan has Asperger's. . . . Instead, it being a network, we decided not to label a main character, for good or for bad. But those elements are in there."[61] Emily Deschanel, who plays Brennan, explained in an interview that she learned about the condition by talking with a psychologist specializing in ASD.[62] Although no episode ever discloses Brennan's diagnosis, it is clear that both the show's writers and the cast have deliberately portrayed Brennan as having autistic character traits.

Not only does Brennan display many autistic characteristics, but her young assistant, Zack Addy, also seems to have Asperger's. Emily Deschanel stated in an interview that the head of the team at the Jeffersonian is not the only autistic in the lab: "If you look at the character of Zack, played by Eric Millegan, he almost definitely has Asperger Syndrome."[63] Brennan's lab assistant is a socially isolated graduate student pursuing two doctorates. With a genius IQ and status as a child prodigy, his interests are at least as intense as those of his beloved mentor, and he may even surpass her in the area of social awkwardness. He needs almost constant social coaching from Jack Hodgins (the team's entomologist). While his eidetic memory gives him savant-level abilities, Zack's poor social skills make it difficult for him to maintain a job: even after he completes his two doctorates, the supervisor at the Jeffersonian initially refuses to hire him—she says that a jury could never take him seriously in court. Bullied relentlessly as a child, he reveals that his parents signed him up for extracurricular activities that they hoped would "help integrate me socially." He is highly attached to his daily routine (the other characters make fun of him for eating the same thing for lunch every day), and the show hints that he struggles with some aspects of self-care (he lives with Hodgins and seems to rely on him heavily for practical support). Many of the show's jokes depend on the neurotypical characters' commentary on interactions between Brennan and her like-minded protégé, and it is clear that she and Zack are separated from the rest of the characters by their intense interests and awkward social skills—the very characteristics that help them to relate to each other and to work well as a crime-solving team.

While Zack's memory and skill with numbers clearly make him an autistic savant figure, the show's main focus is on Brennan's savant skills: she is praised as the best in her field, and her ability to describe victims and crime scene details based only on bones verges on the mystical. When Booth's supervisor at the FBI describes Brennan as "good," Booth immediately responds, "No, she's amazing. Gives me the victim's age, sex, and favorite sport." Booth cannot believe that Brennan can recognize someone simply by looking at a skull: "How did you recognize her before she even had her own face?" "I recognized the underlying architecture of her features. The rest was just window dressing," Brennan explains. Harking back to Watson's comparisons of Holmes's observations to magic, Booth describes Brennan's abilities as supernatural: to find out everything she knows about the crime she must be using a "crystal ball." "It's not magic," Brennan objects, "it's a logical re-creation of events based on evidence."[64] Building on the common stereotype of those on the spectrum as computers, the show implies that Brennan's mind works better than all of the Jeffersonian's expensive technology. When using a computer program to identify a victim, Angela is interrupted by Brennan, who, in a hurry to find the murderer, identifies the victim on the spot. Angela says with exasperation, "Why do we pay eight zillion dollars for this software when we have you?" Laughing as she hurries out the door, Brennan responds, "Under normal circumstances it allows me to take a longer lunch."[65] In short, the show presents Brennan as a crime-solving savant in the style of Sherlock Holmes, as she uses her detail-oriented mind and keen observation skills to solve seemingly impossible cases.

While her savant skills help her to solve crimes, some of her autistic traits limit her abilities as well: it is difficult for Brennan to relate emotionally to other people and to understand what they are thinking—the other characters perceive her as so emotionally disengaged that she is sometimes compared to a sociopath. Brennan's difficulty relating emotionally causes particular problems in dealing with the families of victims. For example, she cannot understand why Booth lies to grieving parents to tell them that their daughter did not suffer: "Those people deserve the truth," she objects.[66] She tells a grieving and crying widow that she cannot identify her husband because "the body was fragmented by the blast. We are still retrieving pieces."[67] In the show's pilot episode, she is not able to see the political danger of accusing a senator of a murder and seems unaware of the so-

Imagining Autism

cial implications of her actions in publicly accusing him. She is also frequently confused when it comes to determining criminal motive: "The evidence said he did it, but I don't know why," she exclaims in frustration.[68] Booth is often left to explain the situation, revealing political and social motivations of which Brennan seems all too often unaware. In fact, the other characters' perception of her as unemotional means that she must constantly defend herself from being compared to a sociopath. When she is stopped at the airport for carrying a human skull, the security officers find her body language difficult to read. The first officer confronts her: "What most people do in this situation, what they do is sweat. You know who doesn't sweat?" "Sociopaths," the second officer says, glowering at Brennan. Clearly angry, Brennan responds, "I'm not a sociopath. I'm an anthropologist with the Jeffersonian."[69] Coaching her on how to interact with a murder victim's family, Booth admonishes her: "It's sad. Try to remember that." Brennan objects: "I'm not a sociopath." Booth responds: "You're bad with people. There's no use being offended by the fact."[70] As in *Sherlock,* the unfortunate labeling of autistic characters as "emotionless" or "sociopaths" could contribute to negative perceptions of people with autism. In any case, Brennan's struggles to relate emotionally to the other characters somewhat hinder her abilities in the field.

In depicting characters on the spectrum, the show makes use of multiple stereotypes regarding ASD: Zack and Brennan are frequently depicted as emotionally cold and generally lacking in common sense. Angela, who works at the Jeffersonian as a forensic artist, serves as the show's "warmhearted" and creative figure: she is frequently juxtaposed with the two autistic characters to humorous effect, often by suggesting that the characters with Asperger's are cold and strange. Such jokes usually build on the all-too-common trope that compares those on the spectrum with aliens and robots:

> Zack: You're supposed to bump my fist with yours.
> Brennan: Why?
> Zack: I'm told this is a widely acknowledged gesture of mutual
>   success.
> Angela: I love it when you two impersonate earthlings.[71]

In the same episode, Brennan is told that her testimony regarding a murder reminds the defense attorney of a "robot."[72] Indeed, Brennan and Zack are frequently assumed to be "abnormal" compared to the show's neurotypical characters. Outnumbered at the autopsy table, Angela jokes uncomfortably, "Can I, as the only normal person in this room, say 'eww'?" Brennan is frequently depicted as "cold" and "hard." Angela feels that Brennan distances herself because of her strong feelings: "You come off a little distant because you connect too much." Brennan responds, "I hate psychology—it's a soft science." Angela's gentle response implies that Brennan comes across as both hard and inhuman: "People are mostly soft." Booth constantly says that Brennan and Zack lack common sense and real-world know-how. He refers to scientists as "squints," mocking their intense scrutiny of the evidence: "This is exactly why squints belong in the lab. You guys don't know anything about the real world."[73] In short, the show depicts characters on the spectrum in part by using common and easily recognizable autism stereotypes.

Another stereotype the show uses in the portrayal of Brennan is that of autism as representing the "extreme male brain": Brennan's sexual relationships often hint that she plays the "masculine" role.[74] Although it is true that ASD is far more often diagnosed in men than in women, the perception that women on the spectrum have more stereotypically masculine traits than their neurotypical counterparts is a common misconception about autism and gender. Certainly, Brennan strongly reflects this misconception. The heroine of *Bones* is definitely not traditionally feminine: she enjoys the shooting range and doing martial arts and is deeply involved in the male-dominated fields of science and law enforcement. In the early seasons of the show, Brennan engages in a stereotypically masculine role in her dating relationships: her relationships tend to be about sex and sex only—Brennan asks that there be no emotional attachments in her dating life. As she explains her sexual relationship with another scientist to a confused Angela, "Our relationship is purely platonic—what we share is the love of science. Neither one of us has the time nor the inclination for emotional attachments."[75] In fact, the show's main juxtaposition—that between Brennan and Booth—is at least partially based on inverted gender stereotypes: the show's writers present the heart, emotion, and gut instinct represented by Booth as directly opposed to the science, logic, and objective evidence represented by Brennan. As Brennan explains to Booth, "You're a heart person. I'm a brain person."[76] Booth sometimes takes on the more stereotypically feminine role in their relationship, even waiting for Brennan to propose marriage to him. Ultimately, Brennan's more stereotypical "masculine" traits and habits invert common gender stereotypes while furthering the misconception that women on the spectrum have many masculine characteristics.

Finally, the show's various plotlines suggest that both of its autistic characters have "criminal minds," aligning its female Sherlock Holmes and her autistic sidekick with the criminals they pursue. Brennan is associated with the criminal underworld on multiple levels. Her parents were both criminals and worked with a gang of professional bank robbers. Once her father comes back into her life, Brennan proposes herself as a possible suspect in a murder he committed. In the eyes of the jury, she is suggestive enough as a killer to be able to create doubt and to get her father acquitted. Indeed, she helps her guilty father evade the law on multiple occasions. Brennan also shares many character traits with the serial killer Christopher Pelant. The extremely intelligent but socially isolated Pelant is a genius computer hacker: his savant-level computer skills allow him to seem omnipresent and omniscient (he can hack and manipulate any system). When he uses those skills to frame Brennan for murder, she is forced to run from the law with the help of her ex-convict father. The episodes in which Pelant frames Brennan are so ambiguous that viewers cannot be certain that Brennan is not the killer—in fact, the members of her own team at the Jeffersonian begin to suspect her of murder. In short, the show repeatedly hints that Brennan, by virtue of her intelligence and interest in crime, would make for a particularly dangerous criminal.

Zack, on the other hand, becomes an actual criminal. Taken in by the false logic and smooth rhetoric of a serial killer, Zack becomes his coconspirator and accomplice. It is interesting to note that Zack describes himself as the serial killer's "apprentice"—he abandons his old mentor, who has been teaching him to solve crimes, in favor of a new mentor, who teaches him how to commit them. The implied comparison between the two mentor figures suggests that Brennan may share some traits with the killer. After discovering his guilt, Brennan convinces Zack to confess to the crime, and he is placed in a mental institution. The show depicts the autistic character's sudden conversion from crime fighter to murderer as a change based completely on logic—Brennan must use a syllogism to demonstrate the fault in the killer's reasoning before Zack expresses any regret for the murder. His anguish at the discovery of his faulty logic, the realization that reason has failed him, seems to move him more than the death he caused. Ultimately, Zack's transformation from awkward savant to dangerous killer seems to build on fears that those who act based on logic rather than emotion must be inhuman and, therefore, dangerous. From allusions that hint at Brennan's fearsome criminal potential to Zack's outright participation in a murder, *Bones* aligns its autistic detective figures with serial killers.

Clearly, the character of the autistic detective has maintained his popularity both in the ongoing adaptations of Conan Doyle's work and in various mystery-solving characters based on Sherlock Holmes. Simultaneously both endearingly popular and socially awkward, both inside and outside of the law, both crime fighter and potential criminal, Holmes is a multifacted hero with a complex legacy. Although Conan Doyle was writing at a time when autism was not yet a diagnostic label, new manifestations of his stories are meeting an audience with an ever-growing awareness of ASD. While the figure of the autistic detective may seem positive on the surface, a closer look reveals that these heroes often encourage dangerous tropes regarding cognitive difference. Depicted as cold and emotionless machines, imagined as puzzles to solve, these figures perpetuate negative depictions of people with autism. Although the autistic crime fighter may seem to help dispel false perceptions of people on the spectrum as violent, Holmes and other characters like him maintain a lingering liminality between the autistic detective and the villains he pursues, suggesting that there is something inherently criminal about any kind of cognitive difference.

TWO

The Autistic Savant: *Pygmalion, Saint Joan,* and the Neurodiversity Movement

For success in science or art, a dash of autism is essential.
—Hans Asperger, "Problems of Infantile Autism"

Genius may be an abnormality.
—Temple Grandin, "Genius May Be an Abnormality: Educating
Students with Asperger's Syndrome, or High Functioning Autism"

As the autistic community searches for historical identity, it is surprising to notice that Bernard Shaw appears on almost every list of famous figures associated with the autism spectrum, from T-shirts displaying his distinctively bearded image to chat about him on the online autistic community "Wrong Planet," he is one of the few figures in literary history whom autism advocates claim with pride.[1] While it would be folly to try to diagnose a dead playwright with a neurological difference, it says something about the way that the public imagines autism (and the way that the autistic community perceives itself) that this playwright is consistently claimed as a person with autism.[2] Indeed, multiple elements of Shaw's plays seem to appeal to the "Wrong Planet" sensibility. Comedies that show iconoclasts applauded for behavior that defies clearly established social norms, a belief in creative evolution that hailed the man who does not adapt to his environment as a prophet, and a penchant for plays that value logic and morality over emotion and aesthetics—all have played a role in Shaw's adoption as one of the historical heroes of the neurodiversity movement, and all point paradoxically to cultural stereotypes about autism at the same time that they indicate the autistic community's growing sense of unique identity. While the neurodiversity movement's surprising appropriation of Shaw and his characters may seem superficially beneficial to public perceptions about autism, proposing an autistic identity for characters such as Saint Joan and Henry Higgins (and possibly even Shaw himself) actually threatens to reaffirm damaging stereotypes of people on the spectrum, perpetuating the erroneous idea that all autistic people are geniuses and savants.

The Saint as Savant: *Saint Joan*

Given the diagnostic criteria for ASD, Shaw stands out as one of the autism community's most unexpected figures. Some of the scientists and inventors claimed by the neurodiversity movement seem like obvious choices for autistic heroes, but Bernard Shaw is a more unusual choice: in fact, it seems that his characters, many of whom adhere to the common stereotype of those with autism as eccentric geniuses, have played more of a role in the later construction of Shaw as "autistic" than the character of the man himself. As popular audiences have begun to recognize autistic traits in Shaw's characters, they have also begun to transpose those characteristics onto the playwright, engaging in a vague conflation of author and character.[3] A survey of characters from Shaw's best-known plays (the ones most familiar to a pop culture audience) betrays a collection of eccentric heroes whose poor social skills (or absolute rejection of standard social norms) allow them to work for social change.[4] Because of differences in social and communication skills, people on the spectrum often feel like (or are described by others as) social outsiders.[5] On the whole, Shaw's comedies celebrate the figure of the social outsider, investing the outcast who turns away from society and makes his or her own way with wit, power, and a happy ending. As Sylvan Barnet explains, "Traditional comedy, conceiving of society as having arrived at a satisfactory fixed or static code, censures deviations, but Shaw, subscribing to an evolving cosmos, insists that a consistent allegiance to a code is necessarily ludicrous for it becomes outdated. His comic hero, then, develops, or adopts, a new realistic morality beyond that of his society's idealism. Shavian comedy is critical not of individuals but of society's norm, insisting that the individual who pierces illusions is not absurd but in line with the process of the world spirit."[6]

The social norms that Shaw's plays critique are often based on emotion, hierarchy, and idealism, while his characters rebel against society by creating a logical plan of action. Through their presentation of heroes who are social outcasts, their celebration of eccentric individuality, and their prioritizing of logical solutions over emotional thinking, Shaw's plays align with cultural stereotypes about people on the spectrum. More importantly, many of Shaw's most brilliant characters lack social skills or reject social norms, and these heroes often struggle against norms perpetuated by huge social institutions. While the larger comic pattern at work in Shaw's canon conveys sentiments that are stereotypically associated with individuals on the spectrum, there are many other reasons why people with autism might identify with his heroes. Unfortunately, the interpretation of characters like Joan and Higgins as autistic also forwards the stereotype of all people on the spectrum as savants.

Shaw's Joan adheres to a long list of Asperger's stereotypes: as an example of the stereotypical eccentric genius, she is also the ultimate social outsider and seems completely oblivious to social hierarchy and the nuanced consequences of opposing it. Shaw describes Joan as a character known for her "originality and oddity" and claims that her age and education left her "disabled . . . when she had to deal with such elaborately artificial structures as the great ecclesiastical and social institutions."[7] When she is betrayed by the people she trusts, Shaw explains that the girl is so socially naive that "she did not understand that they were glad to be rid of her" (17). Faced with complex social forces she cannot comprehend, Joan responds with directness and dangerous honesty. According to Shaw, Joan "lacked . . . knowledge of men's vanities and of the weight and proportion of social forces. She knew nothing of iron hands in velvet gloves: she just used her fists" (22). Shaw claims that Joan's age leads to her dangerous social naïveté, but an overall effect of her characterization is reminiscent of a young woman with Asperger's. Regardless of the reasons for her lack of social awareness, she is a heroine who dies because of her poor social skills. In the preface, Shaw explains that "if she had been old enough to know the effect she was producing on the men whom she humiliated by being right when they were wrong, and had learned to flatter and manage them, she might have lived as long as Queen Elizabeth. But she was too young and rustical and inexperienced to have any such arts" (4). In part, Shaw describes Joan's death as a result of her poor social skills: if Joan had only known how to "flatter and manage" people, the play might have a rather different ending.

Shaw presents Joan as a character whose genius keeps her from adapting socially (certainly, a common stereotype of people with Asperger's). In Shaw's version of the story, it is Joan's overweening intellect that contributes to her social naïveté; thus, it is her intellectual gift that both turns her into a saint and leads to her death. Shaw is quick to label his protagonist as "a genius," going on to explain that "a genius is a person who, seeing farther and probing deeper than other people, has a different set of ethical valuations from theirs, and has energy enough to give effect to this extra vision and its valuations in whatever manner best suits his or her specific talents" (7–8). The emphasis on "different . . . ethical valuation" and "specific talents" suggests both the prioritizing of logic and the narrow field of interest so commonly associated with Asperger's. Shaw repeatedly argues that Joan is the victim of intellectual excess—her nature is too reasonable for her to interact well with other human beings. Shaw explains that "an explanation which amounts to Joan being mentally defective instead of, as she obviously was, mentally excessive, will not wash" (13). Comparing Joan to Socrates in the play's preface, Shaw remarks on the intelligence of both characters as the primary reason for their dangerous inability to adapt socially. Socrates "had no suspicion of the extent to which his mental superiority had roused fear and hatred against him in the hearts of men towards whom he was conscious of nothing but good will and good service" (5). Both Joan and Socrates "combined terrifying ability with a frankness, personal modesty, and benevolence which made the furious dislike to which they fell victims absolutely unreasonable, and therefore inapprehensible by themselves" (5). The phrase "terrifying ability" evokes the shock and wonder aroused by the autistic savant. Both characters are intelligent, but they are unable to understand human motivations that are "unreasonable." In Shaw's mind, both Joan and Socrates prioritize reason over emotion—a common stereotype of people on the spectrum. This mindset creates challenges when it comes to feeling and expressing empathy: acting based solely on reason may blind one to the motives of those who act or make decisions based on emotion. It is this very inability to realize what others are feeling that leads to Joan's death, as her reliance on pure intellect makes her the unwitting victim of powerful social forces.

In line with the stereotype that connects mental disorders with genius and creativity, Joan is accused of madness: Shaw goes to great lengths in the play's preface to prove that her mental differences are not a sign of mental defect. For Shaw, Joan's unorthodox behavior is the result of neither insanity nor divine revelation but is a triumph of human creativity and intellect. Shaw claims that the various interpretations imposed on Joan say little about the maid and more about the ignorance of society. As Shaw puts it, "The test of sanity is not the normality of the method but the reasonableness of the discovery" (12). Shaw is quick to dismiss the various labels applied to his protagonist: as he points out in the preface, people claimed that "she was mad, that she was a liar and impostor, that she was a sorceress. . . . [T]he variety of conclusions reached shew how little our matter-of-fact historians know about other people's minds, or even about their own" (11). Specifically, Shaw claims that people are ignorant about the mind: their inability to understand its workings extends not only to people who deviate from the norm but to their own minds as well. These mysterious workings of the human mind (that aspect of autism that causes people to regard it as a mysterious phenomenon) are an important subject in the play's preface. Joan, like many people with autism, thinks in pictures: "She saw imaginary saints just as some other people see imaginary diagrams and landscapes with numbers dotted about them, and are thereby able to perform feats of arithmetic impossible to non-visualizers" (18). This comparison between Joan's visions and the visualization skills of an autistic savant suggests a reason for her visions that is grounded in logical thought. She reaches the answers to battle strategy via logic, but her subconscious mind renders that information in pictures. Shaw compares her to Newton, another figure popularly diagnosed from beyond the grave (in part because of his visual thinking about mathematical concepts) (12). In short, Shaw lauds Joan's visualization skills as a gift of genius and makes a strong case for her as a sane and rational individual: while Shaw's depiction of Joan draws attention to her status as an eccentric savant (building on the cultural stereotype that connects mental disorders with genius), his defense of Joan also anticipates the neurodiversity movement's advocacy of neurological difference.

Overall, the preface to *Saint Joan* draws attention to the definition of "sanity" as a cultural construct: this very discussion, however, emphasizes Shaw's binary approach to mental difference and emphasizes Joan's role as a savant figure. Shaw points out that society draws the line between "normal" and "mental disorder," an ever-moving boundary that has little to do with individual capacity and more to do with changing social norms. Society, Shaw claims, often gets the definitions and labels wrong when it comes to describing other people's minds: "Society must always draw a line somewhere between allowable conduct and insanity . . . in spite of the risk of mistaking sages for lunatics and saviors for blasphemers" (40). The image of the "idiot savant" haunts Shaw's play, as "sage" and "lunatic" become dangerously close social categories—so close that people cannot tell which label to apply. Regardless of whether one is lunatic, sage, or sage because lunatic (or lunatic because sage), Shaw argues that "society is founded on intolerance" (40). Anyone who is outsider enough to earn any of these labels is likely to suffer for it. Yet Shaw adamantly defends Joan from a socially constructed definition of sanity that would exclude her: "For us to set up our condition as a standard of sanity, and declare Joan mad because she never condescended to it, is to prove that we are not only lost but irredeemable" (17). In Shaw's opinion, Joan is above the norm as opposed to below it: she must condescend to lower her own sanity and mental capacity to meet the social expectations of the other characters. On the other hand, society's inability to accept Joan's elevated status as more (rather than less) "sane" shows not only that society is mistaken in its definition of sanity but also that it will never be equipped to understand these distinctions. Shaw's argument that mental difference is not defect might endear him to proponents of the modern neurodiversity movement, but his description of Joan's character holds her up as a savant who would have to "condescend" to think like the majority. In the end, Joan's characterization as a genius visionary with many characteristics of autism does nothing to dispel stereotypes that are still common today: the person whose mind works differently must be either above or below the other characters around her, either highly prized by society or cast out of society, either prophet or fool. Her mental difference sets her apart. She can be a madwoman or a saint, but she can never be a regular person.[8]

Although Joan's characterization may encourage the stereotypes associated with autistic savant figures, the aspects of Joan's personality that are associated with autism allow her to be a champion for social change. Shaw describes Joan as a "visionary": she has the ability to conceive of a different social order and to lead social evolution in a new direction (14). In a typical Shavian diatribe against the conventional man, Shaw claims that "all evolution in thought and conduct must at first appear as heresy and misconduct" (38). Joan is, of course, guilty of heresy and misconduct. According to Shaw, social and cultural growth requires that one "shock conventional people," and Shaw argues that without a "well informed sense of the value of originality, individuality, and eccentricity, the result will be apparent stagnation" (41). Joan's power lies in being an individual set apart from her society. Her status as an outsider allows her to perceive institutionalized lies and outdated ideologies. According to Christopher Innes, Shaw praised Henrik Ibsen's work because he believed it "exposed all collective abstractions as damaging illusions, and promoted the 'individual will' against 'the tyranny of ideals.'"[9] Joan is a heroine in the style of Ibsen, a protagonist who stands heroically against idealism and social illusions. Although other people see her as delusional, Joan uses logic and reason to fight against the collective delusions perpetuated by her society. While Shaw's depiction of Joan as a visionary genius with autistic traits may play into savant stereotypes, Joan remains a Shavian heroine worth celebrating.

Imagining Autism

The Absentminded Professor as Savant: *Pygmalion*

In recent years, the connection between the brilliant but eccentric Henry Higgins and Asperger's syndrome has become popularized on the Internet: Higgins's status as a linguistic genius clearly connects to the stereotype of all people with autism as savants.[10] *Pygmalion*'s socially awkward hero displays multiple characteristics of the condition: his phonetic abilities are savant level, he seems to feel little empathy for Eliza, his social behavior is often inappropriate, and he is obsessed with his mission to transform the flower girl's language at the expense of everything else.[11] When interacting with other people, Higgins rarely interacts with other people—he is more concerned with the concepts and ideas that pertain to his interest in phonetics. From the very beginning of the play, Higgins is designated as a man apart—and depicted as one who literally stands apart from the crowd. In the opening description of Higgins, "all are peering out gloomily at the rain, except one man with his back turned to the rest, wholly preoccupied with a notebook in which he is writing."[12] This seems like a classic example of someone with AS using a distraction to block out the sensory overload of a noisy and crowded environment, for Higgins is surrounded by "torrents of heavy summer rain. Cab whistles blowing frantically in all directions. Pedestrians running for shelter" (13). Higgins quickly turns from the man with his back to the group, however, into the man who is entertaining the group, as his phonetic skills elicit the surprise and wonder associated with savant figures. When he proves that he can identify people's origins based simply on their accents, the bystanders perceive him as "fortune-telling," claiming that he "know[s] everything" (25). The entertainment value of his special skill is immediately the center of attention: "Do you do this for your living at a music hall?" (25). Higgins also struggles with empathy throughout the play.[13] Shaw describes him as "of the energetic scientific type, heartily, even violently interested in everything that can be studied as a scientific subject, and careless about himself and other people, including their feelings" (34). Shaw's promise in this description is borne out when Higgins proves more interested in Eliza as an experiment than he is interested in her as a human being: he shows little concern for her feelings and is indifferent to her future after his experiment is complete.[14] When Pickering asks, "Does it occur to you, Higgins, that the girl has some feelings?" Higgins's answer is surprisingly blunt, "Oh no, I dont think so" (43).[15] Overall, Higgins's incredible phonetic skills, obsessive nature, and problems with empathy suggest the autistic savant stereotype.

Higgins's socially awkward behavior extends beyond trouble with empathy: his bad manners are constantly critiqued by other characters in the play as his savant skills combine with social eccentricity to form the classic Asperger's stereotype.[16] One of the ongoing jokes in *Pygmalion* is the comic irony that arises when a character with poor social skills attempts to teach manners to someone else. Higgins lectures Eliza on the importance of napkins, but the housekeeper must remind him to use them himself: "Might I ask you not to come down to breakfast in your dressing-gown, or at any rate not to use it as a napkin to the extent you do, sir" (52).[17] Mrs. Higgins is constantly commenting on her son's lack of manners: "Im sorry to say that my celebrated son has no manners" (70). Higgins admits that (like many people with AS) he cannot make small talk: "Nonsense. I know I have no small talk; but people dont mind" (68). Physically clumsy, Higgins always seems to be slamming objects about—he handles doors and furniture almost as roughly as he handles Eliza's feelings.[18] Mrs. Higgins's at-home begins when "the door is opened violently; and Higgins enters with his hat on" (67). He does not remember to take his hat off indoors, and his mother has to take it off for him (67). Although Higgins has come to his mother's home to explain that Eliza is making a practice social call, he apparently has no intention of staying for visitors and makes a run for the door when guests are announced, shouting "'Oh Lord!' [He rises: snatches his hat from the table; and makes for the door; but before he reaches it his mother introduces him]" (70). Trapped in the unexpected social encounter, he physically backs away from the guests and stumbles through an uncomfortable greeting:

> Mrs Eynsford Hill. Your celebrated son! I have so longed to meet you, Professor Higgins.
> Higgins. [glumly, making no movement in her direction] Delighted.
> [He backs against the piano and bows brusquely]. (70)[19]

Even the minute details of the stage directions connect Higgins with Asperger's. During his mother's at home, he is constantly berated for fidgeting with the coins and keys in his pocket, and he cannot seem to stop pacing, whistling, and grinding his teeth—all examples of the self-stimulating behaviors associated with ASD.[20] When the role is performed according to Shaw's description of Higgins and the character is not romanticized as a leading man (a practice that Shaw abhorred), audience members may recognize Higgins as being on the spectrum: according to Rodelle Weintraub, the 2004 Shaw Festival Theatre production "gave the audience a Higgins that might have pleased Shaw. Rather than being a handsome, sexy hero, Higgins was a balding, middle-aged eccentric linguist utterly lacking in social skills."[21] When asked in an audience talk-back about the decision to depict Higgins as having Asperger's, artistic director Jackie Maxwell stated that the association between Higgins and AS was not deliberate.[22] Not only does Higgins have many characteristics of AS, but audiences and readers have sometimes identified him as an autistic character, perhaps because he adheres to the savant stereotype so pervasive in popular culture.

In Higgins, Shaw offers a more negative portrayal of a character with autistic tendencies: in the play's preface, however, Shaw excuses Higgins on the basis of his intellectual achievements, explaining that he is socially inept (like Joan and Socrates) because of his intelligence rather than in spite of it. Again, the savant is excused on the basis of his genius. In the play, Higgins comes across as self-involved, obsessive, pedantic, and uncompassionate. Yet Shaw describes Higgins in the preface as "the hero" of the play: he claims that "phoneticians . . . are among the most important people in England at present," and Shaw based the characterization at least partly on phonetics expert Henry Sweet, whom he admired (5, 9). In the preface, Shaw praises Sweet's work and uses Sweet's expertise in his subject to excuse him for his poor social skills. As compared to other, more likable professors, Sweet "lacked their sweetness of character: he was about as conciliatory to conventional mortals as Ibsen" (6). Even this comment shows Shaw's praise: Sweet is unconventional and like Ibsen. Shaw argues that Sweet's inability to get along with his colleagues at Oxford was one of the main reasons that his brilliant work was overlooked in England while his work was praised abroad: "Nothing could bring the man himself into any sort of compliance with the university to which he nevertheless clung by divine right" (6). While Shaw claimed that "Oxford is quite right in demanding a certain social amenity from its nurslings," he felt that the dismissal of Sweet's work was a terrible mistake (8). Because of his lack of social skills, Professor Sweet "might as well have been the Sybil who tore up the leaves of prophecy that nobody would attend to" (7). For Shaw, Sweet was a near-mystic figure, and his intelligence and expertise in his subject were the main reasons he struggled socially: "I well know how hard it is for a man of genius with a seriously underrated subject to maintain serene and kindly relations with the men who underrate it. . . . [S]till, if he overwhelms them with wrath and disdain, he cannot expect them to heap honors on him" (8). The description is similar to what Shaw writes about Joan and Socrates in the preface to *Saint Joan:* the visionary is cast out because he speaks the truth about a subject that others do not value. Shaw describes Sweet (and Higgins), like Joan, as struggling socially because of great intelligence. In spite of his inability to establish relationships with the other characters in the play, Higgins remains a genius. The negative aspects of his character, like Sweet's, are presented as being balanced out by his savant skills, and he is excused from bad social behavior because of academic brilliance.

Clearly, both Joan and Higgins are savant figures who could be seen as possessing autistic traits—and one damaging stereotype about autism is the public perception that all autistic people are savants.[23] Although some might find validation or comfort in statements about the potential academic or intellectual prowess of those on the spectrum (such as the words of Hans Asperger and Temple Grandin that open this chapter), both the Supercrip and savant figures suggest that people with disabilities are worthy only if they overcome or overcompensate for characteristics that may form an integral part of personal identity.[24] It is not surprising that people on the spectrum have banded together to oppose and rewrite negative stereotypes perpetuated by the majority culture. Yet the self-advocacy of autistic adults has been surprisingly ambiguous, and it is not always clear if self-construction within the neurodiversity movement is dismissing the cultural stereotypes perpetuated about ASD or attempting to embrace them. Ultimately, the autism community's willingness to embrace savant figures such as Joan and Higgins only furthers misconceptions about people on the spectrum.

Indeed, Shaw himself is a figure that perpetuates the genius stereotype and could be seen as a kind of literary savant. No doubt one reason for the public diagnosis of Shaw is that he was a man of great intellect and great accomplishment. As such, he joins a growing list of positive role models for those who accept autism as a part of personal identity. It also seems likely that Shaw was chosen because his public persona often presented him as an outsider with a unique (and strongly held) perspective. His name is recognizable as a symbol of "eccentric genius," the hallmark of the Asperger's stereotype forwarded by the media. Even as his characters tread the line between social outcast and celebrated hero, between sage and lunatic, the public conception of Shaw, with his comic words of wisdom and idiosyncratic beliefs on a wide variety of topics, could be seen as haunted by legends of "wise fools" and "idiots savant." Such an ambiguous position sets one apart as a "genius" while simultaneously rendering one an outsider. Such titles offer both praise and dismissal—while Shakespeare's wise fools might speak prophetic truth, they are rarely heeded by the other characters. In a discussion thread on "Wrong Planet" in 2011, a member writes, "I was just thinking about George Bernard Shaw's famous quotation in relation to Aspieness [slang for Asperger's]. . . . The reasonable man adapts himself to the world; the unreasonable one persists in trying to adapt the world to himself. Therefore all progress depends on the unreasonable man."[25] The maxim from *Man and Superman* led to discussion responses that ranged from praising other famous figures believed to be on the spectrum to contemplating the potentially "unreasonable" social behavior of autistic people. One poster responds, "Since Autistics tend to want the world to adapt to them (though they view this 'adaptation' to be the way 'the world ought to be' to begin with), they are often viewed by those who readily accept that which is already 'acceptable' to society as 'unreasonable.'"[26] Like his characters, Shaw gained a reputation for genius partially because of his radical beliefs, his confrontational willingness to speak the truth, and his ability to resist the allure of group ideologies—his own ability to be "unreasonable" in the face of social norms. It seems clear why such a figure is appealing as a romanticized vision of the strengths that autism could lend to a powerful personality— yet while autism advocates may delight in Shaw's eccentricity as a public figure, the popular conception of him as an outcast genius only serves to reinforce the savant stereotype already pervasive in media depictions of ASD.

While claiming Shaw and his characters as in some way autistic may do some superficially positive work for the place of autism in popular culture, it simultaneously perpetuates the savant stereotype. In many ways, the autistic community's claiming of Shaw and his characters merely furthers the false binary propagated by seemingly "objective" medical discourse and blatantly fictionalized media representations.[27] Medical discourse constructs a definition of autism using the language of "deficit" and "loss" ("a deficit in social skills"), while the media construct autism in terms of fantastic excess (the savant and his compensation cure).[28] Neither extreme is an accurate representation. Again and again, Shaw's depiction of eccentric characters blames social deficit on intellectual excess and claims the compensation of savant skills as a recompense for social disability. Furthermore, if the claiming of Shaw and figures like him is intended to combat the stereotype of all people with Asperger's as geniuses, the community is choosing the wrong figures and drawing attention to the wrong set of characters. While Shavian geniuses and visionaries may present a picture of life on the spectrum that is largely positive, such a vision is obviously one-sided. As Sharon Snyder and David Mitchell explain, those who "fill in an alternative 'positive' content of disability experience . . . merely replace one form of historical simplification with another."[29] Although the opposite of deficit and loss is gain, the experience of living with autism is more complex than either. As for Joan and Higgins, they are characters who express Shaw's "major themes: the fallacies of idealism being ridiculed or demolished . . . while the moral primacy of the individual will forms the basis for the concept of Superman."[30] In the end, describing Bernard Shaw as a person with autism and looking to his plays for autistic role models yields to the Superman and his unattainable power. Like any minority group subject to stereotyping, adults with autism have internalized some of the cultural stereotypes that surround them: perhaps they are even deliberately embracing some of those stereotypes. Certainly, when Shaw's characters display signs of autism, those signs are paired with savant skills, incredible intellect, and brilliant wit. The Shavian Superman may be on the spectrum, but he is a Superman still.

THREE

The Autistic Victim: *Of Mice and Men* and *Flowers for Algernon*

We must be concerned not merely about who murdered them, but about the system, the way of life, the philosophy which produced the murderers.
—Martin Luther King Jr., "Eulogy for the Martyred Children"

Autistic people are particularly likely to be the victims of filicide.[1] The collection *Loud Hands: Autistic People, Speaking,* edited by Julia Bascom and published by the Autistic Self Advocacy Network in 2012, is dedicated to thirty-six people, all of them disabled (most of them autistic), all of them killed by caregivers or family members (most of them parents). Neurodiversity.com, dedicated to autism-related issues and managed by Kathleen Seidel, maintains a list of names under the heading "Murder of Autistic Persons."[2] The list is long. Such cases often garner great attention from the media—but the focus is rarely on the autistic victim.[3] As Stuart Murray notes, "In the majority of these cases the focus of the media coverage is not on the child who has died, but rather on the parent."[4] Media coverage of these "mercy killings" often solicit sympathy for the killer.[5] To give only one example, after Daniela Dawes killed her ten-year-old son, Jason, ABC reported that "Jason Dawes was diagnosed as autistic when he was 18 months old. At the age of 10 he had the mental age of a 3-year-old. He couldn't speak and he needed constant help to eat, bathe, and go to the toilet. Most of that responsibility fell to his mother, Daniela Dawes. . . . It all got too much for her on August the fourth last year. That day she suffocated her son and then tried to kill herself."[6] When the victim of the crime is disabled, the killer may even be more likely to receive a reduced sentence. (Dawes's sentence was reduced: she pleaded guilty to murder in 2004 but was "ultimately sentenced to a five-year good-behavior bond.")[7] Media coverage that is sympathetic to autistic filicide, presenting parents as overwhelmed by their children's care or depicting murder as an act of mercy (highlighting the pain the disabled child was believed to be suffering), works together with reduced sentences to suggest a lack of cultural value placed on autistic personhood. In this chapter, I want to explore the fluid boundary between fiction and reality in literature about autistic characters in order to contemplate the various ways in which reality influences fiction (and fiction influences reality) in cultural discourses about characters (and people) with autistic characteristics. I am not arguing that any real-life tragedy was inspired by any fictional event, only that assumptions that devalue autistic identity and stereotypes that create fear and discrimination may be in dialogue between media interpretations of actual events and depictions of characters in fictional works. Fictional depictions found in literary texts and the public interpretation of actual events become mutually sustaining social artifacts that forge a cultural connection between autism and death. The interconnection of the "cure or kill" trope of disability studies and real-life events tragically reinforces cultural attitudes that regard neurotypical subjectivity as the only subjectivity.[8]

Of Mice and Men and Autistic Filicide

Some might argue that actual deaths have little to do with fictional depictions of people on the spectrum: the Texas legal system's appropriation and interpretation of Steinbeck's novella *Of Mice and Men* is a reminder of the powerful impact that fictional representations of disability can have on the actual perceptions of cognitively disabled subjectivity. In 2002 the U.S. Supreme Court ruled that individuals with intellectual disability (those with IQs measured to be below the average range) could not receive the death penalty.[9] The state of Texas, however, has continued to execute individuals who qualify as intellectually disabled under guidelines established by the American Association on Intellectual and Developmental Disabilities.[10] Instead of using clinical tests developed by psychologists to diagnose intellectual disability, Texas courts use characteristics known as "the Briseño factors."[11] This group of criteria was developed by the Texas Court of Criminal Appeals and is based on Steinbeck's character Lennie Small.[12] As the court explains, "Most Texas citizens might agree that Steinbeck's Lennie should, by virtue of his lack of reasoning ability and adaptive skills, be exempt" from the death penalty.[13] The literary character has become adapted into law, as the court rules that individuals judged to be less impaired than the fictional Lennie may be executed, while those judged to be more impaired than the literary character may not.[14] Steinbeck's son has objected strenuously to this use of his father's novella: "I had no idea that the great state of Texas would use a fictional character that my father created . . . as a benchmark to identify whether defendants with intellectual disability should live or die."[15] The Texas law using a literary character to define intellectual disability is a startling reminder of the influence that fictional depictions can have on public opinions. Indeed, *Of Mice and Men* is so deeply woven into our cultural narratives of disability and euthanasia that it has sometimes been taught in classes on medical ethics, forming part of the education of another professional group called upon to make life and death decisions.[16] Steinbeck's fictional account of a cognitively disabled man influencing death penalty laws in Texas shows that literary depictions of disabled subjectivity can have a strong influence on public policy.

Although *Of Mice and Men* is a staple of the U.S. high school curriculum and the book has received abundant attention from literary critics, the novella has seldom received analysis from a disability studies perspective: this dearth of disability approaches to the novella may be connected to Lennie's perceived lack of subjectivity as a cognitively disabled character. As Sally Chivers argues, "Though overtly 'about' disability, Steinbeck's novella *Of Mice and Men* has largely escaped notice in the emerging field of disability studies, likely because of its simple moral lesson that leaves little room for complex analysis."[17] In fact, Steinbeck's presentation of Lennie as a character lacking in human subjectivity may motivate this avoidance on the part of disability studies scholars. One dangerous cultural perception that ignores autistic subjectivity is the tendency to see autistic characters (and people) only as they relate to neurotypicals. Many disability studies critics have noted that disabled characters in literary works and films are often minor characters: while they may prove central to the plot, these figures generally appear on the margins of the story. This is a particularly pervasive and significant facet of characterization for figures with intellectual disabilities, reflecting real-life perceptions that deny the subjectivity of those with cognitive differences. While Lennie is a major character, he is completely subordinated to George in the course of the novella's plot: the reader is subtly guided to empathize with George and to see Lennie only through his relationship with his neurotypical friend. As Patrick McDonagh explains, "In literature characters with intellectual disability are rarely considered on their own terms so much as in their relationships to other people. The same holds true beyond the text."[18] Disability studies scholar Licia Carlson, who specializes in intellectual disability, is often disturbed when people ask her if she has a disabled family member: "As I have delved deeper into the margins of philosophy, this relatively benign question has come to represent far more troubling beliefs that I have encountered. First, the intellectually disabled are not persons. They are owed respect and justice only by virtue of their relationship to non-disabled family members who are persons."[19] In other words, a disability studies reading of Lennie as autistic requires a critical approach to a character deemed (in literary and cultural discourses) as a virtual nonentity, and a lack of critical attention to his perceived absence or vacancy in the narrative may be part of larger cultural trends that categorically deny cognitively disabled subjectivity.

No literary critic has ever suggested that Lennie may be on the autism spectrum; it is clear, however, that autistic traits are key to Lennie's character. Reading Lennie as autistic gives his death an uncomfortably contemporary political dimension in relation to recent media depictions of autistic filicide and raises moral questions regarding public perceptions of autistic subjectivity.[20] It is clear that Lennie adheres to many of the stereotypes commonly perpetuated about people with intellectual disability. However, Lennie is also depicted as a recognizably autistic character. At least one theatrical production has made the decision to represent Lennie as overtly autistic, clarifying the exact nature of his intellectual disability for the audience.[21] Certainly, Lennie's special interest in animals is one of the defining attributes of his character. He talks endlessly about his desire to own rabbits: "I wish't we'd get the rabbits pretty soon, George."[22] He also engages in stimming: when overstimulated or stressed, Lennie "flapped his big hands" or "rocked himself back and forth" (67, 83). He relies strongly on ritual and routine (especially the ritual of George repeatedly narrating the story of their imagined farm).[23] His social naïveté, trusting nature, and intellectual disability present serious challenges to his self-care skills (it is likely that he could not find and maintain work without George's help). Furthermore, Lennie's sensory difference leads to the novella's climactic conflict, as his desire for sensory stimulation (stroking soft animals or materials) ultimately results in an accidental death.[24] While studies have shown that it is virtually unheard of for autistic sensory issues to contribute to violent behavior, Steinbeck's popular novella offers sensory integration dysfunction as the primary cause in a murder.[25] Although this turn of events is extremely improbable, it may give modern readers (who are generally more aware of autistic traits than a 1930s audience would have been) a feeling of unease, causing them to perceive people on the spectrum as potentially dangerous. Ultimately, Lennie's death is "authorized" by cultural discourses that depict autistic people as violent and threatening because of a perceived lack of human subjectivity.

Multiple stereotypes regarding autism and intellectual disability help to reduce the reader's perception of Lennie's subjectivity and thus to validate the supposed heroism of George's mercy killing.[26] For example, Steinbeck depicts Lennie as both childlike and unusually large and strong.[27] During the early 1900s, "popular discussions of intellectual disability constructed it in two ways: the body could be seen as physically incompetent, a reflection of the mind's vacancy, or it could become dangerously healthy, an exemplar of the body without a mind to control it."[28] Although autism conveys no particular physical attributes, public perceptions of those on the spectrum as unusually large and strong are still prevalent today.[29] Benjy Compson of *The Sound and the Fury* (see the discussion in chapter 4) is another autistic character who is depicted as being an unusually large man (he is much taller than his caregiver, Luster, and Faulkner compares him to a lumbering bear). Indeed, Faulkner's description of Benjy is remarkably similar to Steinbeck's description of Lennie.[30] Steinbeck describes Lennie as "a huge man, shapeless of face, with large, pale eyes, with wide, sloping shoulders; he walked heavily, dragging his feet a little, the way a bear drags his paws. His arms did not swing at his sides, but hung loosely" (2). As Martin Halliwell argues, "Lennie's 'shapeless' features and 'heavy' walk mark him out as an idiot figure, with his large size, his proximity to animals (bear) and objects (pendulum) reinforcing his lack of freewill and rationality."[31] A plethora of stereotypes combine in Steinbeck's description: the autistic Lennie is unusually large, animal-like, mechanical, clumsy, and symbolically deprived of "freewill and rationality." Indeed, Lennie's strong connection with (and frequent comparison to) animals is an example of an overarching literary trend: "The relationship between intellectual disability and animality has a long history."[32] As many critics have noted, Steinbeck constantly compares Lennie to animals throughout the novella.[33] This literary depiction participates in a larger philosophical trend: "Animal rights theorists have paid special attention to those with cognitive disabilities. Some have averred that we need to parse our moral universe so that 'normal' human and nonhuman beings who possess the capacity for reason constitute one category, while nonhuman animals and intellectually subpar humans together constitute another. If these philosophers are right, then people who are lacking the capacity . . . for rational deliberation cannot be our equals—they are non-persons. . . . The controversy indicates the extent to which the moral status of individuals with cognitive disabilities remains unsettled."[34] Writing in 2009, Carlson noted that even with an ever-increasing awareness of disability rights, "when I looked for contemporary discussions about this group [people with intellectual disabilities], most of the references I found were in discussions of animal rights, asking pointedly whether the severely mentally retarded can be distinguished from

The Autistic Victim

non-human animals in any meaningful sense."[35] These stereotypes (dangerous uncontrollable size and animal metaphors) work together in forming the literary (and cultural) texts that reduce Lennie's perceived subjectivity and humanity, thus "authorizing" Lennie's autistic filicide.

In the novella, Steinbeck builds on common stereotypes of mental disability to transform an actual murder that he witnessed into a fictional tale: these alterations to the real-life events work to reduce Lennie's subjectivity and agency. In reality, Steinbeck's Lennie was based on a man whom Steinbeck had known in his own days working as a migrant worker: "The characters are composites to some extent. Lennie was a real person. He's in an insane asylum in California right now. I worked alongside him for many weeks. He didn't kill a girl. He killed a ranch foreman. Got sore because the boss had fired his pal and stuck a pitchfork right through his stomach. I hate to tell you how many times. I saw him do it. We couldn't stop him until it was too late."[36] The actual event on which Steinbeck's work was based was wildly different from the situation presented in the novella. In reality, the murder had a different motive (in Steinbeck's opinion, the man committed murder because "the boss had fired his pal"), the victim of the crime is altered (the foreman is killed, not his wife), the manner of death is more overtly violent (a deliberate stabbing as opposed to an accident), and the disability status of the killer is highly ambiguous (Steinbeck perceived the man as having some kind of intellectual disability, although his depiction of Lennie highlights traits strongly associated in the public mind with autism). By altering the perceived level of violence and the motive for the murder, Steinbeck clearly depicts the crime in the novella as accidental rather than deliberate, thus creating an ambiguous moral dilemma that has tortured generations of high school students. More importantly, Steinbeck's alterations of his real-life source material highlight Lennie's disability and difference. The change of perceived motive for the crime—a move from social motivation to sensory motivation—emphasizes Lennie's fundamental Otherness: neurotypical readers are not likely to share Lennie's intense sensory responses. Significantly, Steinbeck presents Lennie's sensory issues as a force that controls his character. A murder driven by sensory needs greatly reduces Lennie's agency: he seems to be controlled by his impairment. In short, Steinbeck alters his real-life source material in ways that highlight Lennie's autistic nature and that may reduce the character's subjectivity.

However, the most telling alteration from the real-life case is that of the gender of the victim: the circumstances surrounding the death of Curley's wife invoke stereotypical fears of disabled sexuality, depicting sexuality as an uncontrollable force that overrides Lennie's agency. The fear of disabled sexuality has a long cultural lineage, and the eugenics movement of the early twentieth century created an environment that only served to reinforce "societal fears that cognitively disabled men are always potentially violent sexual predators."[37] During this time period, "sexual criminality was seen as synonymous with cognitive impairment."[38] Indeed, many literary critics have noted the implied potential for sexual violence underlying the accidental death in Steinbeck's novella. Although Lennie's encounter with Curley's wife is clearly not a rape, "the implication of sexual danger exists at the level of word transfer: petting animals versus petting women changes the whole nature of the event."[39] Leo Gurko agrees: "Lennie is . . . presented as a violent sexual predator."[40] In fact, one of the official "articles of belief" (published in 1912) justifying the eugenics movement stated that "feeble-minded persons, especially females, have abnormally strong sex drives which they are unable to control."[41] Unfortunately, these stereotypes regarding disabled sexuality have persisted into modern discourses in various ways. There are still false rumors on the Internet that men with Asperger's are more likely to commit rape than their neurotypical counterparts, although there is no evidence to support such claims (these rumors may be based on a misplaced fear that difficulty decoding social cues might result in an inability to recognize a woman's lack of consent). Sensory issues that involve hypersensitivity to touch may also be misinterpreted or falsely sexualized. As Halliwell argues, "Lennie's love of fur and soft material is certainly an indication of his polymorphous sexuality."[42] Interpreting Lennie as autistic, I would argue that his intense desire for this kind of sensory input is a result of sensory integration needs that have little or no relationship to sexuality.[43] In general, cultural depictions of people on the spectrum display the two stereotypical extremes accorded by our society to disabled sexuality in general (people with disabilities are imagined as either asexual or as hypersexual/sexually deviant).[44] While the stereotype of the asexual savant has been more popular in the past two decades (think of television characters such as Spencer Reid and Dr. Sheldon Cooper of *The Big Bang Theory*), people with cognitive impairments were more likely to be imagined as hypersexual in the 1920s and 1930s. Clearly, these attitudes contributed to the widespread sterilization and institutionalization of people with mental disabilities during this era.[45]

In fact, the implied potential for sexual violence in Lennie's depiction is reinforced by the proposed punishment for his crime: Curley and the other ranch workers threaten to lynch the cognitively disabled man, thus intertwining cultural narratives of eugenics and ableism with historical discourses surrounding rape and racism. According to Michelle Jarman, in "the early twentieth century . . . discourses surrounding white-on-black lynching and the eugenic castration of cognitively disabled men," while forming "distinct historical practices, . . . are actually profoundly interconnected."[46] Jarman goes on to explore the "link . . . between eugenic narratives of abnormal sexuality and the rape stories used to mobilize racist mob violence," explaining that "the 'black rapist' and the sexually aggressive 'moron' represented tangible threats to the sanctity of white domesticity. White men . . . cast themselves as chivalrous heroes who rescued 'their' women and families by eliminating these menaces."[47] Like the imaginary threat to women supposedly posed by victims of lynching, the popular construction of cognitively disabled men as hypersexualized set up a particular minority group as a perceived threat to a normative ideal of white heterosexual marriage.[48] It is significant that Lennie (as a representative of disabled sexuality) kills a married woman rather than a single one, as he symbolically comes between Curley and his wife. In Steinbeck's novella, however, it is George who is depicted as heroic, as his killing of his friend serves to protect normative sexuality from the uncontrollable and hypersexualized disabled body, symbolically "protecting" his society from the possibility that Lennie will pass on a genetic legacy of mental disability. Overall, the fictional female victim draws attention to larger cultural fears of disabled sexuality and ultimately suggests that Lennie, driven by sexual need, is out of control and lacking in agency.

Yet George's act of euthanasia is culturally authorized by more than just hints of potential sexual violence: animal metaphors are again brought into play to justify his actions and to present Lennie as lacking in human subjectivity. Edward E. Waldron has noted that "Steinbeck uses Candy's early behavior toward his dog as both a foreshadowing and an example against which to measure George's behavior toward Lennie."[49] As Stephanie Jensen-Moulton explains, "In the novel, Steinbeck does not afford Lennie fully human stature. He is cruelly executed in exactly the same manner as Candy's old dog."[50] Approval of these actions is directly provided by Slim, "the prince of the ranch" whose word is "law." Slim approves of both the killing of Candy's dog and George's execution of Lennie: "This confirmation of the necessity of his action might not comfort George, but it does affirm for the reader the lightness of George's action in the value scheme of the novel."[51] Waldron and Jensen-Moulton have both noted that Steinbeck's use of animal imagery is an underlying argument for Lennie's death. According to Waldron, "A point often made by proponents of active euthanasia for hopelessly dying patients is that we accept such actions on behalf of animals in our society."[52] In sum, Lennie's comparison to animals validates his death by denying that people with cognitive disabilities have human subjectivity.

Ultimately, Lennie's death might serve as a theoretical example of the ways in which the cultural denial of autistic subjectivity informs violence: the death of a cognitively disabled person may be read through the lens of euthanasia regardless of circumstance. The belief that there is no subjectivity within the intellectually disabled body, that the autistic body is an empty frame that must inevitably be suffering, seems to underpin common responses to Steinbeck's novella. George's killing of Lennie is most often understood as a form of euthanasia.[53] Waldron's interpretation is typical of this common approach: "George knows that Lennie will die as the result of his killing Curley's wife, either by being blasted by Curley and the other hands or by being locked up in an institution. Lennie is, in effect, 'terminally ill,' that is, he faces imminent death. George chooses to provide a more tolerable form of dying for his friend."[54] As a matter of fact, Lennie isn't terminally ill. He is about to be lynched. What if Lennie were not disabled but were instead part of another cultural minority group? If Lennie were African American, would his white friend George be portrayed as a hero for shooting him in order to prevent a lynching?[55] If we imagine Lennie as part of a different cultural group, the pivotal role of society and discrimination in George's "merciful" decision is suddenly all too apparent. As Jarman explains, our society views racial issues as "volatile, divisive, and political," while disability issues are generally viewed as "medical and individual."[56] The political and public aspect of Lennie's death (threatened lynching) is obfuscated in critical discussions of Steinbeck's work because readers and critics usually focus on the isolated and private aspect of Lennie's death (what is culturally read as euthanasia). Such an approach denies disability as a social and political issue, insisting that impairment be read as a private tragedy.[57]

Furthermore, stereotypes about autism work in subtle ways to culturally authorize George's criminal act. Lennie is depicted as being unable to understand the full magnitude of what he has done and as having so little control that he may not be able to prevent doing it again in the future. In effect, the novella is *only* able to present mercy killing as a viable moral option because Lennie is disabled— the plot of the novella simply would not make sense in our cultural imagination if Lennie were neurotypical. George kills his autistic friend because Lennie faces social discrimination that the novella presents as natural, justified, and unchangeable. In fact, the novella was first titled *Something That Happened*: "Steinbeck was not interested in exploring the reasons why events transpired in a particular way, but tried to focus on a particular occurrence and its consequences."[58] Of course, Lennie's death, while depicted as though divorced from both past and future, an unpreventable tragedy in which no other course is possible, is not just "something that happened" but a choice that George (and Steinbeck) make as a result of a certain set of cultural ideologies. Because the autistic victim is presented as being without true subjectivity, readers may falsely perceive George's choice as the only option when in fact other options exist. Shouldn't George try to stop the mob? Or try to turn his friend in to authorities who will prevent the mob violence? Or even try to help his friend escape because George knows that the court system will not render true justice? On a larger scale, the novella does not address the role of good care, education, and therapy for Lennie. Lennie's material conditions and socioeconomic status come into play here: George cannot afford to find appropriate care and therapy.[59] Shouldn't those circumstances be changed? Placing Lennie in an institution is also disregarded as a viable option because psychiatric institutions are perceived to be places of suffering. Shouldn't such institutions be changed? If a jury is perceived as being unable to render true justice for Lennie, shouldn't the prejudices of the jury be changed? George finds that shooting his autistic friend is easier than answering any of these questions.

If Lennie is an autistic character, then his death at George's hands gains contemporary relevance in comparison to recent media depictions of autistic filicide: media representations of these tragedies broach the division between literary fiction and reality, as these cultural texts (televised reports, newspaper articles, and online blogs) deny autistic subjectivity and assume the lens of euthanasia. George is Lennie's only "family," and Steinbeck presents him as both guardian and father figure for his infantilized friend:

> George's voice became deeper. He repeated his words rhythmically as though he had said them many times before. "Guys like us, that work on ranches, are the loneliest guys in the world. They got no family. They don't belong no place. . . ."
> Lennie broke in. *"But not us! An' why? Because . . . because I got you to look after me, and you got me to look after you, and that's why."* (14–15, second ellipses in the original)

Violence against people with autism is often perpetrated by family members.[60] Rosemarie Garland-Thomson has written about "the cultural logic of euthanasia": "The logic of 'cure or kill,' accompanied by today's faith in technology, is that if the disabled body cannot be normalized, it must be eliminated. If it does not respond to being improved, if it refuses to register the success of the rescuer's moral or technological efforts, the disabled body becomes intolerable, a witness to the human inability to perfect the world."[61] Many readers see George, in his role as both father and killer, as Lennie's "rescuer."[62] The critical history of Steinbeck's work seems to affirm the supposition that Lennie is without subjectivity, that he does not exist without his neurotypical friend. In the end, the ethical debate that has engaged generations of critics (and generations of high school students) is not really about Lennie's death so much as it is about George's decision.

"Up and Down" the Spectrum:
Autistic Fictions in *Flowers for Algernon*

Daniel Keyes's *Flowers for Algernon* is another iconic classroom text that treats cognitive disability and engages with various autistic fictions.[63] Although Charlie Gordon, the tale's protagonist, is specifically described as having phenylketonuria (PKU), his story builds on cultural myths about intellectual disability (and intellectual ability) that reflect current stereotypes about the autism spectrum.[64] Specifically, the imaginary "cure" for intellectual disability that increases Charlie's IQ moves him from one set of autism stereotypes to another, merely shifting his place on the larger spectrum of neurodiversity rather than rendering him neurotypical. In other words, Charlie moves from representing stereotypes commonly associated with intellectual disability to embodying stereotypes associated with the genius autistic savant. Keyes's novel devalues both ends of the "spectrum," presenting the intellectually disabled Charlie as a child worthy of pity and the savant Charlie as egocentric, didactic, and unempathetic.[65] Both sets of stereotypes work to reduce the subjectivity of those with cognitive differences (whether they have PKU, autism spectrum disorder, or some other form of cognitive disability). While the novel depicts both ends of the spectrum in damaging and stereotypical ways, it ultimately prioritizes the traits more often associated with the "higher functioning" end of the autism spectrum, reflecting larger cultural controversies regarding disability representation and oppression (including some controversies within the autism community itself).

First, Charlie's depiction as an intellectually disabled character is riddled with damaging stereotypes: in this novel, intellectually disabled people are assumed to be both lazy and lacking in human subjectivity. The novel is written in first person, with Charlie narrating his story through the progress reports he writes for his doctors. The early reports demonstrate poor spelling and punctuation in an attempt to realistically portray intellectual disability. This use of "dialect" could be seen as offensive: the spelling and grammar errors that are meant to indicate cognitive disability are a kind of performance—a way for the neurotypical writer to assume rhetorical blackface.[66] Other characters frequently speak in front of Charlie as though he were not present—he is assumed to lack understanding (and therefore subjectivity): "People have always spoken and acted as if I weren't there, as if they never cared what I overheard."[67] In his journal, Charlie uses asterisks to indicate the words he does not understand: "Most people of his low ment** are host** and uncoop** they are usually dull and apathet** and hard to reach. Charlie has a good natcher and hes intristed and eeger to please" (8–9). Here the reader has to fill in the terms that Charlie does not comprehend: "Most people of his low mentality are hostile and uncooperative. They are usually dull and apathetic and hard to reach." Charlie is chosen for the experimental procedure because he is perceived as ambitious and hardworking, two characteristics that Professor Nemur believes most individuals with intellectual disability lack. Nemur's attitude perpetuates the false stereotype that those with cognitive disabilities are lazy rather than impaired. Charlie's ambition to learn and his caring manner are both presented as being unusual for someone with an intellectual disability, thus making him an "overcomer" figure who stands out in Nemur's mind.

Like Lennie, the intellectually disabled Charlie is aligned with animals, and he is depicted as a childlike "innocent": such representations work to decrease the perceived subjectivity of those with intellectual disability. Charlie's sympathy for the lab rat Algernon is clear: "I dont think its right to make you pass a test to eat. How would Burt [the graduate assistant conducting the experiments] like to have to pass a test every time he wants to eat. I think Ill be frends with Algernon" (31). In many ways, the book makes it seem as though the "childlike" and "innocent" Charlie is unable to feel the abuse and bullying that the other characters heap upon him, suggesting that intellectually disabled people are so socially unaware that they don't feel the pain of mockery and rejection. Charlie does not realize when he is being bullied and believes that his abusers are his friends: "He really pulled a Charlie Gordon that time. I dont know why they say it but they always laff and I laff too" (23). Brent Walter Cline argues that the novel forwards "the pity-inducing trope of infantilizing the mentally disabled" and notes that "even the laudable, intelligent Charlie cannot accept the full humanity of the pre-operative Charlie."[68] Indeed, when Charlie begins to return to his old self, he says that "the child in me is reclaiming my mind," thus denying the full subjectivity and adulthood of his former self (298). When Charlie later realizes that a coworker has used him to help embezzle money from the boss, he is stricken with guilt. However, Dr. Strauss tries to convince Charlie that when he was intellectually disabled he lacked agency (and therefore responsibility). As Charlie relates, Dr. Strauss tells him that "I'm no more to blame than the knife is to blame in a stabbing or the car in a collision" (89). All of these stereotypes work to reduce Charlie's subjectivity.

Even though the novel was published thirty years after *Of Mice and Men*, the fear of disabled sexuality is alive and well in *Flowers for Algernon*: Charlie is presented as both sexual threat and potential victim of filicide. Rose, Charlie's mother, is afraid that he will sexually assault his neurotypical sister Norma: "If you ever touch a girl, I'll put you away in a cage, like an animal, for the rest of your life. Do you hear me?" (112). After the operation, Charlie doubts himself, fearing that the cultural stigma regarding disabled sexuality could be true: "I wondered if I had ever done anything to justify my mother's fear. There were no such memories, but how could I be sure there weren't horrible thoughts repressed behind the barriers of my tortured conscience? . . . Possibly I will never know. Whatever the truth is, I must not hate Rose for protecting Norma. I must understand the way she saw it. Unless I forgive her, I will have nothing" (275). By claiming that Charlie must understand and forgive his mother for her actions, the novel seems to authorize them: even Charlie sees the intellectually disabled version of himself as a potential sexual threat. The novel is also haunted by threats of filicide. Throwing her teenaged son out of the house, Charlie's mother screams, "He's better off dead. He'll never be able to live a normal life" (184). She also threatens her son with a knife: "On the way out, Charlie sees on the kitchen table the long carving knife she cuts roasts with, and he senses vaguely that she wanted to hurt him" (184–185). These threats indicate the lack of subjectivity and value that Rose Gordon attributes to her intellectually disabled child. Overall, these stereotypes (Charlie is presented as lacking in ambition and emotion, as having a connection to animals, as being simultaneously a sexual threat and a childlike victim) reduce Charlie's perceived subjectivity.

Furthermore, the postoperative Charlie is not neurotypical—the experimental "cure" seems to have transformed the young man with PKU into an autistic savant, complete with all of the common Asperger's stereotypes. The experiment moves Charlie from intellectual disability to social disability, embracing the stereotype that presents "excessive" intelligence as a social problem.[69] Charlie now has a variety of savant skills (he is a polyglot and has an eidetic memory, as well as having high-level skills in neuroscience and math), but they seemingly come at a price—these skills are the "compensation cure" for Charlie's social disability.[70] The novel presents Charlie as being socially awkward because he is *too* smart. Charlie struggles to make conversation at a party: "I started out the evening with every intention of being pleasant and making friends. But these days I have trouble getting through to people. . . . [A]ny attempt at conversation usually fades away in a minute or two, and the barriers go up" (242). The genius savant may be boring his listeners with pedantic monologues: "The same thing happened when I tried to discuss Chaucer with an American literature specialist, questioned an Orientalist about the Trobriand Islanders. . . . They would always find excuses to slip away, afraid to reveal the narrowness of their knowledge" (98). What Charlie does not seem to realize is that an American literature specialist is not going to be interested in Chaucer: he probably finds Charlie's choice of subject boring. While Charlie perceives others as trying to hide their lack of knowledge, they may in truth simply be uninterested in the highly specialized subjects he pursues. As Burt explains to Charlie, "You're lopsided. You know things. You see things. But you haven't developed understanding, or—I have to use the word—tolerance" (152). Indeed, most of the understanding (and tolerance) that the new Charlie seems to lack is in the area of social skills.

The "new" Charlie is rigid, rule bound, obsessed with his work, and separated from the people around him by his intense interests: all are common Asperger's stereotypes that seem to come into play as a result of Charlie's increased intelligence. Charlie's girlfriend, Fay, clearly perceives him as rigid and rule bound. She describes Charlie's new lifestyle: "Everything is too neat and straight and you're all boxed in" (193). Charlie's interpretations are always rule bound and literal: "It's a lie. . . . Things just don't happen that way. . . . [E]ven in the world of make-believe there have to be rules" (77). The giant maze he builds for Algernon is exactly the kind of unusual hobby stereotypically associated with the autism spectrum: "I'm going to move most of the furniture out of the second bedroom and use the room for Algernon. I plan to build him a three-dimensional maze out of scrap plastic" (172). Charlie's newfound love of scientific pursuits is clearly his true passion: "They all think I'm killing myself at this pace, but what they don't understand is that I'm living at a peak of clarity and beauty I never knew existed. Every part of me is attuned to the work. I soak it up into my pores during the day, and at night—in the moments before I pass off into sleep—ideas explode into my head like fireworks. . . . This is joy. . . . I am in love with what I am doing" (240–241). However, Charlie chooses his work over his relationship with Fay: "I've had a cot moved into the lab. She's become too possessive and re-

Imagining Autism

sentful of my work" (236). Charlie has segued from the stereotype of the cognitively disabled as hypersexual to the stereotype of the asexual savant. Overall, Charlie's depiction suggests that Asperger's traits are commonly aligned in the cultural imagination with increased intelligence.

In addition, the novel plays on stereotypes suggesting that high intelligence prevents people from being emotionally engaged and empathetic, falsely presenting reason and emotion as opposing binaries: the other characters perceive the genius Charlie as unempathetic and egocentric. Alice, Charlie's current love interest and former teacher, emphasizes the novel's sharp division between reason and emotion: "Charlie, you amaze me. In some ways you're so advanced, and yet when it comes to making a decision, you're still a child. . . . [T]he answer can't be found in books. . . . You've got to find the answer inside you—*feel* the right thing to do" (91). Charlie's new genius status does not prevent the other characters from viewing him as childlike. He is still mentally disabled, and the characters around him recognize his disability status by treating him like a child. Charlie resents this treatment and accuses Alice of treating him as though he were "emotionally retarded" (92). His choice of terminology reminds the reader that his disability label has followed him even after the operation. Dr. Nemur clearly feels that Charlie's increased intelligence has made him less empathetic and emotionally engaged: "This experiment was calculated to raise your intelligence. . . . We had no control over what happened to your personality, and you've developed from a likeable, retarded young man into an arrogant, self-centered, antisocial bastard" (246). In addition, Charlie's newfound intelligence seems to naturally lead to self-absorption: "I was an arrogant, self-centered bastard. Unlike [the old] Charlie, I was incapable of making friends or thinking about other people and their problems. I was interested in myself, and myself only" (252–253). Even Charlie perceives the savant version of himself as rude and egotistical, thus connecting his depiction with negative stereotypes frequently associated with Asperger's syndrome.

Furthermore, his newfound savant skills separate Charlie from other people: the genius Charlie is presented as being incapable of love—especially of the romantic relationship he desires with Alice. Where Charlie was once perceived as a sexual threat (a person driven by uncontrolled and excessive sexual desire), he is now unable to act on his desires to consummate his relationship with Alice (he is hindered by uncontrolled intellect and excessive thought). Again, Charlie's logical, systematic knowledge is presented as being opposed to emotion (and especially romantic love): "I had no way of knowing what she expected of me.

This was far from the clear lines of problem-solving and the systematic acquisition of knowledge. I kept telling myself that the sweating palms, the tightness in my chest, the desire to put my arms around her were merely biochemical reactions" (99). Not only is Charlie uncertain of how to maintain a sexual relationship with Alice, but he feels that his intelligence separates him from everyone around him: "This intelligence has driven a wedge between me and all the people I knew and loved. . . . Now, I'm more alone than ever before" (107). Alice seems to agree that conversation (and connection) with the savant Charlie is nearly impossible: "These days I can't talk to you. All I can do is nod my head and pretend I understand all about cultural variants, and neo-Boulean [sic] mathematics, and post-symbolic logic" (124). In the end, one of the moral lessons that Keyes presents is that being too intelligent is socially, emotionally, and psychologically damaging: excessive intelligence is presented as a potential *cause* of mental disability. Charlie comes to believe that "intelligence and education that hasn't been tempered by human affection isn't worth a damn. . . . [I]ntelligence is one of the greatest human gifts. But all too often a search for knowledge drives out the search for love. . . . [I]ntelligence without the ability to give and receive affection leads to mental and moral breakdown, to neurosis, and possibly even psychosis. And I say that the mind absorbed in and involved in itself as a self-centered end, to the exclusion of human relationships, can only lead to violence and pain" (249). In this passage, "intelligence and education" are presented as being directly opposed to "the search for love." The result of intelligence without human connection is mental illness (and mental illness that is falsely linked to morality): Charlie's intelligence results in "mental and moral breakdown, . . . neurosis, and possibly even psychosis." Charlie's intelligence has also resulted in "the exclusion of human relationships," which makes him "self-centered" and which contributes to "violence." In short, Charlie's transformation only moves him from one set of negative stereotypes about cognitive disability to another, shifting him from the intellectually disabled childlike innocent to the cold and uncaring genius savant.

Because Keyes depicts the intellectually disabled Charlie as lacking in human subjectivity, the return of Charlie's intellectual disability is treated as the tragic death of his genius alter ego: this devaluing of the "lower-functioning" manifestation of cognitive difference—the reader's presumed (and Charlie's own) preference for the "higher-functioning" Charlie—points to the possibility for discrimination within the autism community itself and hints at larger issues in disability representation.[71] In the world of the novel, Charlie's eventual return to his old self, to his original identity, to the way he was born is presented as tragic. The return of his intellectual disability is described using images of darkness and death. He refers to Warren, the institution where he will live after the failed experiment, as having "the feeling . . . of living death—or worse, of never having been fully alive and knowing" (230). Visiting the institution is like "ordering my coffin, to sit in before I died" (220).[72]

Flowers for Algernon has been praised as a work of advocacy for those with intellectual disabilities; as the *New York Times* put it, "The obvious part is the message: We must respect life, respect one another, be kind to those less fortunate than ourselves."[73] But as Cline has noted, while "the text seemingly brims with advocacy for the mentally disabled . . . readings that suggest the inherent dignity of the mentally disabled . . . ignore the idea that when mental disability 'returns' to the novel, it operates as an inevitable force that threatens the distinct personality of the novel's hero."[74] I would argue that Charlie is always "mentally disabled"—he merely moves from a state in which intellectual disability causes his primary impairments to a state in which social disability is his primary impairment. His final return to intellectual disability serves to "rank" these impairments: Charlie's movement from "high-functioning" stereotypes to "low-functioning" stereotypes is culturally interpreted as tragedy, even though he actually returns to his original disability identity. Even within the autism community, debates about functioning levels can create division, strife, and discrimination. Questions of representation (Who can call themselves autistic? Who speaks for nonverbal people? Who represents intellectually disabled people in scholarly conversations about intellectual disability?) become heated and contested areas.[75] Just as people with physical disabilities have sometimes tried to differentiate themselves from those with cognitive disabilities, those with cognitive disabilities may internalize mainstream culture's attitudes and try to differentiate themselves from those who are perceived as "lower functioning."[76] The characterization of Charlie fictionally dramatizes the presence of ableist attitudes among disabled people, as the "high-functioning" Charlie regards his return to intellectual disability as tragedy.

In the end, *Of Mice and Men* and *Flowers for Algernon* are both classic classroom texts that suggest the cultural ubiquity of perceptions that devalue autistic subjectivity, revealing the underlying cultural assumptions that connect autism with notions of curing and killing. Lennie's autistic filicide is a reminder of the way in which fictional depictions of life on the spectrum can become interwoven with public representations of actual events, of the way in which these two discourses can work together to sustain perceptions that devalue autistic personhood and equate cognitive disability with death. *Flowers for Algernon* further demonstrates the ways in which the "cure or kill" trope is a constant threat to disabled characters (and perhaps to disabled people): when Charlie Gordon's "cure" fails to render him neurotypical, the reader is invited to see him as metaphorically dying—disappearing into the realm of intellectual disability. These novels show the strong legacy in our literature of interweaving cognitive disability with violence, representing larger cultural myths about autism, curing, and killing.

FOUR

The Autistic Gothic:
To Kill a Mockingbird,
The Glass Menagerie, and
The Sound and the Fury

> Mr. Underwood simply figured it was a sin to kill cripples, be they
> standing, sitting, or escaping.
> —Harper Lee, *To Kill a Mockingbird*

Some characters with autism appear to be locked within themselves, confined by a tragic interiority, unable to communicate. The ghostly figure of Arthur "Boo" Radley from *To Kill a Mockingbird,* the painfully awkward Laura of *The Glass Menagerie,* and the silent, childlike Benjy of *The Sound and the Fury* are all outsiders who prove central. Indeed, these works present autistic characters as empty reflections, able only to point outward to the needs of nondisabled characters.[1] The strong network of associations in these works connecting race, disability, and socioeconomic class show that these characters' apparently central place in the narrative is the ultimate marginalization. As the monolithic nature of the narrative replaces one group with another, what appears on the surface to be empathy and tolerance suggests further stereotyping and discrimination. These "monstrous" figures either unite the family unit or destroy it, either strengthen the community with their outcast status or symbolize the community's ultimate decay by remaining within it. In the end, the Gothic mode proves to be the ideal genre for symbolically representing cultural anxieties and fears that interweave autism, family, and tragedy.

The Autistic Specter: Disability in *To Kill a Mockingbird*

Although *To Kill a Mockingbird* has traditionally been understood as a novel about race, it is also crucially a novel about disability.[2] Specifically, disabled figures in the novel are presented as a source of Gothic monstrosity. Images of disability are central to Lee's symbolic patterns and narrative structures: in fact, the novel is the story of how Jem became disabled.[3] The adult Scout begins her narration: "When he was nearly thirteen, my brother Jem got his arm badly broken at the elbow. When it healed, and Jem's fears of never being able to play football were assuaged, he was seldom self-conscious about his injury. His left arm was somewhat shorter than his right; when he stood or walked, the back of his hand was at right angles to his body, his thumb parallel to his thigh. He couldn't have cared less, so long as he could pass and punt."[4] The novel opens with an image of disability that "passes" as able-bodied. While the young Jem is relieved that this injury will not limit his involvement in the world of sports, it is symbolically significant that Scout recounts the story of how Jem became "crippled," incurring a disability that mirrors that of the novel's central disabled figure, Tom Robinson.[5] Like Jem, Tom sustained an injury that made one arm shorter than the other: "His left arm was fully twelve inches shorter than his right, and hung dead at his side. It ended in a small shriveled hand, and from as far away as the balcony I could see that it was no use to him" (212). The symbolic connections here are blatant—the emotional events surrounding Tom's trial have a profound effect on Jem, and that emotional change, the symbolic movement from boy to man, the charge of bearing witness to injustice and tragedy, leaves a permanent mark (both emotional and physical) on Atticus's son. Thus, Jem's injury mirrors Tom's: both men have a left arm that is shorter than the right. The left side of the body, long symbolically represented as the "sinister side" in literary works, is frequently figured as a representation of evil, while the right side of the body is symbolically associated with justice and morality. Thus, it is significant that the villainous Bob Ewell is left-handed, that the heroic Atticus "always shoots a little to the right," and that the innocent Tom is stronger on the right side of his body than on the left. Ewell is involved in injuring both characters (Tom through the accusation of rape and Jem by literally breaking his arm). More importantly, Jem is emotionally changed (perhaps emotionally impaired?) by the injustice he witnesses at Tom's trial, and this has a lasting effect on the young man. Thus, the novel depicts Jem's injury as Tom Robinson's injury—both figuratively and physically. While Scout begins her narration by telling readers that she will relate the story of how her brother broke his arm, Jem tells her that the story should really start with the tale of yet another disabled character: "I maintain that the Ewells started it all, but Jem, who was four years my senior, said it started long before that. He said it began the summer Dill came to us, when Dill first gave us the idea of making Boo Radley come out" (3). Thus, the disabled figure of Arthur "Boo" Radley also frames the story, and the tale of the recluse's "coming out" becomes entangled with the tale of Jem's injury. Arthur's ghostly appearance brings the novel's obsession with disability and disabled figures firmly into the Gothic realm.

Although it is not overtly stated in the novel, many readers have felt that the character of Arthur Radley represents an autistic presence in Lee's narrative: his central role in the narrative interweaves cultural fears about autism with southern Gothic myth.[6] The popular alignment of Radley with the autism spectrum has become so common that one can find multiple websites discussing the subject (although there has been no scholarly examination of Arthur Radley as an autistic character).[7] Most recently, award-winning British playwright Mike Kenny has written a play entitled *Boo* that retells *To Kill a Mockingbird* from Radley's perspective and that overtly depicts Arthur as a character with Asperger's.[8] In one recent production, the role was played by Jonathan Ide, an actor with Asperger's syndrome (this is perhaps the first professional theatrical production in which an autistic character was played by an autistic actor).[9] While the adults in Lee's novel seem to believe that Radley has some form of posttraumatic stress resulting from an abusive relationship with his father (and that this trauma explains his unusual behavior), many details of characterization suggest that Radley's traits could be better explained as autistic.

Arthur exhibits unusual body language, intense sensory sensitivity, and a communication style that is largely nonverbal. When he appears at the end of the novel, he speaks only a single sentence, "Will you take me home?" (320). When he does speak, he speaks too softly: "He almost whispered it" (320).[10] When the other characters address him directly, he does not respond. He communicates mostly through gestures; for example, Scout intuits from a nod that he wants to "say good night to Jem" (319). Earlier in the novel, Arthur communicates his compassion for the children without words: by giving them gifts, by mending Jem's torn pants, and by giving Scout a blanket when she is cold. Like the autistic child narrator of *Extremely Loud and Incredibly Close,* he uses objects (such as a broken pocket watch, soap dolls, and a ball of twine) to communicate.[11] Overall, Arthur's nonverbal communication style suggests that he may be on the spectrum. Arthur's body language is also unusual. When he appears at the end of the novel, he initially hovers in the corner and later waits for Scout to guide him through the house. At first, he remains standing while everyone else sits: "Mr. Tate sat in Jem's desk chair. He waited until Atticus returned and settled himself. I wondered why Atticus had not brought a chair for the man in the corner. . . . This one was probably more comfortable where he was" (306). Arthur's unusual gait ("shuffling," "uneasy steps") and hesitation in moving through the environment ("every move he made was uncertain") suggest dyspraxia (developmental motor problems that are common in those on the autism spectrum). When Arthur "shuffled to his feet . . . every move he made was uncertain, as if he were not sure his hands and feet could make proper contact with the things he touched" (319). Scout discovers that Arthur's body language requires careful interpreting both because it is different from other people's and because it is his primary means of communication: "I was beginning to learn his body English. His hand tightened on mine and he indicated that he wanted to leave. I led him to the front porch, where his uneasy steps halted" (320). Arthur asks Scout (with both body language and words) to guide him through her home and later to lead him back to his own house. Dyspraxia can make it difficult to navigate a new place (the Finch home) or even a familiar one (the street that lies between the Finch and Radley houses). Furthermore, Arthur's intense light sensitivity is not adequately explained by a life lived indoors (the Radley house does, contrary to the children's beliefs, have lights). His sensory sensitivity is distinctively autistic: "I wondered why Atticus was inviting us to the front porch instead of the living room, then I understood. The living room lights were awfully strong" (313). Scout helps to keep Arthur away from the lights: "I led him to the chair farthest from Atticus and Mr. Tate. It was in deep shadow. Boo would feel more comfortable in the dark" (313). Overall, Arthur's behavior at the end of the novel strongly suggests that he is on the autism spectrum.

In addition, Arthur's social behavior, his decision to live as a recluse, and his family's attitude toward him could all be explained as being autism related. Although the events of his life are retold as a part of neighborhood rumor and therefore are not completely explained, Arthur Radley seems to have pronounced social difficulties. Indeed, Miss Maudie recalls Arthur as socially awkward: "I remember Arthur Radley when he was a boy. He always spoke nicely to me, no matter what folks said he did. Spoke as nicely as he knew how" (51). Miss Maudie's comment implies that Arthur did not speak as well or as politely as expected, but he did the best he could. As a teenager, he gets in trouble with the law, apparently as a result of peer pressure: "When the younger Radley boy was in his teens he became acquainted with some of the Cunninghams from Old Sarum. . . . Nobody in Maycomb had nerve enough to tell Mr. Radley that his boy was in with the wrong crowd" (10–11). It is hard to imagine the timid man who appears later in the novel as a ringleader for a group of teenagers—it seems far more likely that Arthur is a man who could not distinguish "the wrong crowd" and does not have the social skills to know whom he can trust. Whatever the cause of Arthur's behavior, his father asks the local police to let him keep his son at home rather than sending him to "the state industrial school." The boy's teenaged hijinks are not a major crime—and while there is no justification for keeping someone sequestered at home for twenty-five years, the young man's disappearance from the public life of the town leaves many questions unanswered. One must wonder if Arthur Radley wants to leave the house: has he decided to stay inside as a result of sensory and social problems? This seems to be Miss Maudie's interpretation: "Arthur Radley just stays in the house, that's all. . . . Wouldn't you stay in the house if you didn't want to come out?" (49). The Radley family's motives are unclear: they may see themselves as "locking him up," as "protecting him" from the outside world, or as "hiding" his cognitive difference from the neighbors. After his father dies, Arthur's older brother moves back home. While the neighborhood children assume it is so that the family can continue to "keep Boo locked up," it seems more probable that Nathan has returned home to help care for his disabled brother.

In fact, the children's circumscribed world is bordered by disability on both sides: the novel presents Mrs. Dubose as a "heroic overcomer," feeding into cultural discourses that depict disability as a personal tragedy that one must battle and conquer: she is as much a Gothic figure as "Boo," frightening the children with her physical appearance and harsh attitude. The liminality of the novel's disabled figures is symbolically represented by Jem and Scout's neighborhood boundaries: "When I was almost six and Jem was nearly ten, our summertime boundaries (within calling distance of Calpurnia) were Mrs. Henry Lafayette Dubose's house two doors to the north of us, and the Radley Place three doors to the south. We were never tempted to break them. The Radley Place was inhabited by an unknown entity the mere description of whom was enough to make us behave for days on end; Mrs. Dubose was plain hell" (7). Like Arthur Radley, Mrs. Dubose serves as both boundary and boogeyman: her liminal status marks the outside edge of Jem and Scout's community. The social and cultural world of the novel is constructed based on the disabled Others it marginalizes and excludes. Indeed, the novel highlights the fact that the very act of social inclusion implies that someone else must be excluded. Gossip about the Radley place is a way for the children to bond through small talk: "When Walter caught up with us, Jem made pleasant conversation with him. 'A hain't lives there,' he said cordially, pointing to the Radley house" (26). Society is created by excluding people like Arthur Radley. *To Kill a Mockingbird* is primarily a story about the community of Maycomb, and the novel has a powerful social focus; thus, it is significant that the children's world is bounded by disabled figures (and Gothic monsters) on both ends of the street.[12]

Although Mrs. Dubose's illness is not identified in the novel, she uses a wheelchair, experiences seizures, and takes morphine: Atticus interprets her place in the novel as a disabled subject, presenting her to the children as a heroic overcomer—an interpretation very different from Scout and Jem's perception of her as a monstrous Other. From the perspective of the child narrator, Mrs. Dubose has a great deal to "overcome." Scout expresses horror and fear when she sees Mrs. Dubose's disabled body, particularly when she witnesses her seizures:

> She was horrible. Her face was the color of a dirty pillow-case, and the corners of her mouth glistened with wet, which inched like a glacier down the deep grooves enclosing her chin. . . . Her bottom plate was not in, and her upper lip protruded; from time to time she would draw her nether lip to her upper plate and carry her chin with it. This made the wet move faster.
>
> I didn't look any more than I had to. (122)

While Scout responds to Mrs. Dubose with horror, Atticus depicts their elderly neighbor as simultaneously both victim and hero. He tells Jem that Mrs. Dubose should not be held responsible for her racist attitudes and rude behavior because of her disability. As a matter of fact, Atticus acts as though her status as disabled removes her human agency completely: "Jem, she's old and ill. You can't hold her responsible for what she says and does" (121). Specifically, the novel depicts her as heroically overcoming the pain of her terminal illness by refusing palliative measures: "She's not suffering any more. She was sick for a long time. . . . Mrs. Dubose was a morphine addict. . . . She said she was going to leave this world beholden to nothing and nobody. Jem, when you're sick as she was, it's all right to take anything to make it easier, but it wasn't all right for her" (127). Atticus imagines Mrs. Dubose's death as a merciful release from suffering (Atticus's attitude inadvertently aligns with our culture's belief that it is "better to be dead than disabled"). He also praises her stoicism in choosing to endure unnecessary pain: "She was a great lady. . . . I wanted you to see something about her—I wanted you to see what real courage is, instead of getting the idea that courage is a man with a gun in his hand. It's when you know you're licked before you begin but you begin anyway and you see it through no matter what. . . . She was the bravest person I ever knew" (128). The image of "a man with a gun in his hand" is evocative of Atticus's earlier warning to the children not to kill innocent mockingbirds. Ultimately, Mrs. Dubose's character conjoins multiple (and conflicting) literary stereotypes regarding disability: she is both triumphant hero and suffering victim, both social boundary and moral center.

The depiction of the supposedly monstrous Arthur Radley also invokes multiple autism stereotypes: although the novel portrays Arthur as someone who acts out of compassion for children, Lee symbolically links his lack of visible outward emotion to violent behavior. According to Miss Stephanie Crawford, he stabs his father with a pair of scissors with absolutely no show of emotion:

> Boo was sitting in the livingroom cutting some items from *The Maycomb Tribune* to paste in his scrapbook. His father entered the room. As Mr. Radley passed by, Boo drove the scissors into his parent's leg, pulled them out, wiped them on his pants, and resumed his activities.
>
> Mrs. Radley ran screaming into the street that Arthur was killing them all, but when the sheriff arrived he found Boo still sitting in the livingroom, cutting up the *Tribune*. He was thirty-three years old then. (10–11)

Although the idea that people on the spectrum do not feel emotion is a false and damaging one, it is sometimes true that they express emotion in unexpected ways or that their emotions may not be outwardly apparent to others. While the attack on his father reveals that there must be strong emotions inside, Arthur's outward demeanor shows nothing to the other characters around him: he simply returns calmly to his activities. Indeed, the very activity in which he is engaged suggests emotional and social disengagement. Scrapbooking might be considered an unusual hobby for a thirty-three-year-old man—particularly one who never leaves the house (Arthur's only participation in the community is by chronicling its events). When the authorities again suggest that Arthur be institutionalized, his father again intervenes (in spite of the fact that his son has just attacked him): "Boo wasn't crazy, he was high-strung at times. It was all right to shut him up, Mr. Radley conceded, but insisted that Boo not be charged with anything: he was not a criminal" (12). Although Mr. Radley may be concerned about the family's reputation in the Maycomb community, he may also have a protective motive in mind, feeling that it is better to keep his son at home with the family. Furthermore, Arthur shows no emotion after killing Bob Ewell: even though he acts in defense of the children, one would generally expect this violent encounter to elicit some kind of visible emotional response. Overall, Lee's portrayal of Arthur as unemotional is intertwined with the depiction of violence—his dearth of outwardly apparent emotion seems implicated in his violent behavior.

The ghostly figure of Arthur Radley also plays on other common autism myths: Lee depicts him as an enigmatic source of fascination and wonder, presents him as an autistic adult who is childlike and immature, and suggests that he is "locked away" from the rest of the world by an imaginary boundary. The children are certainly captivated by Arthur: "The Radley Place fascinated Dill. In spite of our warnings and explanations it drew him as the moon draws water, but drew him no nearer than the light-pole on the corner, a safe distance from the Radley gate. There he would stand, his arm around the fat pole, staring and wondering" (9). Dill stops where the light (representing the children's known world) ends, too afraid to venture into the (literally and figuratively) dark Radley world. Yet what is in the dark is enticingly mysterious to him, and he is too entranced to stay away from the Gothic allure of the Radley house. The children are so fascinated with their reclusive neighbor that they use Arthur as a form of entertainment, making up a play about his life and performing it on the front lawn (an activity Jem describes as "playing Boo Radley") (43). The adults are also curious about him—and not just the gossipy Stephanie Crawford: even Miss Maudie would like to see the adult Arthur. After Scout nearly sees Arthur during the fire that destroys Miss Maudie's house, Miss Maudie confesses: "Tell you the truth, I'd like to've been with you. And I'd've had sense enough to turn around, too" (83).

Not only is Arthur a source of mystery and wonder for the neurotypical neighbors, but he is also consistently depicted as childlike. He speaks to Scout "in the voice of a child afraid of the dark" and lets the third grader guide him by holding his hand (320). Lee's most common adjective for Arthur is "timid" (310, 320). When the children discuss the gifts left in the tree, Jem wonders if the tree's hole might be "some grown person's . . . hidin' place," but Scout responds that "grown folks don't have hidin' places" (38–39). Although Radley protects the children by rescuing them from Bob Ewell, he is himself depicted as childlike and in need of rescuing (Sheriff Tate implies that he must hide the truth of Ewell's death in order to protect Arthur from public attention). Finally, Arthur's reclusiveness, his defining attribute in the novel, becomes the ultimate symbol of autistic otherness and separation, as his home represents the invisible social barrier that is so often imagined to surround and entrap those on the spectrum.

There is an enclosing finality in the last time Scout sees Arthur: "He gently released my hand, opened the door, went inside, and shut the door behind him. I never saw him again" (320). His mysterious separation itself becomes a symbol of autism. Thus, the book relies on multiple autism stereotypes in the construction of Arthur's character.

The novel strongly aligns autism (and disability at large) with its Gothic motifs, presenting autism as mysterious, dangerous, and supernatural. Certainly, *To Kill a Mockingbird* participates in the southern Gothic tradition—especially through the children's conception of Arthur Radley as a frightening ghoul.[13] From the twisted tree of the novel's cover illustration (evocative both of the mockingbird metaphor and of the southern Gothic tradition more generally) to the final chapter's climax on Halloween night (an appropriate day for the conclusion of a child's Gothic tale), Boo Radley is a prominent part of the novel's Gothic motifs (he leaves gifts for the children in the spooky tree near the Radley lot and finally comes out on Halloween night). The children imagine Arthur as a supernatural being, a ghostly figure that menaces the neighborhood in the night:

> Inside the house lived a malevolent phantom. People said he existed, but Jem and I had never seen him. People said he went out at night when the moon was down, and peeped in windows. When people's azaleas froze in a cold snap, it was because he had breathed on them. Any stealthy small crimes committed in Maycomb were his work. Once the town was terrorized by a series of morbid nocturnal events: people's chickens and household pets were found mutilated; although the culprit was Crazy Addie, who eventually drowned himself in Barker's Eddy, people still looked at the Radley Place, unwilling to discard their initial suspicions. (9)

Like a coven of witches, Arthur Radley is reputed to poison everything around him: "From the Radley chickenyard tall pecan trees shook their fruit into the schoolyard, but the nuts lay untouched by the children: Radley pecans would kill you" (9).[14] As Claudia Durst Johnson explains, "The children, and even some of the town's adults, view Boo Radley as a ghost or vampire or witch to whom they attribute bloodlettings and blood sucking, as well as a host of minor incidents, unnatural and foul. . . . This monster, whose face reportedly looks like a skull, is a horror to behold."[15] Indeed, Jem describes Arthur as looking something like Frankenstein's monster: "Boo was about six-and-a-half-feet tall. . . . [H]e dined on raw squirrels and any cats he could catch, that's why his hands were bloodstained—if you ate an animal raw, you could never wash the blood off. There was a long jagged scar that ran across his face; what teeth he had were yellow and rotten; his eyes popped, and he drooled most of the time" (14).[16] The children's stories about Arthur eventually tip over into comic excess: they imagine him as a cannibal (Dill says that Mrs. Radley "lost most of her teeth, her hair, and her right forefinger. . . . Boo bit it off one night when he couldn't find any cats and squirrels to eat" [44]) and cast him as the dénouement in one of Poe's macabre tales ("maybe he died and they stuffed him up the chimney" [48]). But it is important to remember that the adults in the novel are also afraid of Arthur and imagine him as a potentially threatening outsider: "Miss Stephanie Crawford said she woke up in the middle of the night one time and saw him looking straight through the window at her . . . said his head was like a skull lookin' at her" (14). Miss Crawford describes Arthur as both Peeping Tom and memento mori, mixing hints of potential sexual threat with a Gothic emblem of death. Even the trustworthy and fair-minded Atticus, who usually insists that the children refer to "Mr. Arthur" respectfully, once slips and uses the belittling nickname "Boo" (81). Overall, the autistic image of Arthur Radley is strongly aligned with the novel's Gothic motifs: Arthur becomes a kind of boogeyman, inspiring fear in his community through his absence and silence. His separation from the social life of the community results in his demonization, and his demonization results in his further separation from the social life of the community.

Lee's Gothic depiction of autism reflects larger cultural anxieties about autistic difference. The Gothic mode is centrally concerned with interrogating the boundaries of the human, and the frequent dehumanization of autistic people in literary works and cultural representations has a clear parallel in the Gothic examination of the division between natural and supernatural. When disability appears in Gothic texts, "the classic Gothic binary—Self-human-known-Good/Other-inhuman-unknown-evil—is repackaged as the binary of Enlightenment medicine: health/pathology, with pathology as the code for otherness and all it represents."[17] While pathology can become conflated with Otherness in Gothic texts, this is even more common in depictions of autism. Because people perceive the condition itself as unexplainable and therefore mysterious (a clear etiology has not been definitively proven), the supposedly "unknown" nature of autism naturally lends itself to the Gothic mode. As Kate Ferguson Ellis puts it, "Not knowing is the primary source of Gothic terror."[18] The Gothic also commonly explores a set of motifs that overlap with autism in the cultural imagination. The Gothic is often concerned with familial decay, focusing on the "failed home . . . as the site of terror."[19]

Unfortunately, one common stereotype that is particularly prevalent in the media is the depiction of autism as a personal tragedy that destroys families.[20] As Bradley Shaw notes, "Boo's history is a family's horror story."[21] The Gothic mode is invested in exploring "social relations and social institutions," as well as in examining "the anticonventional vision of reality" that may work outside of such institutions.[22] This makes it a perfect venue for the exploration of social disability (and of those characters who act outside of social norms). The Radley home clearly fits the Gothic motif of the "architecture of fear," in which the haunted house holds "forbidden secrets."[23] The secret, ineffable "family tragedy" of autism is hidden and silenced within the confines of the Radley house. The Gothic mode is "preoccup[ied] at its innermost core with taboos."[24] The taboo includes those realities "which offend, which are suppressed, which are generally swept under the carpet in the interests of social and psychological equilibrium."[25] There can be no doubt that our culture treats autism as taboo. As David Mitchell and Sharon Snyder explain, disability is rarely discussed openly because of "the socially 'forbidden' nature of the topic."[26] Finally, the Gothic tradition focuses on themes such as "the black-and-white tone of 'unmerited persecution'; the insistence on the potential finality of imprisonment; the note of half-gasping, half-gloating voyeurism."[27] One cannot help but notice that autistic texts are overrun with characters who either feel that they are the object of "unmerited persecution" or actually are the object of unmerited persecution (see chapters 3 and 6). Other texts include characters who have been committed to a psychiatric institution and view it as a form of imprisonment (see chapter 6 and the discussion of *The Sound and the Fury* below). Other cultural representations of autism capitalize on sensationalism, fascination, and the role of the neurotypical voyeur (see chapters 1, 2, and 6). Thus, it is perhaps unsurprising that Lee represents autism in the Gothic mode.

In the case of *To Kill a Mockingbird*, the novel's Gothic themes intertwine with Atticus's mockingbird metaphor: these motifs work together to present the novel's critique of the social system. As Ruth Bienstock Anolik notes, "The Gothic adventure is the journey of the normative, enlightened Self as it encounters the unknown. . . . [T]he Gothic presents human difference as monstrous, and then, paradoxically, subverts the categories of exclusion to argue for the humanity of the monster."[28] This is exactly what happens when Scout stands on

The Autistic Gothic

Arthur Radley's porch at the conclusion of the novel: "Atticus was right. One time he said you never really know a man until you stand in his shoes and walk around in them. Just standing on the Radley porch was enough" (322). Looking at the world from a new perspective ("I had never seen our neighborhood from this angle" [321]), Scout suddenly realizes that the Gothic monster is in fact a man. Through the trial of Tom Robinson, Jem's service to Mrs. Dubose, and Atticus's explanations regarding Arthur Radley, the children ostensibly learn to appreciate the perspective of the disabled Other. Miss Maudie explains Atticus's reasoning in forbidding the children to kill mockingbirds: "Mockingbirds don't do one thing but make music for us to enjoy. They don't eat up people's gardens, don't nest in corncribs, they don't do one thing but sing their hearts out for us. That's why it's a sin to kill a mockingbird" (103).[29] Significantly, all of the novel's metaphorical mockingbirds (Tom Robinson, Arthur Radley, and Mrs. Dubose) are disabled characters, and these characters become an exercise in empathy and charity for the privileged Scout and Jem.

While the novel's message is overtly one of acceptance and tolerance, many critics have noted that the book is racist on multiple levels: the novel's childish and shallow approach to the dynamics of racism in the Deep South is parallel to its facile treatment of disability.[30] Mitchell and Snyder argue that *Mockingbird* is *directly about* making the terrain of disability and disabled people less alien."[31] This agenda must fail, however, on the same merits as its racial one, for the novel offers only "the simplistic and racist exploration of race."[32] Indeed, the novel's African American characters are dehumanized and are frequently described in animalistic terms. As Jennifer Murray notes,

> Scout's description of a black boy as "rich chocolate with flaring nostrils and beautiful teeth" (161) smacks of animal imagery, as does the description of Tom Robinson: "Tom was a black-velvet Negro, not shiny, but soft black velvet. The whites of his eyes shone in his face, and when he spoke we saw flashes of his teeth. If he had been whole, he would have been a fine specimen of a man" (192). Regardless of the health and implicit quality of the "specimens" under study, the description focuses on difference in such a way that the physical is implicitly seen through the lens of evaluation of the workhorse, judging its worth through its skin and teeth.[33]

The novel also offers an unrealistic depiction of the fight for civil rights by presenting a white hero (Atticus) who champions the black community, thus implying that African Americans are passive victims in need of white heroes.[34] As Isaac Saney argues, "Perhaps the most egregious characteristic of the novel is the denial of the historical agency of Black people. They are robbed of their role as subjects of history, reduced to mere objects who are passive hapless victims; mere spectators and bystanders in the struggle against their own oppression and exploitation."[35] In a novel about "standing in other people's shoes," Tom's own perspective is omitted completely: "*To Kill a Mockingbird* is the white 'get-out-of-jail-free' card. . . . Keeping the Maycomb jury out but failing to win an acquittal for Tom Robinson . . . is grounds for an overwhelming number of readers of the novel to champion Atticus. . . . What *To Kill a Mockingbird* misses completely is the anguish of Tom Robinson."[36]

As the novel's depictions of race and disability overlap, the conflation of all forms of Otherness becomes a part of the book's oppressive subtext.[37] This conflation of race and disability is representative of a larger cultural trend, the "critical tendency to see the diseased or disabled body as the code for 'another Other,' gesturing to differences of race, class, gender. . . . [I]n fact, the critical displacement of the disabled or diseased body reflects the invisibility of disability in 'polite' society."[38] All outsiders of the Maycomb community are grouped together as "mockingbirds," placed into a group of victims in need of the (presumed white, able-bodied, and privileged) reader's pity and rescue.[39] The idea that the neurotypical Scout can understand Arthur's autistic perspective simply by standing on his porch seems facile. Furthermore, her presumed change of perspective is a passive one, doing nothing to include Arthur in the community or to reduce the prejudice against him.[40] As with Atticus's ineffectual defense of Tom Robinson, the novel's efforts to understand and to foster empathy for its autistic character fall far short of real acceptance. No matter how long Scout stands on his porch, readers are likely to leave the novel remembering "Boo" as a Gothic monster whose overpowering Otherness unites the Maycomb community with his symbolic outsider status.

The Unspeakable Disability: Familial Decay in *The Glass Menagerie*

While Arthur Radley unites the community (and the Finch family) through his exclusion and absence, Laura Wingfield seems to create disunity in her family simply through her presence. Laura's social awkwardness symbolizes the downfall of an entire culture: the aristocratic South represented by her aging southern belle mother, who has been transported from her peaceful porch to a rundown

St. Louis apartment. Although Tennessee Williams's play initially seems to demonstrate sympathy for Laura, inviting the audience to share in her autistic perspective, his reliance on stereotypes casts Laura as fragile and needy—her inability to survive in the "real world" ultimately leads to her family's tragic downfall. Less overtly Gothic than Harper Lee's novel, Williams's nostalgic play subtly symbolizes the decay of the Wingfield family through the autistic Laura's inability to connect socially.

Although critics of Williams's work have long acknowledged *The Glass Menagerie* as an autobiographical play in which the timid and painfully shy Laura Wingfield represents Williams's sister Rose, it is only recently that critics and audiences have begun to think of Laura (and Rose) as autistic.[41] During Williams's lifetime, Rose was diagnosed as schizophrenic: she was institutionalized and later lobotomized. Many of Rose's traits, however, suggest Asperger's syndrome (a diagnosis that did not exist in the 1940s) rather than schizophrenia: she had unusual rituals and routines (Williams described her "peculiar habit of setting a pitcher of ice-water outside her door, each night when she retired"), she went through a phase in which she ate only Campbell's tomato soup (she also collected the labels), she engaged in echolalia (frequently repeating phrases such as "tragic, just tragic"), and she struggled socially (one young man who dated Rose described her as "very awkward, I remember her standing in the shadow in the dining room, unable or unwilling to come in—and, as I recall, she never spoke at all").[42] Tragically, Rose's lobotomy may be representative of the treatment received by an entire generation of autistic people: as Roy Richard Grinker explains, the 1940s were an era in which "children were being lobotomized, especially those who were described as living in fantasy worlds—children then called schizophrenics, but who would today almost certainly be called autistic."[43] Considering Rose's strong autistic traits, it is unsurprising to find that Laura, a character based on Williams's sister, also has many autistic tendencies.

From the very beginning, the play invites the viewer to participate in Laura's autistic perspective, emphasizing her narrow interests, her sensory sensitivities, and her social struggles: at first glance, this treatment seems sympathetic to Laura, encouraging audience empathy. For example, Laura's special interest is represented in the play's title. This prioritizing of Laura's interest (making her collection of glass animals both the title and symbolic center of the play) aligns well with an autistic main character. In addition, Williams's script encourages the use of stage technology (the screen projecting words and images onto the stage wall, as well as lighting choices) to emphasize Laura's sensory perceptions and social experiences. For example, when Amanda (Laura's mother) and Laura discuss the typing school that Laura attended, the screen behind the two women visually suggests the sensory overload that overwhelmed Laura at school, as the stage directions call for the image of "a swarm of typewriters."[44] When Tom (Laura's brother) and Amanda have a fight, the lighting accentuates Laura's sensory distress at the loud and angry voices: *"Before the lights come up again, the violent voices of Tom and Amanda are heard. They are quarreling behind the portieres. In front of them stands Laura with clenched hands and panicky expression. A clear pool of light is on her figure throughout this scene"* (38). The spotlight also suggests Laura's social isolation: she is excluded from the fight, not participating in the angry conversation but merely overhearing it. Indeed, the stage directions emphasize that Laura's sensory integration issues are an important part of multiple scenes: she customarily responds to the sound of slamming doors (or other loud noises) by screaming or huddling in the fetal position on the sofa. The screen is also used to communicate Laura's panic during social situations. When Jim O'Connor, the gentleman caller, knocks on the door, Laura's response is augmented by the screen: "[panicky]: Oh, Mother—*you* answer the door! . . . Oh, Mother, please answer the door, don't make me do it! . . . [Legend on screen: 'Terror!']" (74). The message on the screen helps to emphasize the sense of dread that Laura feels in this particular social situation. Overall, Williams uses multiple stage devices to emphasize Laura's distinctively autistic reactions to the events around her, ostensibly creating audience sympathy.

Williams also accentuates Laura's poor social skills and narrow interests by consistently comparing her to Amanda, her socialite mother, and Jim, her gregarious suitor: Laura's fundamental difference from her mother is a symbol of Gothic decay, and her inability to make social connections leads to the downfall of the Wingfield family. Unfortunately, Laura's mother places great emphasis on the social aspects of life and perceives her daughter's introverted interests and social awkwardness as signs of failure. Amanda constantly tells stories about the social escapades of her youth, emphasizing that she has succeeded where Laura fails: "One Sunday afternoon in Blue Mountain—your mother received—seventeen!—gentleman callers! Why, sometimes there weren't chairs enough to accommodate them all" (26). Amanda devalues Laura's interests (the glass collection and her phonograph records) and feels that her daughter fails at every social situation: "I put her in business college—a dismal failure! Frightened her so it made her sick at the stomach. I took her over to the Young People's League at the church. Another fiasco. She spoke to nobody, nobody spoke to her. Now all she does is fool with those pieces of glass and play those worn-out records. What kind of a life is that for a girl to lead?" (53). Divorced from the social realm, Laura's fixation on objects and music seems pointless to her mother. In fact, Amanda refuses to acknowledge that there could be any value or satisfaction in Laura's interests: "So what are we going to do the rest of our lives? Stay home and watch the parades go by? Amuse ourselves with the glass menagerie, darling? Eternally play those worn-out phonograph records your father left as a painful reminder of him?" (34). Amanda believes that a suitor is the answer to all her daughter's problems; however, the suitor is as gregarious as Amanda and therefore extremely ill suited to Laura. Jim values "social poise! Being able to square up to people and hold your own on any social level" (77). He values and admires the very thing that Laura lacks—she cannot succeed in his world. As Clay Morton notes, Laura has "severe difficulty initiating and maintaining conversations" with Jim.[45] She is unable to make small talk, and there are long pauses in her exchanges:

Jim: You don't smoke, do you?
[*She looks up, smiling, not hearing the question. . . .*]
Jim: Would you—care for a—mint?
[*She doesn't seem to hear him. . . .*] (107)

Not only does Laura struggle with conversational reciprocity, but Williams also describes Laura's body language as "nervous," "stiff," and "awkward" (29, 74). In other words, Laura's ways of socializing are vastly different from those valued by her chatty mother and confident suitor. Because the social domain is central to Amanda's worldview, Laura, the unsociable daughter, is presented as the ultimate failure. Overall, the play draws attention to Laura's poor social skills by comparing her to the play's more outgoing characters: her inability to carry on in the socialite role prescribed for her by her mother's society represents the decline of the Wingfield family.

The autism stereotypes that Laura's character displays suggest that she is weak and unable to provide the familial legacy her mother has envisioned: although Williams describes her as a supernatural being from another world, she is also presented as a helpless victim. Indeed, Laura's helplessness, fragility, and victimization are central to her character.[46] Williams's stage directions refer to "the lovely fragility of glass which is her image" (9). Like the glass unicorn to which she is compared, Laura is a beautiful but impossible "monster." Again, the use of lighting draws attention to her isolation, depicting her as mystical and otherworldly: "The light upon Laura should be distinct from the others, having a peculiar pristine clarity such as light used in early religious portraits of female saints or madonnas" (10). Laura's nickname, "Blue Roses," also indicates her fundamental eccentricity—a blue rose is as impossible as a unicorn. As Jim puts it, "Being different is nothing to be ashamed of. Because other people are not such wonderful people. They're one hundred times one thousand. You're one times one! They walk all over the earth. You just stay here. They're common as—weeds, but—you—well, you're—*Blue Roses!*" (106). As Robert Cardullo points out, this moniker "suggests the oxymoronic existence of Laura Wingfield, a young woman of this world who simultaneously, like the lovely but easily broken creatures of her glass menagerie, seems physically unfit for, or unadapted to, an earthly life."[47] Like the parents of many autistic children, Amanda worries about Laura's ability to take care of herself when her mother is gone: "What are we going to do, what is going to become of us, what is the future?" (30). Her attempt to match Laura with a husband is part of her ongoing mission to make sure that her disabled daughter will be provided for and taken care of in the future.[48] She confronts Tom with her concerns: "We have to be making some plans and provisions for her. She's older than you, two years, and nothing has happened. She just drifts along doing nothing. It frightens me terribly how she just drifts along" (52). The sense that Laura lacks direction and needs someone else to care for her clearly aligns with popular representations of adults on the spectrum. Indeed, Amanda makes Tom feel guilty for failing to take responsibility for his autistic sister: "Don't think about us, a mother deserted, an unmarried sister who's crippled and has no job! Don't let anything interfere with your selfish pleasure!" (114). The play presents Laura as a burden to her neurotypical family.[49] Symbolically, Laura needs the light/redemption of a neurotypical romance and marriage (when Jim speaks, his "warmth and charm . . . lights her inwardly with altar candles" [97]). After Jim leaves at the end of the play, Tom tells Laura to "blow out your candles" (115): the play ends in darkness, with the image of Laura eternally waiting for someone to rescue her from her isolation. Thus, the play depicts Laura as helpless, as a beautiful "monster," a creature too fragile for the real world.

Williams's presentation of her special interests as a means of escape also contributes to the perception that Laura cannot adapt to the world outside of the Wingfield apartment: familial degeneration, a loss of legacy and future, is presented as a direct result of Laura's "childlike" nature and inability to care for herself. The depiction of special interests as a means of escape is a recurring theme in literature involving autistic characters (e.g., Lisbeth's use of math and numbers in *The Girl with the Dragon Tattoo*). Williams presents Laura's devotion to her interests as a ritual that relieves her fear and anxiety. Laura can only answer the door after turning on her music: "A faraway, scratchy rendition of 'Dardanella' softens the air and gives her strength to move through it" (75). As soon as Jim walks into the apartment, she immediately "returns through the portieres, darts to the Victrola, winds it frantically and turns it on" (75). When Jim speaks to her, she "picks up a piece from the glass menagerie collection, and turns it in her hands to cover her tumult" (97). Signi Falk describes "the little glass ornaments and phonograph records" as Laura's "escape."[50] Morton agrees: "These interests serve as coping mechanisms; when faced with anxiety, Laura inevitably retreats to them."[51] Clearly, this is a reductive understanding of the true purpose and scope of special interests.[52] The other characters perceive Laura as childish, feeding into yet another stereotype: "How old are you, Laura? . . . I thought you were an adult; it seems that I was mistaken" (30). Her perspective is generally ignored, especially by her mother. When Laura refuses to answer the door, her mother perceives her behavior as trivial: "What is the matter with you, you silly thing? . . . I told you I wasn't going to humor you, Laura. Why have you chosen this moment to lose your mind?" (75). In sum, the fragile and needy Laura, consistently imagined as a child in need of protection, clearly represents the stereotype of the autistic "victim": her weakness and fragility ultimately contribute to the social decline of her once aristocratic family.

Critics have frequently noted that Laura's physical disability symbolizes her emotional state. It is also important to notice, however, that the disability that can be named, spoken about, and rendered visible is used to talk about a disability that cannot be named, spoken about, or rendered visible: the inability and unwillingness to discuss Laura's mental disability represents autism as an unspeakable fear. Throughout the play, Laura's "crippled" leg allows the characters (and, later, readers) to talk about a cognitive disability that represents the ultimate cultural taboo.[53] As Williams describes Laura's physical disability, "A childhood illness has left her crippled, one leg slightly shorter than the other, and held in a brace. . . . Stemming from this, Laura's separation increases until she is like a piece of her own glass collection, too exquisitely fragile to move from the shelf" (5). Williams describes Laura's physical disability as the source of her unusual behavior, deflecting the effects of mental disability into the physically visible realm. Indeed, Laura's mother forbids her from talking about either of her disabilities: "Nonsense! Laura, I've told you never, never to use that word. Why, you're not crippled. You just have a little defect—hardly noticeable, even!" (36). Ironically, her mother suggests a compensation cure for her leg that is made impossible by her other (unspoken) disability: "When people have some slight disadvantage like that, they cultivate other things to make up for it—develop charm—and vivacity—and—charm! That's all you have to do!" (36). Of course, social behavior is the last way the autistic Laura is likely to "make up for" her perceived physical deficits. What starts out as a speech on Laura's leg quickly turns into an attack on her social skills. The focus on Laura's physical disability serves to remind the audience of her taboo mental disability.

In an era before the diagnosis existed, Tom and Amanda have no words with which to adequately describe or encounter AS, and while it is clear that Laura has some kind of undiagnosed mental disorder, they avoid alluding to her cognitive disability in any way, always talking around the subject of Laura's mental disability rather than talking about it—but the Gothic taboo, the one subject they can never talk about, eventually becomes the symbolic downfall of their entire family. Even though Amanda considers talking about her daughter's physical disability to be "rude" or "inappropriate," talking about her mental disability is absolutely forbidden:

> Amanda: Don't say crippled! You know that I never allow that word to be used!
> Tom: But face facts, mother. She is and—that's not all—
> Amanda: What do you mean, "not all"?
> Tom: Laura is very different from other girls.
> Amanda: I think the difference is all to her advantage.
> Tom: Not quite all—in the eyes of the world—strangers—she's terribly shy and lives in a world of her own and those things make her seem a little peculiar to people outside the house.
> Amanda: Don't say peculiar. (65–66)

As is so often the case in *The Glass Menagerie*, a conversation about Laura's limp (the physical disability that can be named and articulated) becomes a conversation about Laura's autism (an invisible disability that has no name and cannot be articulated). Although Amanda regards both topics (limp and autism) as inappropriate, she would rather discuss the physical disability than the mental one. While she tries to stop Tom from using words such as "crippled" and "peculiar," it is clear that she is able to at least acknowledge the existence of Laura's limp, while her daughter's mental disability is met with denial. When Tom tries to segue from physical disability to mental disability, Amanda initially refuses to engage him, pretending that she does not understand what he is alluding to: "What do you mean, 'not all'?" (65). This defense of feigned ignorance is immediately followed by an overly positive response to Laura's cognitive difference that ignores her social impairments: "I think the difference is all to her advantage" (65). Finally, Amanda is resigned to trying to "unname" Laura's mental disability in the same way she has "unnamed" her physical one. She struggles to take away from Tom the words that he uses to indicate a disability without a name: "Don't say peculiar" (66). Jim and Laura also have a conversation about autism that is not about autism:

> Laura: I wasn't acquainted with many people. . . . I—I—never have
>   had much luck at—making friends.
> Jim: I don't see why you wouldn't.
> Laura: Well, I—started out badly.
> Jim: You mean being—
> Laura: Yes, it sort of—stood between me—
> Jim: You shouldn't have let it! (93–94)

Talking about Laura's limp is uncomfortable, but talking about Laura's mental disorder is downright impossible. When Jim says, "You mean being—" the reader is meant to fill in "crippled." But what is really under discussion, Laura's difficulties in the social realm, is more about her mental disorder than her limp. This conversation reveals two levels of social obfuscation surrounding Laura's autism in this play. Her unspeakable mental disorder is replaced with the only slightly more socially acceptable physical disability. In the first couple of sentences, Laura's dashes indicate every time she thinks about mentioning her disability but then hesitates. "I—I—never have had much luck" and "Well, I—started out badly" relay in their embarrassment and hesitation the words that are not said: "I was crippled, so I never have had much luck" and "Well, I was crippled, so I started out badly." Overall, the play layers symbolic disabilities, covering the supposedly unspeakable and incomprehensible "tragedy" of autism with the socially unacceptable but at least socially legible image of the cripple.

Indeed, Laura's narrative is deeply interwoven with cultural discourses of tragedy, pity, and "overcoming": her inability to overcome her autism is presented as a moral failing that leads to the demise of the Wingfield family. Historically, physical disabilities have often been used in literature to represent moral failings or character flaws: the outward difference symbolizes inner wickedness or shortcoming.[54] In *The Glass Menagerie,* however, the character flaw that so many critics see as being symbolized by Laura's limp is conflated with her autism (which the limp also symbolically represents). Thus, Laura's limp simultaneously points readers to mental disorder and character flaw, ultimately conflating and connecting the two. This symbolic overlap mirrors the real-life tendency to see mental disorders not as neurologically determined disabilities but as a sign of moral failing on the part of the mentally disabled—an indication of weakness, selfishness, or a lack of self-control. The other characters blame Laura for her social impairments and find fault with her for her inability to overcome these impairments:

> Jim: You were shy with people!
> Laura: I tried not to be but never could—
> Jim: Overcome it?
> Laura: No, I—I never could! (94)

Laura is, of course, more than shy: she is afraid to even open the door when Jim comes to call. The idea that her "shyness" is a fault that she must overcome shows both the way that the gravity of her disability is underestimated and the manner in which her fundamental character is devalued and presented as "flawed." Jim attempts to comfort Laura by mitigating the impact of her social disability: "I guess being shy is something you have to work out of kind of gradually. . . . And everybody has problems, not just you, but practically everybody has got some problems. You think of yourself as having the only problems, as being the only one who is disappointed. But just look around you and you'll see lots of people as disappointed as you are" (94). Jim implies that Laura will overcome her mental disability if she just "works" at it. Such words come across as naive and ironic in Williams's play, since the audience has already seen the true depth of Laura's social terror. From there, he segues into the trite commonplace that "everyone is disabled." While true on at least a theoretical level, some disabled people regard this sentiment as offensive because it mitigates the real-world challenges and social stigma they face on a daily basis.[55] Next, Jim offers his own diagnosis to replace the implied narrative of mental disability that is never spoken in the play: "You know what I judge to be the trouble with you? Inferiority complex! . . . I understand it because I had it too. Although my case was not so aggravated as yours seems to be. I had it until I took up public speaking, developed my voice, and learned that I had an aptitude for science" (99). As disability scholars have frequently noted, disability always contains a preinscribed narrative, the demand for story, the able-bodied interpreter's desire to know "how you became this way."[56] Again, the emphasis of Jim's "diagnosis" is placed on overcoming— it is a personal character flaw in Laura if she does not overcome her "inferiority complex" by taking a course in public speaking. While stage technology that emphasizes Laura's autistic perspective initially invites audiences to empathize with Laura, the final trajectory of the plot blames her (and autism) for her family's degeneration.

In the end, Williams's choice to depict his autistic sister as physically disabled and to exclude discussion of Laura's mental disability from the play subtly indicates the social forces involved in the real-life silencing of Rose Williams: after all, the taboos of the stage reflect the taboos of real life. Although Williams deeply regretted his mother's decision to have his sister lobotomized (he was not consulted before the operation), he censors the narrative of mental disability in his own work, choosing a physical disability to symbolically stand in for the "unspeakable" truth. Williams interpreted Rose's lobotomy as an attempt to silence his sister: in a 1981 interview, he reported that when his sister began talking about masturbation, his mother, Edwina Williams, "rushed to the head doctor, and she said, 'Do anything, *anything* to shut her up!'"[57] The fear of disabled sexuality (and especially of cognitively disabled sexuality) is here intertwined with the need for censorship (as in *Of Mice and Men* and *The Sound and the Fury*, cognitively disabled sexuality is assumed to be inappropriate, dangerous, and/ or violent). Silenced by the lobotomy (Williams described her as "tragically becalmed"), Rose no longer spoke in ways that her mother found dangerously unsettling.[58] However, the representation of Rose's mental disability is also metaphorically "silenced" in Williams's play. Although disability is often taboo, the play presents mental disability as the most socially unacceptable form of difference. Laura can say "I'm crippled," but she could never say "I'm crazy."[59] Presenting disability as taboo, connecting blame and familial fall, Williams's play adopts Gothic symbols and themes to surround the autistic Laura: a beautiful monster made of glass, she is not of this world—and her inability to engage with other people ensures the decay of her family and the end of her mother's aristocratic legacy. The tone of nostalgia that overwhelms Williams's play reminds the audience that Williams was writing autobiographically, that the fragile Laura represents a real-life woman, and that *The Glass Menagerie* fictionalizes the Williams family's own encounter with the fearsome cultural taboos surrounding autism spectrum disorder.[60]

"theres a curse on us": The Autistic Gothic in *The Sound and the Fury*

Literary critics have diagnosed Benjy Compson as autistic more often than any other character in the English literary canon.[61] Although it is clear that Benjy is nonverbal and intellectually disabled, Faulkner's depiction of the Compson family's youngest son allows for a variety of potential disability identities. When Faulknerians abandon outdated and offensive terms such as "idiot," "retarded," and "fool" (although, unfortunately, these are the terms most popular in the many critical discussions of Benjy), "autistic" is often the scholarly diagnosis of choice.[62] Sara McLaughlin, Mark Decker, Ineke Bockting, Patrick Samway and Gentry Silver, and Jesse Bering all describe Benjy as autistic.[63] However, other critics, such as David Mitchell, Sharon Snyder, and Michael Bérubé, identify Benjy as having Down syndrome.[64] The case for both conditions is compelling. Certainly, Faulkner was aware of the existence of autistic individuals—it seems likely that Faulkner either knew (or knew of) Eugene Hoskins, an autistic savant who spent his days doing calendar calculations at Oxford, Mississippi's local train station.[65] Benjy has many autistic traits: he has intense sensory perceptions, he rarely makes eye contact, he flaps his hands, and he avoids physical touch.[66] If the other characters deviate from his routine even slightly, his meltdown (crying, wailing, screaming) is immediate.[67] He thinks literally (he only knows one meaning for the word "Caddy"), he has intense interests (his obsession with fire, water, and other outdoor elements), and his narrative mostly repeats the words of other characters (a kind of internal, literary echolalia).[68] On the other hand, there is strong biographical evidence that Benjy's character was based on a real-life figure—a neighbor of Faulkner's who had Down syndrome.[69] As Samway and Silver explain, Benjy "is perhaps based on Edwin, the brother of Miss Annie Chandler, Faulkner's first-grade teacher. . . . Once, as Faulkner was reading the novel to Phil Stone, his friend automatically connected Benjy with Edwin Chandler."[70] In the scholarly squabble over Benjy's diagnosis, critics have overlooked the fact that the narrator of the first section of *The Sound and the Fury* could in fact have characteristics of both conditions (it is possible for someone to be diagnosed with both Down syndrome and autism).[71] It is most likely, however, that Faulkner had no particular disability in mind: his own comments on the character in interviews suggest an attempt to represent an amorphous intellectual disability.[72] Whatever disability identity readers may assign to Benjy, his cognitive difference symbolizes the Compson family's fall from their aristocratic status.[73] Indeed, the other characters interpret Benjy's mental disability as a supernatural "curse" on the entire Compson household: this curse comes to symbolically join multiple Gothic motifs in the novel, bringing together images of incest, suicide, and institutionalization, as Benjy's autism comes to represent the novel's obsession with isolation and interiority.

First, it is clear that the other characters in the novel regard autism as a curse on the Compson family at large, harking back to medieval interpretations of disability as supernatural in origin. Benjy's mother is insistent that her youngest son's disability is "a judgment on me."[74] Specifically, she views having an autistic son as a punishment for sin: "what have I done to have been given children like these Benjamin was punishment enough" (102). Even looking at Benjy is imagined to be unlucky. As Roskus says, *"Folks don't like to look at a looney. Taint no luck in it"* (19). Roskus also imagines that Benjy has supernatural and prophetic powers: "He know lot more than folks thinks. . . . He knowed they time was coming, like that pointer done. He could tell you when hisn coming, if he could talk. Or yours. Or mine" (31). Frony worries that Luster will be hurt by sharing a bed with Benjy: "You take Luster outen that bed, mammy. . . . That boy conjure him" (31). Because Benjy intuits Caddy's loss of virginity, Quentin feels that this shows a kind of prophetic power in his "innocent" and "childlike" brother, "lying on the ground under the window bellowing. He took one look at her and knew. Out of the mouths of babes" (100). Versh aligns Benjy's imagined supernatural power with that of a mythical conjurer with the ability to spread his curse to others:

> Versh said, Your name Benjamin now. You know how come your name Benjamin now. They making a bluegum out of you. Mammy say in old time your granpaw changed nigger's name, and he turn preacher, and when they look at him, he bluegum too. Didn't use to be bluegum, neither. And when family woman look him in the eye in the full of the moon, chile born bluegum. And one evening, when they was about a dozen them bluegum chillen running around the place, he never come home. Possum hunters found him in the woods, et clean. And you know who et him. Them bluegum chillen did. (69)

Versh compares Benjy to the monstrous preacher (a man reputed to create cannibal children simply by looking at his pregnant parishioners). Although Versh is clearly wrong about Benjy's supernatural influence, he may be partially right about the significance of his change in name. Benjy's name is an unstable entity in *The Sound and the Fury*: he is first named "Maury" (for his mother's brother), but Mrs. Compson later changes his name to "Benjamin" when his intellectual disability is discovered. Although his mother insists that he should have no nickname, most of the characters call him "Benjy," and his brother Jason later calls him "Ben." This multiplicity of names suggests Benjy's unstable identity. His change of name is an attempt to deny his place in the family: it is his mother's symbolic rejection of his role as a Compson and an attempt to cast out the family "curse."[75]

Indeed, the other characters frequently express fear and anxiety regarding Benjy's place in the family in part because they feel that the curse that his autism represents may have the ability to spread to other members of the household. Although Mrs. Compson regards the discovery of Benjy's autism as the first sign of a familial curse, she eventually applies this supernatural explanation to her other children as well, "talking about how her own flesh and blood rose up to curse her" (181). Jason fears that the public perception of Benjy's autism will lead other people to perceive the entire Compson family as "crazy": "And there I was, without any hat, looking like I was crazy too. Like a man would naturally think, one of them is crazy and another one drowned himself and the other one was turned out into the street by her husband, what's the reason the rest of them are not crazy too" (233). Autism is cited here as the harbinger of family tragedy— Jason implies that it is the original curse that has spread to the rest of the household, symbolically presaging Quentin's suicide and Caddy's promiscuity. In Jason's mind, the whole Compson house is made "mad" by Benjy's presence within it: "Then play with him and keep him quiet. . . . Do I have to work all day and then come home to a mad house" (66). Mrs. Compson tells her husband that the promiscuity of the adult Caddy "corrupts the very air your children breathe Jason you must let me go away I cannot stand it let me have Jason and you keep the others they're not my flesh and blood like he is strangers nothing of mine and I am afraid of them I can take Jason and go where we are not known I'll go down on my knees and pray for the absolution of my sins that he may escape this curse try to forget that the others ever were" (104). In this passage, Caddy's sexuality is as much a curse as Benjy's disability: the two are equated with each other. Overall, the other characters view the presence of an autistic within the Compson household as a supernatural sign of the family's downfall.

Specifically, this familial curse is symbolically aligned with Quentin's incestuous desire for his sister: autism, the stereotypical cultural symbol of imprisoning interiority, stands in for incest, the Gothic sign of a family that turns dangerously inward. This idea of a familial curse marked by the appearance of autism reappears in Quentin's relationship with Caddy. As Quentin says to his sister: "theres a curse on us its not our fault is it our fault" (158). That this curse is supernatural (perhaps even demonic) is implied by Quentin's later biblical reference: "until all cedars came to have that vivid dead smell of perfume that Benjy hated so. Just by imagining the clump it seemed to me that I could hear whispers secret surges smell the beating of hot blood under wild unsecret flesh watching against red eyelids the swine untethered in pairs rushing coupled into the sea" (176). Caddy, always associated with trees in Faulkner's text (Benjy's constant refrain is "Caddy smelled like trees"), has covered her natural scent with a perfume (representing her promiscuity). It is Caddy's "hot blood" that is "under wild unsecret flesh," and her sexuality is like "the swine untethered in pairs rushing coupled into the sea." The biblical story in which Jesus casts demons into a herd of swine, which then run into the sea (Matthew 8:30–32), connects the novel's motifs of supernatural curse, incest, and exorcism with Quentin's fantasies of drowning himself. When Quentin tells his father that he has consummated his incestuous desire for his sister, his father sees the lie for what it is: "you wanted to sublimate a piece of natural human folly into a horror and then exorcise it with truth" (177). The older Compson seems able to intuit his son's convoluted thinking: while Caddy's promiscuity is an act of "folly," incest with her brother would be an act of "horror"—but it would be a horror that Quentin could control by "exorcising" it through his confession to his father. As Faulkner explains it, Quentin "loved not his sister's body but some concept of Compson honor" (appendix). In Quentin's mind, for Caddy to sleep with him would be more honorable than for her to sleep with someone outside of the Compson line. As Quentin explains it to his father: "it was to isolate her out of the loud world so that it would have to flee us of necessity and then the sound of it would be as though it had never been" (177). Quentin wants Caddy to himself, separated from the "loud world," isolated from everyone else.

This fantasy of total isolation underpins both cultural myths about autism and the cultural taboo of incest: in Faulkner's novel, autism and incest are interwoven with other Gothic motifs such as suicide and imprisonment. Autistic people are often imagined as cut off from everyone else, trapped in their own world by an invisible barrier. Incest, like autism, is a powerful cultural myth of imprisoning interiority. Frank Whigham explains brother-sister incest as both a psychological and a social turn inward: "The taboo is cast as a denial but functions as a positive pressure outward"; thus, incest "looks like a desire but functions as a hostile withdrawal inward."[76] In other words, the "denial" of potential partners within the family unit naturally makes one move "outward" in search of other partners.[77] Hence, the "desire" of incest is really a "withdrawal" into the self.[78] Unable to consummate his incestuous desire for Caddy, Quentin eventually drowns himself, casting his own demons into the sea. His suicide (unfulfilled desire turned violently inward) is yet another symbol of the terrible interiority that entraps Faulkner's characters.

Benjy also desires his sister Caddy, but in a very different way: Caddy is the only character who treats Benjy with respect and love, and after she leaves the Compson household, Benjy perpetually searches the grounds for his "lost" sister. When he does leave the Compson yard (the gate has been left open), he attempts to ask a neighbor girl about Caddy: "They came on. I opened the gate and they stopped, turning. I was trying to say, and I caught her, trying to say, and she screamed and I was trying to say and trying" (53). Because Benjy is nonverbal and is often misinterpreted, this is construed by the girl (and by Benjy's family) as an attempted sexual assault (see chapter 3's discussion of autism and fears of sexual threat). Benjy's search for Caddy ultimately leads to his castration—he is prevented from connecting with a woman outside of the family when the love he seeks (the motherly care and affection of his older sister) is really within the family itself. Partially as a result of this episode, Jason later commits Benjy to an institution. The institution marks a lack of freedom for Benjy and represents the imprisoning interiority that haunts the entire Compson family. In the end, the "curse" of the Compsons is represented as threefold: the curse is biological (autism), sexual (incest), and social (the downfall of the family). All of these "curses" are symbolic and metaphorical representations of isolation and interiority: autism, incest, suicide, and institutionalization all become Gothic symbols entangled in the family's destruction.

Of course, Faulkner's presentation of Benjy as a symbol (rather than as a representation of an actual person) is built on dehumanizing stereotypes: Faulkner's narrative can only present Benjy as a curse because it ignores his status as a person. *The Sound and the Fury* depicts Benjy as a narrative voice that records and repeats rather than as a character who thinks and feels. Indeed, Benjy seems completely without interiority: "Ben sat, tranquil and empty" (284). His attempts to communicate are seen merely as hollow sound: "Suddenly he wept, a slow bellowing sound, meaningless and sustained" (285). Because Faulkner presents Benjy as being without feeling, all that can matter about Benjy is what he represents for other people, as they project their own meanings and interpretations onto him: "Then Ben wailed again, hopeless and prolonged. It was nothing. Just sound. It might have been all time and injustice and sorrow become vocal for an instant by a conjunction of planets" (288). Benjy is here presented as a kind of "Everyman" figure: because he is no one, he can be everyone ("all time and injustice and sorrow"). But the sound of a human being weeping is never just sound. Again, Benjy cannot be himself but must represent all humanity: "But he bellowed slowly, abjectly, without tears; the grave hopeless sound of all voiceless misery under the sun" (316). Benjy's expression of pain is not particular to him—according to Faulkner, it is not one individual's pain but the misery of all humanity. Even though he cannot speak, the other characters are constantly telling him to be quiet ("Hush, Benjy"). The youngest Compson is thus doubly silenced: the other characters do not understand his attempts to communicate because he is nonverbal, but they also do not recognize his attempts to communicate because they are not willing to "listen."

The novel ends with a famous final scene, a climactic encounter with Benjy that encapsulates the ways that autistic characters are used to symbolize supposedly universal neurotypical concerns. When Luster deviates from Benjy's routine and turns the carriage to the left instead of the right, the novel ends with a scene of full-blown autistic meltdown:

> Luster hit Queenie again and swung her to the left at the monument.
> For an instant Ben sat in an utter hiatus. Then he bellowed. Bellow on bellow, his voice mounted, with scarce interval for breath. There was more than astonishment in it, it was horror; shock; agony eyeless, tongueless; just sound, and Luster's eyes backrolling for a white instant . . . with Ben's voice mounting toward its unbelievable crescendo . . . (320)

Once the carriage can be turned around and Benjy's routine route is put back in place, order is restored: "his eyes were empty and blue and serene again as cornice and façade flowed smoothly once more from left to right, post and tree, window and doorway and signboard each in its ordered place" (320). In the novel's memorable final scene, Benjy's individual pain is presented as a symbol of the Compson family's social destruction: his autistic meltdown symbolizes the disintegration of the neurotypical Compson world—the fragile line between order and chaos.

In conclusion, *To Kill a Mockingbird, The Glass Menagerie,* and *The Sound and the Fury* present autistic characters as symbols of disunity and disruption within the family and/or community, linking autistic characters with Gothic symbols and motifs. All three works treat themes of isolation in relation to cognitive disability: Arthur lives out his reclusive life watching the neighborhood through the windows of the Radley house; Laura chooses to remain isolated in the family's run-down St. Louis apartment; and Benjy is confined to the Compson grounds, following the world through the gaps in the fence. All three works also highlight the autistic struggle to communicate with the neurotypical world: Arthur seldom speaks at all, leaving Scout to intuit his perspective by standing on his porch; Laura's awkward halts and conversation gaps fail to communicate her true feelings; and Benjy's vocalizations are regarded as "just sound." These works are also connected in their use of autistic characters to stand in for other issues (such as race and socioeconomic class): Arthur Radley's outsider status is conflated with the role of race in Tom Robinson's trial, while the aristocratic downfall of Laura's and Benjy's families is linked (in Laura's case subtly but in Benjy's case more overtly) to their autism. Each figure is presented as a "monster": Arthur and Benjy both frighten the neighborhood children, while Laura is the fragile and otherworldly unicorn so easily broken by careless hands. Although Arthur helps to unite the Finch family, saving Jem and Scout from Ewell, Laura and Benjy are imagined as the figures who bring about their families' final destruction. All three texts serve to remind readers of the powerful connections forged between autism and family in the cultural imagination, presenting people on the spectrum as Gothic monstrosities, emblems of outsiders who either pull the family together or pull it apart.

FIVE

The Autistic Child Narrator: *Extremely Loud and Incredibly Close* and *The Curious Incident of the Dog in the Night-Time*

> Our situation is the following. We are standing in front of a closed box which we cannot open, and we try hard to discover about what is and is not in it.
>
> —Albert Einstein, "Letter to John Moffat"

Many literary critics have noted the increase in fictional depictions of autism in recent years. *Extremely Loud and Incredibly Close* and *The Curious Incident of the Dog in the Night-Time* are both best sellers narrated by autistic child detectives. Jonathan Safran Foer's novel follows the adventures of the precocious Oskar Schell as he travels around New York looking for clues, attempting to solve the puzzle of his father's mysterious key. Mark Haddon's more lighthearted novel is narrated by Christopher Boone, a fifteen-year-old autistic savant who is trying to solve the canine murder mystery of Wellington, the neighbor's poodle. In spite of the sharp difference in tone between the two novels, both characters come from families that are torn apart by tragedy and strife (indeed, the humorous tone of Haddon's novel can only be sustained because Christopher is often unaware of the pathos that surrounds him). Both child narrators also function in their fictional worlds as symbols for larger social concerns: Oskar's unspoken disability and struggle to communicate symbolize the larger cultural trauma surrounding 9/11, while Christopher's autistic characteristics are stereotypically represented as the cause of his family's drama. Ultimately, both characters become symbols that reflect outward—these autistic children stand in for larger cultural anxieties regarding the instability of the postmodern family and the struggle to establish emotional connections in a postmodern world.[1]

Private Disability, Public Tragedy:
Extremely Loud and Incredibly Close

Extremely Loud and Incredibly Close is a novel about the search for absent family members, for stories in silences, for unfinished conversations and undelivered messages. The symbol at the center of the novel, the hidden answering machine, holds the words of a desperate but deceased father, a message that his child heard but failed to answer, words that form half of a vital but incomplete conversation. Indeed, *Extremely Loud and Incredibly Close* is a novel obsessed with incomplete acts of communication, fascinated with words and messages that never reach their destinations.[2] In fact, if "communication" is defined as the sending and receiving of a message that is mutually understood by both speaker and listener, then there is seldom any true communication among the characters. It is fitting, then, that the child narrator, Oskar Schell, seems to have a communication disorder. Although Jonathan Safran Foer has stated that it was not his explicit intent to create Oskar as an autistic character, this has been a common interpretation of the novel—so pervasive, in fact, that the director of the film adaptation did extensive research on Asperger's syndrome in order to prepare for filming.[3] Whatever the author's intent, the reading public has consistently found autism in this novel, perhaps because so many of the themes in the book—an inability to communicate, a breakdown in the family, and an isolated child facing an internal struggle—are tropes that our culture stereotypically associates with the autism spectrum.[4] Ultimately, autism stereotypes encapsulate forces that drive the narrative on a symbolic level: like the father's unanswered final message, autism becomes a symbol of disunity in communication, and the novel offers the condition as a metaphor for the neurotypical struggle to communicate in a postmodern world. Emphasizing the stereotypes of autism as "tragic" and "ineffable," Oskar's autistic traits symbolically underpin the novel's plot, as the "ineffable tragedy" of autism stands in for the tragic events of 9/11, so that the autistic child who is unable to communicate, unable to answer the vital message of his father, reflects a mourning nation unable to find words in the face of tragedy.

Although readers were quick to diagnose the precocious boy detective as being on the spectrum, the growing body of critical literature on *Extremely Loud and Incredibly Close* does not even address the possibility. Yet Oskar clearly displays many autistic traits: he struggles with social skills and displays an intense interest in numbers. The other characters often perceive his behavior as both socially inappropriate and age inappropriate: Oskar is socially naive in spite of his intellectual sophistication. For example, his mother is upset when he gives a key to their apartment to the mailwoman: "But you can't give a key to a stranger," she says, clearly aghast. "Fortunately, Alicia isn't a stranger," Oskar responds.[5] His inability to distinguish, even at the age of nine, between "trusted friend," "acquaintance," and "stranger" is certainly reminiscent of some people with AS. He has a hard time socializing at school, frequently spending recess in the library. He describes himself as "unpopular," and the other students bully him because they perceive him as different: "Jimmy Synder raised his hand. I called on him. He asked, 'Why are you so weird?' I asked if his question was rhetorical. Mr. Keegan told him to go to Principal Buddy's office. Some of the kids cracked up. I knew they were cracking up in the bad way, which is at me" (189). The inability to recognize rhetorical questions is, of course, a classic autism stereotype. Adults are equally likely to find Oskar socially awkward: "Ada told me, 'Oskar, I think you made Gail quite uncomfortable.' 'What do you mean?' 'I could tell that she felt embarrassed.' 'I was just trying to be nice.' 'You might have tried too hard'" (150). Oskar tells his psychiatrist, "I'm not very good with people" (201). In short, the other characters frequently perceive Oskar's behavior as socially inappropriate; specifically, they comment on his tendency to think literally and on the wide disparity between his intellectual knowledge and his social skills. In addition, Oskar's detail-oriented mind seems particularly fixated on numbers: "I figured that if you included everything—from bicycle locks to roof latches to places for cufflinks—there are probably about 18 locks for every person in New York City, which would mean about 162 million locks" (41). Oskar counts (and remembers) the number of stairs leading up to his home: "I ran up the 105 stairs to our apartment" (11). He is particular about always knowing the time: "I know that it was 10:18 when I got home because I look at my watch a lot" (14). Both his unusual social behavior and his intense interest in numbers suggest autistic tendencies.

In addition to being socially awkward and having strong but narrow interests, Oskar has a hard time understanding his own emotions and relating to (and communicating with) others on an emotional level. When interacting with one of the many Mr. Blacks that he meets, Oskar remarks, "I couldn't tell what he was feeling, because I couldn't speak the language of his feelings" (239). He keeps a "feeling book" in which he writes down his emotions, and some of his fantastic "inventions" involve ways to make his own emotions more apparent or to help him interpret the emotions of others. For example, he imagines a shower that reveals people's feelings:

> What if the water that came out of the shower was treated with a chemical that responded to a combination of things. . . . [I]f you were extremely excited your skin would turn green, and if you were angry you'd turn red, obviously. . . . Everyone could know what everyone else felt, and we could be more careful with each other. . . . Another reason it would be a good invention is that there are so many times when you know you're feeling a lot of something, but you don't know what the something is. Am I frustrated? Am I actually just panicky? (163)

The fantasy suggests a boy who has a difficult time interpreting emotions but who wants to connect with others. Recognizing his own tendency to be blunt, he imagines that if he could recognize what other people are feeling, he could "be more careful" of their emotions. Oskar has an intense desire to establish relationships with other people, but it is a desire that seems constantly thwarted throughout the novel: "I bumped into a googolplex people. . . . I wanted to hear their heartbeats, and I wanted them to hear mine" (288). He displays the autistic desire to catalog in his idea to invent a book that "listed every word in every language. It wouldn't be a very useful book, but you could hold it and know that everything you could possibly say was in your hands" (316). Oskar seems to believe that holding "every word" would reassure him even when he struggles to communicate. His constant yearning for human connections but his simultaneous struggle to create and maintain them suggests a common autism stereotype.

Oskar clearly has intense sensory reactions and engages in stimming behaviors. Indeed, the world as Oskar describes it is an intensely sensory world. Oskar finds physical contact with objects reassuring, a way of physically mapping out the sensory environment: "I touched all the keys that I could reach, and that made me feel OK, for some reason" (39). He reacts strongly to physical touch: "Grandma started touching me again, which was annoying, even though I didn't want it to be" (6). His favorite form of stimming is to shake his tambourine as he travels around New York, most likely because he finds the repetitive motion and sound calming: "I shook my tambourine the whole time, because even though I was going through different neighborhoods, I was still me" (88).[6]

Oskar here describes stimming as a form of sensory engagement and bodily feedback. This description reminds me of autistic author and poet Tito Mukhopadhyay's explanation of hand flapping: "I flap to know that I have arms."[7] The issue here is stimming being used as a means of gaining knowledge of one's self. Even the title of the novel could be seen as pointing to sensory issues, as many of the noises in Oskar's world seem "extremely loud," and his physical contact with people often feels "incredibly close." When he is with his father, Oskar describes their connection in sensory terms: "I tucked my body incredibly close into his" (13). Later, he describes his encounter with Abby Black in the same way: "Her face came incredibly close to my face" (97). Noises only seem to have one volume for Oskar: extremely loud. To give only a few examples, "an extremely loud siren would go off," "the man in the other room called again, this time extremely loudly," and "a car drove by that was playing music extremely loudly, and it vibrated my heart" (38, 93, 195). This constant repetition of the terms "extremely loud" and "incredibly close" is a measure of how intense the world seems from Oskar's autistic perspective.

In fact, Oskar's autistic traits (the sharp juxtaposition between logical/bodily understanding and emotional understanding) represent the mourning nation's struggle to reconcile logical knowledge and sensory experiences with tragedy's emotional impact. While the novel presents the sensory world as immediate, strong, and abrasive, Oskar's engagement with the emotional world functions on strikingly different terms, as the novel frequently juxtaposes sensory and logical apprehension with emotional apprehension. On a symbolic level, the narrative uses the intense sensory reactions associated with ASD to suggest the nation's intense emotional reaction to the attacks on 9/11. Oskar describes seeing the site of his father's death through a viewing lens on the top of the Empire State Building: "When the metal lids opened, I could see things that were far away incredibly close, like the Woolworth Building, and Union Square, and the gigantic hole where the World Trade Center was" (245). Emotionally speaking, "the gigantic hole where the World Trade Center was" is simultaneously both "far away" and "incredibly close." This passage describes the emotional immediacy of his father's death with the exact same terms used to describe Oskar's sensory reaction to physical touch. The novel equates sensory overload and mourning, presenting grief as an overwhelming force that causes disorientation and pain. Foer also juxtaposes Oskar's strong reliance on math and logic with his growing emotional awareness. Describing the symbolic key that he hopes will unlock the answers to his father's secrets, Oskar remarks, "Even though I knew that there were 161,999,999 locks in New York that it didn't open, I still felt like it opened everything" (200). While Oskar can estimate numerically approximately how many locks in New York City will not fit the key, he feels on an emotional level that the key must open all of the secrets in the city, for it has the potential to unlock the secret most important to him—the way to be closer to his late father. The sharp juxtaposition between what Oskar can apprehend with his senses or with logic (both areas in which autism is imagined to create excess) as opposed to what he can understand on an emotional level (an area in which people with autism sometimes struggle) mirrors the neurotypical reader's confusion in trying to grasp the lack of logic in tragedy and to apprehend the sensory horror of the burning towers. Appropriating an autistic narrative voice allows the novel to explore the complex feelings of the neurotypical audience in stark black and white, rendering the natural human response to tragedy more simplistically comprehensible by relying on a false understanding of ASD that depends on divisive binaries (logical vs. emotional, concrete vs. abstract).

These simplistic binaries are not the only autism stereotypes forwarded by the novel: an interpretation of Oskar as autistic reveals that a plethora of stereotypes is built into his character. In keeping with the stereotype of those on the spectrum as "inhuman," Oskar imagines himself as a computer: "I handed him my card and told him, 'Greetings. Gerald. I. Am. Oskar.' He asked me why I was talking like that. I told him, 'Oskar's CPU is a neural-net processor. A learning computer. The more contact he has with humans, the more he learns'" (5). The larger implication in the playful encounter with Gerald seems to be that Oskar is a computer learning social skills by studying humans. Oskar also uses imagery that suggests the stereotype of the autistic person as separated from the rest of the world. He repeatedly describes himself as insular, wrapped in an invisible cocoon that separates him emotionally and socially from everyone else: "I zipped myself all the way into the sleeping bag of myself" (37). Oskar uses metaphors that describe his brain as busy and his thought process as extremely fast paced (indeed, as too fast paced): "I stayed there for a bit, trying to catch up with my brain" (46). His mind needs to be in constant motion: "I needed to do something, like sharks, who die if they don't swim, which I know about" (87). Oskar imagines the comfort of his father's presence as the force that can slow down his wild and whirling thoughts: "Being with him made my brain quiet. I didn't have to invent a thing" (12). These metaphors also hint at the imagined danger of the autistic mind, as Oskar suggests that his brain, if left bored or idle, would simply self-destruct. He imagines his mind as an uncontrollable and potentially destructive force caught in a perseverative loop: "I started inventing things, and then I couldn't stop, like beavers, which I know about. People think they cut down trees so they can build dams, but in reality it's because their teeth never stop growing, and if they didn't constantly file them down by cutting through all of those trees, their teeth would start to grow into their own faces, which would kill them. That's how my brain was" (36). Foer presents Oskar's thoughts as a form of repetitive perseveration that he cannot control: once Oskar starts to imagine ("inventing"), he finds that he is unable to stop his fixation. Oskar's inability to "turn his mind off" or to "slow his mind down" is here imagined as leading to self-destruction: if he doesn't "file" his brain down with creative exercise, it will become a dangerous force. The idea of the brain as a sharp-edged weapon that turns on the self is certainly a disturbing one—and it points directly to our culture's false construction of the autistic mind as dangerous and out of control. In short, all of these stereotypes—the autistic person as a computer learning socialization, the autistic child as insulated from the world in an isolating cocoon, the autistic mind as a source of danger and disorder—are an inherent part of Oskar's characterization.

Indeed, the film adaptation of *Extremely Loud and Incredibly Close* deliberately portrays Oskar as stereotypically autistic: although the film leaves his diagnostic status ambiguous, it uses Oskar's AS as a primary obstacle in his quest, presenting an unrealistic narrative in which Oskar is able to overcome his sensory issues and autistic traits through courage and determination.[8] While actor Thomas Horn does an excellent job of portraying Oskar's autistic body language and vocal inflection, the clichéd plotline of overcoming disability reduces the complex novel into an overly simplified film. Although the director, Stephen Daldry, acknowledges that he researched AS and chose to depict Oskar as autistic (in an interview, Daldry describes Oskar as "somewhere on the autism spectrum"), the film avoids a direct diagnosis.[9] In the film, Oskar tells Abby Black, "People tell me I'm very odd all the time. I got tested once to see if I had Asperger's disease. Dad said it is for people who are smarter than everyone else but can't run straight. The tests weren't definitive."[10] But while the film shies away from labeling its protagonist, Oskar's body language clearly signals to viewers that he is on the spectrum.[11] In the opening of the film, he refuses to play on the playground. When his father encourages him to try the swings, Oskar backs away, holding his hands over his ears and shouting, "Don't be disappointed in me." Oskar is afraid of the kinesthetic stimulation offered by the swings, but he shows that reaction by covering his ears. The instinctive defense against sensory overload (covering his ears even in the absence of sound) is a gesture that is easily recognizable to viewers who know a child on the spectrum.[12] Oskar displays this characteristic gesture throughout the film whenever he feels afraid or overwhelmed. For example, when he imagines his father falling from the World Trade Center, he huddles on the bathroom floor with his hands over his ears. In the end, the film's implicit disclosure (we know that Oskar has autism, but we do not know that Oskar has autism) allows the film to use the idea of "overcoming" Asperger's as a guiding concept in its plot while avoiding potential critique for depicting a character on the spectrum in an unrealistic way.

Ultimately, the film presents Oskar's quest to find the lock as an exercise in overcoming his autistic traits and sensory issues. Oskar thinks of the search for the lock as another expedition planned for him by his father, and he claims that "nothing was going to stop me, not even me." In other words, he feels that he must overcome a part of himself in order to succeed on his quest. In the film, AS is simplified into a series of phobias over which Oskar must triumph.[13] Specifically, his father had designed Oskar's previous expeditions to encourage him to speak more: "Dad designed my expeditions so that I had to talk to people, which he knows I had a hard time doing." Traveling throughout New York also presents major challenges. As Oskar walks down the street, the film offers a montage designed to suggest sensory overload. His hands pressed firmly over his ears, Oskar stands in the middle of a crowded intersection, apparently unaware of the danger posed by the moving vehicles around him. As he spins in a circle, the camera circles around him in the opposite direction, suggesting confusion and disorientation. The background noise of the street increases suddenly, and Oskar's voice, already speaking in rapid panic, increases sharply in volume—by the end of the sequence, he is shouting. Behind him, we see a blurry montage of the various items he lists: "running people, airplanes, tall things, things you can get stuck in . . . loud things, screaming, crying, towers, tunnels, loud things, things with lights." The combination of shouting, spinning, and fast-paced montage mimics the disorientation, confusion, and panic caused by sensory overload. Although some of the "phobias" listed clearly relate to his father's death ("airplanes," "towers"), others are sensory issues commonly associated with the autism spectrum ("loud things," "things with lights"), and it seems worth noting that one of the most common sensory triggers for autistic people (loud noises) is important enough for Oskar to list it twice. Oskar tracks his progress in overcoming these sensory issues throughout the course of his quest, admitting that "I still feel scared every time I go into a strange place, and I'm still scared every time I leave home." Oskar's grandfather Thomas tells him that "sometimes we have to face our fears." In fact, the film simplifies Thomas's complex reasons for abandoning his wife and unborn child in order to fit this facile theme: "I was too afraid to be a father," he tells his grandson, expressing the regret that presumably comes when one gives in to one's fears. This simplistic reduction of AS into a series of phobias that need to be overcome offers a fundamentally false picture of autistic experience, underplaying the true intensity of sensory responses, suggesting that one can "cure" oneself of autism through courage, and, ultimately, representing autism not as a facet of human identity but as a problem that must be solved. In short, the film's presentation of Asperger's as a matter of cowardice and weakness is a false and damaging one. Although the film initially seems to affirm Oskar's autistic traits as a part of his identity, its final scene dramatically undercuts this message. In a conversation from the book that is made even more poignant by the explicit decision to play Oskar as autistic, Oskar tells his mother, "I promise I'll be a better son. I'll be normal." His mother immediately reassures him that he is "wonderful." Through his mother's reassurance, the film superficially affirms Oskar's autistic identity: there is no need for him to try to be neurotypical. At the end of the film, however, Oskar finds a note that his father had hidden for him on the playground swings. The final image is one of Oskar swinging with apparent pleasure. The film's ultimate message seems to be that AS can be overcome through courage, that Oskar's adventures in the film have "cured" his sensory issues, and that his father's love has enabled him to overcome his disability.

Although there isn't enough information provided on Oskar's father and grandfather to do anything more than conjecture, the novel hints that Oskar may have inherited his autistic tendencies from them: certainly, both grandfather and grandson have a communication disorder, leaving a symbolic stigma on the men in the Schell family. The exact nature of the grandfather's communication disorder, however, remains unclear. The novel never adequately explains the silence of Oskar's grandfather Thomas, who communicates by writing: some readers might assume that this is a response to the trauma of the bombing he survived at Dresden. Although Thomas communicated by speaking earlier in his life, he no longer speaks.[14] In any case, Thomas desperately wants to connect with his grandson but is initially unable to do so. Thomas learns everything he can about the boy by watching him: "I learned his life from a distance, when he went to school, when he came home, where his friends lived, what stores he liked to go to, I followed him all over the city" (278). The grandfather's unidentified communication disorder (his inability to communicate by speaking on a literal level) becomes a symbol of his inability to communicate and connect with others on a metaphorical/emotional level. He is separated from Oskar by far more than spoken words: his abandonment of his own son and his personal history of emotional trauma make it difficult for him to connect with Oskar. Whatever his communication disorder may be, Thomas's disability makes him subject to the same dehumanizing stereotypes as his grandson. Oskar attempts to engage Thomas in conversation: "I tried to think of something I could ask him that he couldn't not know the answer to. 'Are you a human being?' He flipped back and pointed at 'I'm sorry'" (238). Because of his disability, Thomas presents himself as less than human. If Oskar's father isn't autistic, he does sometimes come across as pedantic, detail oriented, and uncommunicative (all common stereotypes of people with AS). His habit of marking up the *New York Times* with a red pen is definitely a gesture of nonreciprocal communication—no one sees or responds to his proofreading marks. Indeed, Oskar's mother has a conversation with him about his father's nature that plays on the autistic stereotypes of missing the big picture and misunderstanding metaphorical language. In this humorous exchange, Oskar professes his preference for definite, literal answers: "'What's wrong with definitivity?,' 'Dad sometimes missed the forest for the trees.' 'What forest?' 'Nothing'" (43). When his mother explains that his father often missed the big picture because of his detail-oriented mind, Oskar is confused by the figurative language—his literal-minded question ("What forest?") suggests that Oskar, like his father, cannot see the big picture. In short, both father and grandfather display at least a few autistic traits: certainly, it is significant that both grandfather and grandson have a communication disorder.

Overall, the primary connection between Oskar and his grandfather, a communication disability, is symbolic of larger incomplete acts of communication among the neurotypical characters in the novel. Indeed, Foer uses these communication disorders as symbols of the wider misunderstanding and miscommunication that form an inevitable part of the human condition. The novel as a whole highlights nonreciprocal acts of communication to suggest the nation's inability to fully articulate the grief caused by the events of the 9/11 terrorist attacks. Although some verbal people on the spectrum prioritize nonreciprocal monologues over more conventional two-sided conversation, *Extremely Loud and Incredibly Close* uses disabled characters to suggest a world in which truly reciprocal conversations are impossible (for neurotypical and autistic alike).[15] In a novel in which nonreciprocal communication abounds, it seems that the characters cannot fully connect with each other.[16] Foer's fictionalized New York emphasizes the impossibility of complete communication and understanding, as his characters fundamentally struggle with the speech act, increasingly discovering the disposable, transitory nature of words.[17] Again and again, words in this novel prove empty and futile.

Foer's use of magical realism to describe the grandfather's writing (a plethora of words that cover every surface of the apartment) allows him to explore the transitory and incomplete nature of all human communication. The many pages filled with the grandfather's writing eventually become trash, as his words are recycled for other purposes: "I might rip out a page—'I'm sorry this is the smallest I've got'—to wipe up some mess, or empty a whole day to pack up the emergency light bulbs. . . . I made a fire and used my laughter for kindling 'Ha ha ha!' 'Ha ha ha!' 'Ha ha ha!'" (28). The idea of laughter being burned suggests both the impermanence of words and the sentiments they express. Thomas claims that he uses not just words but "a whole day" to pack up a box of lightbulbs, as though the words he has written represent life itself. Since Thomas communicates by writing, his words are easily erased. His wife relates how transitory his many messages to her really are: "When your grandfather left me forty years ago, I erased all of his writing. I washed the words from the mirrors and the floors. I painted over the walls. I cleaned the shower curtains. I even refinished the floors. It took me as long as I had known him to get rid of all of his words" (233). The novel prioritizes the difficulty of the speech act, recognizing the precarious nature of spoken communication and of words themselves. Oskar's grandfather contemplates the difficulty of expressing oneself through words: "I took the world into me, rearranged it, and sent it back out as a question: 'Do you like me?'" (117). But even the grandfather's transitory and ineffective acts of communication still hold some power to communicate with others: "She cried and cried and cried, there weren't any napkins nearby, so I ripped the page from the book—'I don't speak. I'm sorry.'—and used it to dry her cheeks, my explanation and apology ran down her face like mascara" (32). Thomas's words describing his disability run down his wife's face like tears, reminding the reader that Thomas's communication disorder places great stress on their relationship. His desperate effort to call his wife on the phone after forty years of absence is rendered completely inarticulate: "I knew it wouldn't help, I knew no good would come of it, but I stood there in the middle of the airport, at the beginning of the century, at the end of my life, and I told her everything. . . . I broke my life down into letters, for love pressed '5, 6, 8, 3' for death '3, 3, 2, 8, 4'" (269).[18] Every string of numbers is followed by either a question mark or an exclamation point. He is asking for answers. He is shouting, frantic to communicate with her after finding out about their son's death. Thomas realizes that the message he is sending to his wife cannot possibly be received and understood—she will not know that "5, 6, 8, 3" is "love." The gesture is necessarily nonreciprocal in nature, but the need to tell "everything" "at the end of my life" is an overwhelming imperative: the message, regarding love and death, is vital, and Thomas feels that he is running out of time to tell it. Yet the three pages of inarticulate numbers that follow are indecipherable to both his wife and the reader: the message is not received on either end, suggesting on a wider scale the inability to communicate with each other, especially about the ideas ("death," "love") that we may perceive as most essential. Thomas also frequently writes unanswered letters (and sometimes simply mails empty envelopes or writes letters that are never read).[19] He travels back to New York with suitcases full of unmailed letters addressed to his dead son. Airport security is clearly confused by this kind of baggage: "'That's a lot of paper' he said. . . . The guard looked at the other guard and they shared a smile, I don't mind if smiles come at my expense, it's a small price to pay, they let me through, not because they believed me but because they didn't want to try to understand me" (268). Like the other characters in the novel, the guards fail to realize the magnitude of what Thomas is communicating with these collected letters. Like the majority of the people Thomas encounters, they do not spend time trying to understand a man who struggles to communicate. The image of his son's empty coffin full of unsent, unread letters is the ultimate symbol of the message that cannot be delivered. When Oskar asks what he is putting in the coffin, Thomas writes, "Things I wasn't able to tell him" (322). Just as Oskar's father is trying to get a message to his son via the answering machine, his own father, Thomas, is trying to get a message to his son via letters he can't send—there is a breakdown in communication in both generations of the Schell family, as both grandfather and father struggle to communicate with loved ones beyond the ultimate barrier of death.

Throughout the novel, the image of the grandfather running out of space for his writing symbolizes the struggle to convey all of the truly important messages before one's death, especially to family: "I have so much to tell you, the problem isn't that I'm running out of time, I'm running out of room, this book is filling up, there couldn't be enough pages. . . . But there's too much to express. I'm sorry" (132).[20] Specifically, Thomas focuses on "room" as the problem in his struggle to communicate as opposed to "time": perhaps even if he had a longer life, he would still not be able to articulate everything he needs to convey in a way that would allow the message to be received. Again, the manipulation of the text itself visually represents the novel's thematic problem—by the time the narrative reaches this passage, the font and spacing have been getting smaller for the past several pages: "I went into the room and got this daybook from the closet, this book that is nearly out of pages. . . . I didn't know how to hold him, I'm running out of room. . . . Poor child, telling everything to a stranger. . . . I wanted to give him an infinitely long blank book and the rest of time" (280). The daybook that he uses to communicate becomes a symbol of Thomas's life—as a grandfather, he is "running out of room," and if he could give one gift to Oskar, it would be "an infinitely long blank book and the rest of time." But even "the rest of time" is not enough to ensure communication in *Extremely Loud and Incredibly Close*—one also needs infinite space for writing. Further, Thomas's inability to relate to Oskar, to negotiate his relationship with him on a physical level ("I didn't know how to hold him"), is equated to "running out of room," to the inability to communicate what he wants Oskar to know. Finally, Thomas's words, now written on top of each other, become completely indecipherable (289). This goes on for three unreadable pages, the amount of repetition and overlay causing the print to become more dense and illegible with every page. On these pages, the novel's illegible message is unable to communicate with readers, thus equating the Schell family's private sorrow with the "unreadable" and "unutterable" story of 9/11.[21] The characters' inability to communicate with each other ultimately becomes the novel's inability to communicate its ineffable subject matter.

Oskar's grandmother also engages in her own form of nonreciprocal communication—reading and listening without comprehension. In an effort to improve her English, Thomas brings her magazines and newspapers from the airport: "I used to ride the bus there at the end of every week, to take the magazines and newspapers that people left behind when they got on their planes, your mother reads and reads and reads, she wants English, as much as she can get her hands on . . . so I started bringing a knapsack, which I would stuff with as much as would fit, it got heavy, my shoulders burned with English" (108–109). Yet the book later reveals that because of her visual impairment, Oskar's grandmother may not be able to read any of the copious words piled into her husband's knapsack. As a couple in which one partner communicates by writing while the other cannot read, their marriage is fundamentally based on miscommunication: every week, he brings her a surfeit of messages that she cannot receive. Thomas later reflects on all the written messages she must have misunderstood, "the letters I wrote without response. . . . But worse—it's unspeakable, write it!—

Imagining Autism

I realized that your mother couldn't see the emptiness, she couldn't see anything. . . . All of the words I'd written to her over all of those years, had I never said anything to her at all?" (124). Ironically, the idea that he has unwittingly been miscommunicating with his wife for all these years is, in Thomas's mind, "unspeakable"—a message so terrible that it cannot be communicated. Eventually, the couple separate after they fail to agree about whether their marriage is "something" or "nothing": "It wasn't until last night, our last night together, that the inevitable question finally arose, I told her 'something' by covering her face with my hands and then lifting them like a marriage veil. 'We must be'" (110–111). Over sixty-five pages later, his wife relates the same story from her perspective, revealing she was unable to interpret this crucial message:

> What are we? Something or nothing?
> He covered my face with his hands and lifted them off.
> I did not know what that meant. (178)

Overall, the image of the silent husband writing to his blind wife represents the failure of communication so common to human relationships.

In addition, the postmodern style of the novel emphasizes repetition in both narrative and motif, reflecting nonreciprocal acts of communication and the repetitive nature of autism itself. The form letter Oskar receives in response to his letter to Stephen Hawking appears throughout the novel. Oskar's letters ostensibly go nowhere and reach no audience: the repetitive response he receives is only the empty, formulaic words of a form letter (communication that is not real communication):

> Thank you for your letter. Because of the large volume of mail I receive, I am unable to write personal responses. Nevertheless, know that I read and save every letter, with the hope of one day being able to give each the proper response it deserves. Until that day,
> Most sincerely,
> Stephen Hawking (106)

The unanswered letters to Hawking emphasize Oskar's isolation and inability to communicate. Indeed, the members of the Schell family are not the only characters in the novel who communicate nonreciprocally. William Black is prevented from receiving his father's final message because of the lost key, thus rendering his father's final act of communication incomplete. Ruth, the eccentric recluse who lives on top of the Empire State Building, might as well be talking to herself:

The Autistic Child Narrator

"She started walking again, and we followed her, but I wondered if she would have kept talking even if we hadn't followed her. I couldn't tell if she was doing what she was doing for us, or for herself, or for some completely other reason" (250). A. R. Black chooses to turn off his hearing aids in order to isolate himself from the world: by closing out spoken communication, he refuses to receive the messages that people might speak to him. He also keeps a copious catalog in which he reduces human beings to a single word, a method of organization that implies the potential failure of language to encapsulate and describe human life: "'I write the name of the person and a one-word biography!' 'Just one word?' 'Everyone gets boiled down to one word!'" (157). Oskar objects to this filing method: "'But he's also probably a husband, or dad, or Beatles fan, or jogger or who knows what else.' 'Sure! You could write a book about Manuel Escobar! And that would leave things out, too! You could write ten books! You could never stop writing!'" (157). Clearly, A. R. Black is familiar with the imprecision and vagueness of language and has reached a point in his life at which he accepts language's inability to fully communicate.

Ultimately, the answering machine that holds the father's dying words is the novel's central symbol of nonreciprocal and incomplete communication.[22] Oskar chooses to communicate this message to his mother in a decidedly nonreciprocal way. The Morse code bracelet he gives her represents two layers of nonreciprocal communication (it does not communicate to his mother the already incomplete message his father gave to him). Basically, the Morse code bracelet takes an incomplete act of communication (the answering machine message) and translates it into another incomplete message (the Morse code bracelet). Although Oskar decides to give this "message" to his mother, he also chooses not to explain it to her and seems to accept that she cannot understand what he is telling her—his gift ultimately becomes an act of self-communication. Of course, the gift of a bracelet from son to mother does communicate something, but the message of love that the mother receives is not the message Oskar sends (Oskar is particularly distressed that his father's last words do not include the words "I love you"). The change of medium (from spoken language, to recorded message, to Morse code, to textile object) represents a variety of ways in which this communicative act is passed on without real comprehension or completion.[23]

Finally, Oskar perceives the mysterious key he finds in his father's closet as an incomplete message from his father. On some level, he hopes that the search for the key will complete the unfinished conversation on the answering machine, giving him a way to respond to his father's words by going on a quest. While the

Imagining Autism

key does turn out to be part of a message from a dead father to his son, it does not unlock a personal message for Oskar. As a part of his quest to find the lock, he is finally able to help a completed message pass between a father and son (between William Black and his father), as well as forging a relationship with his own grandfather. Oskar finally finds reciprocal communication, but he is not a part of it: the message the key unlocks is not for him, and he is still closed out of the conversation at the end of his quest.

When Oskar's letters to Hawking are finally answered at the end of the novel, the response presents a metaphor that further emphasizes the ultimately isolated nature of the human condition, suggesting that all human beings are fundamentally unable to understand other people, to connect with each other, and to communicate—even with the people closest to them, even on the most intimate and important topics.[24] Hawking responds,

> Albert Einstein, a hero of mine, once wrote, "Our situation is the following. We are standing in front of a closed box which we cannot open."
> I'm sure I don't have to tell you that the vast majority of the universe is composed of dark matter. The fragile balance depends on things we'll never be able to see, hear, smell, taste, or touch. Life itself depends on them. (305)

In this metaphor, the universe (and the nature of life itself) is fundamentally unknowable. We can observe the box, but we cannot fully understand what is in it. Life "depends" on those ambiguous things that cannot be apprehended with the senses. We have to try to verify that the contents of the box are there, or are what we think they are, by trying to find traces of their influence elsewhere.

The symbolic box from Hawking's letter closely resembles another symbolic object from earlier in the novel: the frozen can in the story of the sixth borough. According to Oskar's father, what is closed off in the container that cannot be opened (without changing the conditions of the contents) is human communication itself: "Instead she said, 'I love you.' The words traveled the yo-yo, the doll, the diary, the necklace, the quilt, the tea bag, the tennis racket, the hem of the skirt he one day should have pulled from her body. . . . [T]he boy covered his can with a lid, removed the string, and put her love for him on a shelf in his closet. Of course, he never could open the can, because then he would lose its contents" (220). As with the words on the answering machine that traveled through a variety of media (spoken language, recorded message, Morse code, textile object), the words "I love you" are translated through a variety of improbable methods (yo-yo, doll, diary). The method of transmission (a children's string-and-can telephone strung between windows) is a childish parody of Oskar's Morse code bracelet. As with the father's dying words, there is a fear that the message will be lost or mistranslated as it is precariously passed from one medium to another. Ultimately, the words "I love you" become the mysterious matter inside the closed container that can never be opened without altering the contents. In fact, Oskar's father reveals that the boy never opens the can and that it is still there today: "On a frozen shelf, in a closet frozen shut, is a can with a voice in it" (223).

Einstein's metaphor gains a completely different dimension when read in relation to the story of the sixth borough. The need to hold on to the message of love means that it can never be fully heard, fully received, or communicatively complete. The love in the can becomes frozen in time, yet another nonreciprocal act of communication. On a broader scale, the closed box represents the inability of human beings to connect with one another. Metaphorically, autism is often imagined as a closed box, a container that shuts out the rest of the world, shrouding the autistic person in mystery. Such stereotypes undermine the ultimately unknowable and incommunicable nature of human beings more generally by imagining that only autistic people are separated from their fellow human beings. If this novel asks fundamental questions about what it means to speak, to communicate, to be heard, and to connect emotionally, seeing Oskar as an autistic character may help readers to see that these are problems for all people, not just autistic people.

Public Disability, Private Tragedy:
The Curious Incident of the Dog in the Night-Time

Mark Haddon's depiction of Asperger's syndrome has received incredible acclaim: not only is his young adult novel, *The Curious Incident of the Dog in the Night-Time,* increasingly taught in the secondary school classroom, but it is also an award-winning best seller with popular crossover appeal—an appeal based at least partially on the novel's presentation of a disability that has engaged public "fascination."[25] As literary critics have been quick to note, the book never uses the terms "autism" and "Asperger's"—within the pages of the novel itself, Christopher's diagnosis is implicit.[26] However, the book was marketed with the term "Asperger's" on the cover, and an audience with even a glancing familiarity with autism will conclude that Christopher Boone is on the spectrum. While Oskar's disability is covert and private, Christopher's is more externally obvious. Indeed, Christopher's character is a conglomeration of stereotypes, presenting autism as the public eye would imagine it to be: his character is more consistent in sticking to general perceptions of the spectrum than any real individual person could be, resulting in a figure who is overdrawn to the point of potential caricature.[27] His charming narrative voice is simultaneously childlike and complex, rhetorically embodying the seemingly paradoxical "splinter skills" of some autistics.[28] Although the novel builds on autism stereotypes, it does so in a complex and multilayered way, harking back to current cultural readings of Sherlock Holmes as autistic, inverting and parodying the autistic detective tradition. Overall, Haddon's use of this tradition allows him to engage autism as both a source of strength (Christopher contemplates the neurodiversity paradigm by comparing himself to Sherlock Holmes) and a source of potential pain (Christopher's disability is represented as the key to the "mystery" of the trauma and sorrow in his family).

First, Haddon's allusions to Conan Doyle's tales of Sherlock Holmes foreground Christopher's place in the autistic detective tradition: it is implied that Christopher has chosen Sherlock Holmes as a role model because the boy perceives the great detective to be an autistic hero. As the popular culture interpretation of Sherlock Holmes as an autistic figure is becomingly increasingly prevalent, Christopher is a young man growing up in a world in which Holmes represents a particular kind of stereotypical autistic identity. In essence, Christopher's society has already told him that he has something in common with Conan Doyle's famous sleuth. Christopher is clearly aware of his own diagnostic label (he attempts to meet the needs of his presumed neurotypical readers by spending a great deal of the novel explaining how his mind works).[29] Although the diagnosis goes unspoken, part of Christopher's identity as an autistic young person is shaped by the cultural stereotype assuming that differences in sensory perception, attention, and memory make autistic people unusually observant. In a culture in which Holmes could be seen as a potential role model for autistic youngsters, Christopher "claims" Sherlock Holmes as autistic and compares himself to the detective as a way of taking pride in his autistic characteristics. Christopher's desire to be like Holmes is clear: "I also like *The Hound of the Baskervilles* because I like Sherlock Holmes and I think that if I were a proper detective he is the kind of detective I would be."[30] In Christopher's mind, to be recognized as a good detective is one potential way to be successful as an autistic person. Clearly, Christopher is aware of the autistic detective stereotype: it is a fictional role that he is attempting to emulate.

Specifically, Christopher is attracted to aspects of Holmes's character that could be claimed as autistic traits and that could also be described as strengths: through his reading of Holmes's character, Christopher engages the neurodiversity paradigm. Nicola Allen notes that Holmes is a source of inspiration for the boy detective: "For Christopher, the detective figure represents an opportunity for a positive re-reading of his inability to intuit other people's emotions. . . . Throughout, he uses Holmes to represent the ultimate positive incarnation of the triumph of reason over emotion: this allows Christopher to reconfigure his social limitations as strengths."[31] As Christopher explains, Holmes "is very intelligent and he solves the mystery and he says *The world is full of obvious things which nobody by any chance ever observes*. But he notices them, like I do" (91). Recognizing intelligence and a detail-oriented mind as traits commonly associated with the Asperger's stereotype, Christopher feels that these are traits that an autistic person should try to cultivate. As Vivienne Muller explains, "In Sherlock Holmes mysteries there is a . . . reassuring formula based on an anchoring logic and the exercise of acute observational powers. In this they resemble Christopher's own meaning-making mechanisms."[32] The ability to hyperfocus (to concentrate on one subject for a long time) is another autistic characteristic that Christopher admires in Holmes: "Also it says in the book *Sherlock Holmes had, in a very remarkable degree, the power of detaching his mind at will*. And this is like me, too, because if I get really interested in something, like practicing maths . . . I don't notice anything else and Father can be calling me to come and eat my supper and I won't hear him" (91–92). Hyperfocus can, of course, be a potential problem (Christopher admits that being very focused can cause him to ignore his father); however, Christopher's interpretation of Sherlock Holmes allows him to see this skill as a potential source of strength (hyperfocus always allows Holmes to solve the mystery). Thus, reading Conan Doyle's work teaches Christopher to value his autistic traits.

Indeed, Christopher's alignment with Holmes leads him to conceive of common neurotypical characteristics as signs of disability and deficit. Christopher perceives a shorter (and more commonly neurotypical) attention span as a potential limitation. As he explains, "And that is why I am very good at playing chess, because I detach my mind at will and concentrate on the board and after a while the person I am playing will stop concentrating and start scratching their nose, or staring out of the window, and then they will make a mistake and I will win" (92). In fact, Christopher has come to regard the shorter attention span common in neurotypical people as potentially *disabling*: "And that is why I am good at chess and maths and logic, because most people are almost blind and they don't see most things and there is lots of spare capacity in their heads and it is filled with things which aren't connected and are silly, like, 'I'm worried that I might have left the gas cooker on'" (177–178). As Muller points out, "In its representation of other characters, as seen through Christopher's eyes, the text destabilizes the disability/ability binary that often privileges the latter term. Adults for example are portrayed as 'disabled' by emotions such as jealousy in the case of Christopher's father."[33] From Christopher's perspective, better sensory integration makes one "almost blind" and compromises one's ability to "see everything" as an autistic person might (177). In other words, instead of interpreting sensory integration problems as a deficit, Christopher believes that neurotypical vision is deficient (less than the autistic norm). The same applies to the shorter attention span associated with neurotypical thinking: Christopher imagines that neurotypical people have "lots of spare capacity in their heads and it is filled with things which aren't connected and are silly" (178). Christopher's "us versus them" mentality is softened by Haddon's sense of humor: Haddon implies that neurotypical people may have shorter attention spans, but they will be less likely to burn the house down. Christopher also admires Holmes for being logical (rather than emotional or superstitious). Indeed, he imagines Holmes as having the "extreme systematizing brain" that researchers have associated with the autism spectrum.[34] As Christopher explains the connections between Holmes and himself, "*His mind . . . was busy in endeavoring to frame some scheme into which all these strange and apparently disconnected episodes could be fitted.* And that is what I am trying to do by writing this book" (91–92). By attempting to solve the mystery of "who killed Wellington," Christopher imagines himself as turning his "systematizing brain" into a potential strength. When Christopher thinks about traveling to London alone and feels afraid and overwhelmed, he uses Holmes as a role model: "And then I thought that I had to be like Sherlock Holmes and I had to detach my mind at will to a remarkable degree so that I did not notice how much it was hurting inside my head" (164). Thus, Christopher perceives Holmes's ability to be logical and emotionally detached as a strength that he can emulate in a moment of extreme stress.[35] Overall, Christopher's reading of Sherlock Holmes allows him to conceive of his own disability identity in terms of neurodiversity rather than pathology, offering him a positive and empowering vision of his own autistic traits.

But while Christopher takes pride in being like Sherlock Holmes, the larger narrative scope of the book presents Christopher as a humorous parody of the autistic detective tradition. Unlike the structure of a Conan Doyle novel, the layering of mystery in Haddon's plot encourages the implied neurotypical reader to view Christopher condescendingly. Haddon presents his young narrator as lacking the emotional knowledge and social maturity needed to serve as an effective detective figure. In this sense, disability overlaps with Christopher's status as a child narrator, creating a situation in which the reader's knowledge constantly surpasses that of the detective.[36] Indeed, Oskar and Christopher have many similarities as detective figures: both boys are trying to solve an objective, concrete puzzle that symbolizes larger emotional and familial secrets. Readers may assume that Oskar and Christopher cannot fully understand these sensitive issues because they are children—and also because they are autistic. Ultimately, Christopher's role as a detective is an inversion of Sherlock Holmes's role in Conan Doyle's stories. Holmes is always the real mystery of Conan Doyle's tales (his mind is the enigmatic puzzle that the neurotypical reader must work to solve), so a Holmes novel always has two layers of mystery—the mystery of how Holmes's brilliant mind works and the crime Holmes is currently solving. Meanwhile, Holmes is always ahead of the reader—readers cannot hope to make the leaps of deduction that the great detective does. *The Curious Incident of the Dog in the Night-Time* and *Extremely Loud and Incredibly Close,* on the other hand, have three levels of mystery. First, the reader is trying to decode the mind of the autistic child (the workings of the autistic mind are stereotypically depicted as a puzzle). Second, the boy detective is trying to solve his concrete riddle (Oskar attempts to find the lock that will fit his key, while Christopher tries to find Wellington's killer). But a third layer of mystery, a larger emotional mystery, is also playing out around the boy detectives (Oskar must learn to deal with the death of his father, while Christopher discovers that his mother is still alive). The fact that these child detectives pursue the "wrong" mystery (or at least, one that may appear trivial in comparison to the larger emotional lives of their families) allows the neurotypical (and perhaps adult) reader to view their attempts with a certain amount of detached (and potentially condescending) humor. Thus, while Haddon's novel is about the potential strengths and pleasures of autism (those traits that Christopher takes pride in sharing with Holmes), it is also about the potential vulnerability and pain of autism (Christopher is solving the wrong mystery, focusing energy and attention on Wellington and never truly comprehending the personal tragedies taking place in his own home).[37] Christopher stumbles upon the deeper mystery of his mother's absence in the search for Wellington's killer: "I looked at the letter and thought really hard. It was a mystery and I couldn't work it out" (124). Relying on the stereotype of autism as a destroyer of families (see chapter 4's discussion of "monstrous" autistic figures), Haddon's novel presents Christopher's disability as one of the reasons his mother leaves home. Although Christopher reads the letters his mother has sent to explain her motivations, Haddon presents the young detective as somewhat disengaged from this painful revelation (his father's admission that he killed Wellington is presented as more shocking and painful for Christopher than the realization of his mother's abandonment). In the end, both child narrators are detectives who focus on a tangible puzzle at the expense of the big picture: because they are focused on concrete objects and animals they fail to fully see what is going on within their families. In Christopher's case, the novel oversimplistically presents his autism as "the answer" to his mother's mysterious disappearance.[38] While the novel realistically depicts some of the unique difficulties of parenting an autistic child, it also falls back on the cliché of autism as a family tragedy, allowing Christopher's disability to stand in as a symbol for his family's dissolution.

In sum, both Oskar and Christopher are autistic child narrators who represent larger social concerns: while Oskar's autism symbolizes the ineffable tragedy of 9/11, Christopher's autism is symbolically tied to the fragmentation of the postmodern family. Both boy detectives offer in their respective narratives an opportunity to contemplate the neurotypical struggle to establish emotional connections with others, autistic and otherwise. Although both novels avoid "labeling" their protagonists, it is clear that these child narrators capitalize on the current public interest in autism spectrum disorder. Parodying the autistic detective tradition, each child's hyperfocus guides his detail-oriented mind to focus on objects (the key) and animals (the death of Wellington)—"small" mysteries that readers may consider inappropriate or superficial compared to the struggles of the adult (read: neurotypical) world around them. The relative unawareness of the boy detectives could be assumed to be the product of their youth, but it is obviously also associated in the cultural mind with their shared disability. The underlying cultural myth that autism may lead one astray, may cause one to have misplaced priorities or to overlook the power of human relationships, is clearly a motif that is a defining factor in both of these books, contributing to their narrative style and their rhetorical pathos.

SIX

The Autistic Label:
Diagnosing (and Undiagnosing)
the Girl with the Dragon Tattoo

Unspeakably more depends on what things are called than on
what they are.
—Friedrich Nietzsche, *The Gay Science*

At what percentage of tattooed body surface does it stop being fetishism
and become a mental illness?
—Annika Giannini, *The Girl Who Kicked the Hornet's Nest*

The incredibly popular Lisbeth Salander is liminal on every axis. She is cast
as sexually other (bisexual?), physically other (a diminutive boxer?), religiously
other (Satanist?), politically other (anarchist?), legally other (murderer?), and neurologically other (mental disorder?). Part of Lisbeth's sensational appeal is that
she is always "other" than the majority normative reader. Apparently liberated
from the social norms that constrain her many fans, she is free to take revenge
and wreak havoc on the wicked primarily because of her overdetermined status as the ultimate cultural outsider.[1] A character shrouded in silence and mystery, Stieg Larsson's misfit heroine has been one of the most popular characters
in recent fiction—the complex, contentious, and controversial Lisbeth was no
doubt a key factor in making the books in his Millennium Trilogy (*The Girl with
the Dragon Tattoo, The Girl Who Played with Fire,* and *The Girl Who Kicked the Hornet's Nest*) international best sellers. While Larsson's novels are as unrealistic and
sensational as their infamous heroine, these popular books attempt to move beyond the commonplaces of crime fiction, using an autistic detective figure to explore society's attitudes toward mental disability. While Larsson's trilogy superficially critiques social injustice against those with cognitive differences, overtly
presenting an autistic heroine whose predicament reveals the stigma, misconceptions, and abuse that she faces because of her mental disorder, this critique ulti-

mately undermines itself: the books' neurotypical narrative voice, stereotypical metaphors, and conspiracy plotline subtly reinforce the very cultural stigma the books attempt to critique. In the end, the novels are only able to redeem Lisbeth and offer her triumph by denying, erasing, and silencing the narrative about mental disorders and social injustice that they initially espouse.

Diagnosing Lisbeth:
Making Autism Speak in the Millennium Trilogy

Lisbeth's mental health diagnosis (or the lack thereof) is one of the major topics of the Millennium Trilogy, and her ongoing experiences with the diagnostic process lay the groundwork for Larsson's indictment of the mental health care system. Larsson's books never settle on any definitive label for Lisbeth's cognitive difference, although many readers believe that she has Asperger's syndrome.[2] Larsson's novels expend seemingly endless pages searching for the proper diagnosis: other characters suggest a plethora of possibilities (schizophrenic, narcissistic, sociopathic). Paradoxically, Lisbeth becomes a figure who is simultaneously overlabeled and underlabeled—so many diagnoses are suggested that none of them ever become definitive. However, a possible diagnosis of Asperger's syndrome comes up again and again: Mikael Blomkvist, journalist and publisher of *Millennium* magazine, Holger Palmgren, a lawyer who serves as Lisbeth's guardian, and Dr. Anders Jonasson, who performed surgery on Lisbeth after she was shot, all suspect that Lisbeth may be on the spectrum. Palmgren notes that Lisbeth has autistic traits: "I thought she had Asperger's syndrome or something like it. If you read the clinical descriptions of patients diagnosed with Asperger's, there are things that seem to fit Lisbeth very well, but there are just as many symptoms that don't apply at all."[3] Dr. Jonasson argues with the assessment of Lisbeth made by Dr. Peter Teleborian, a psychiatrist and profiler: "Have you ever considered a significantly simpler diagnosis? . . . For example, Asperger's syndrome. Of course, I haven't done a psychiatric evaluation of her, but if I had to hazard a guess, I would consider some form of autism. That would explain her inability to relate to social conventions."[4] And while Teleborian disagrees on the basis of her violent behavior ("I'm sorry, but Asperger's patients do not generally set fire to their parents. Believe me, I've never met such a clearly defined sociopath"), even he later admits that Lisbeth is "almost autistic in her relation to doctors and other figures of authority" (*Hornet's Nest*, 693). Overall, Lisbeth's implicit diagnosis (the other characters suspect that she has autism, but the diagnosis is never confirmed) allows the author to create mystery around Lisbeth's character and to take advantage of the exotic appeal of ASD without opening himself to a critique for his inaccurate and unrealistic depiction of the condition. In fact, the mysterious nature of Lisbeth's mind, her role as an autistic detective (her enigmatic brain is the real mystery), is one of the trilogy's major thematic concerns, as well as a source of exotic appeal for neurotypical readers.

Lisbeth does have many autistic traits: her social struggles and intense interests both suggest that she is on the spectrum.[5] The narrator reveals that when Lisbeth was a child, "the rules for social interaction in school had always baffled her."[6] Dragan Armansky, CEO of Milton Security, decides to try to help her socially: "He thought about his own Muslim upbringing, which had taught him that it was his duty to God to help the outcasts. . . . [H]e recognized Lisbeth Salander as a person in need of resolute help. . . . Over the following months Armansky took Salander under his wing. In truth, he took her on as a small social project" (*Dragon*, 44–45). Armansky views Lisbeth as a social outcast and imagines himself as helping to rehabilitate her socially. She clearly has difficulty making friends and maintaining relationships. Blomkvist tries to explain friendship to her, defining the concept as though for a child: "Friendship—my definition— is built on two things . . . respect and trust. . . . And it has to be mutual" (*Dragon*, 552). Indeed, Blomkvist's interpretation that Lisbeth does not understand friendship seems accurate: "The reference to friendship made her uncomfortable. She didn't know how to respond to it" (*Fire*, 472). Although Lisbeth and the authorities rarely agree, they do agree on one point: she has poor social skills. Lisbeth is described by the police as having a "social handicap" (*Fire*, 310), and she admits to Annika Giannini, her lawyer and Blomkvist's sister, that she is "not good at relationships" (*Hornet's Nest*, 755). Lisbeth's strong interest in computers, research, and hacking is definitely a special interest, for she is intense and obsessive by nature: "The idea that had materialized in some unexplored nook of her brain during the last week at Sandhamn had grown into a manic preoccupation. For four weeks she had isolated herself in her apartment and ignored any communication from Armansky. She had spent twelve hours a day in front of her computer, some days more, and the rest of her waking hours she had brooded over the same problem" (*Dragon*, 604). Completely ignoring her boss, she is "isolated" and "preoccupied" for long days, fascinated with the topic of her research. Overall, these character traits (poor social skills, unusually intense interests) neatly align the crime-solving hacker with the autistic detective tradition.

Even in small details of her characterization, such as her hypersensitivity to touch and her unusual affect, Lisbeth comes across as autistic. The neurotypical characters around her often comment on her atypical body language. Lisbeth speaks "impersonally, without ever smiling or showing any warmth. Or coolness, for that matter" (*Hornet's Nest*, 771). Watching the young woman's face, Giannini refers to "Lisbeth's limited repertoire of expressions" (*Hornet's Nest*, 787). Lisbeth also displays sensory integration issues: specifically, she is hypervigilant about physical touch. Lisbeth instinctively pulls away from anyone who initiates physical contact, as Armansky and Erika Berger, editor in chief of *Millennium* magazine, both discover. Armansky once "tried to give her a hug," but "she had wiggled out of his clumsy embrace" (*Dragon*, 47–48). Berger gets the same reaction: "Berger stood up and went around the table and threw her arms around the girl. Salander squirmed like a worm about to be put on a hook" (*Dragon*, 603). Indeed, Lisbeth's tense body language seems to convey a perpetually defensive posture to the characters around her: "Salander always seemed to mark her private space as hostile territory. . . . To everyone around her it was as good a signal as any: *Don't try to touch me—it will hurt*" (*Hornet's Nest*, 673). When Blomkvist thinks of comforting her, he hesitates because of her strong reaction to physical touch: "He felt that he had to find Salander and hold her close. She would probably bite him if he tried" (*Fire*, 666). Lisbeth's sensory issues (particularly her hypersensitivity to touch) cause other characters to perceive her as defensive and potentially violent: this discomforting effect may be the legacy of the cultural anxiety played out in *Of Mice and Men* (see chapter 3's discussion of false stereotypes connecting sensory issues and violence). In short, Lisbeth displays a surprising number of autistic traits for a character who is never overtly acknowledged as being on the spectrum.

Above all, Lisbeth is a character defined by her silence: while being selectively mute is interpreted by the other characters as an invitation to speak for her (and thus to interpret her intentions and emotions), it also offers opportunities for Larsson to highlight the many ways in which Lisbeth's autistic silence is misunderstood and misinterpreted, thus generating sympathy for her character. Lisbeth is clearly awkward when it comes to conversing with others—even when she wants to converse with them. Dr. Sivarnandan of the Ersta rehabilitation home claims that Lisbeth does not have "the ability to carry on a normal conversation" (*Fire*, 183), Blomkvist notes that when talking to Lisbeth there are frequently "long pauses in the middle of the conversation" (*Dragon*, 374), and Giannini feels that "after a month of conversations" with Lisbeth "their communication was still distinctly one-sided" (*Hornet's Nest*, 241). The lack of reciprocity in Lisbeth's dialogue is distinctively autistic. Lisbeth herself acknowledges that she struggles with conversation: "She . . . had such difficulty talking about herself with people of flesh and blood" (*Hornet's Nest*, 354). As a matter of fact, Lisbeth feels most comfortable chatting with the other computer hackers she knows in an Internet community, a parallel to current autistic culture (in which communication is primarily online). Lisbeth's silence is sometimes a matter of choice, but at other times, she is not able to express herself by speaking even though she may want to do so. For example, she is unable to thank Giannini: "She looked as though she wanted to say something but could not find the words. . . . Lisbeth stood at the curb and watched Giannini drive away until her tail lights disappeared around the corner. 'Thanks,' she said at last" (*Hornet's Nest*, 756). Her silence is misunderstood and is constantly interpreted by the other characters as a sign of low IQ, lack of emotion, or deliberate rudeness. For example, after trying to engage her in conversation, Officer Hans Faste of the Violent Crimes Division concludes that "she's fucking retarded" (*Hornet's Nest*, 572). Armansky knows her well but still finds her lack of greetings and farewells offensive: "'Have you got a job for me?' she asked without any greeting." Armansky responds with sarcasm: "Hi. Great to see you. I thought you died or something" (*Dragon*, 289). At school, her silence is read as insanity and ignorance: "Her classmates thought she was crazy and treated her accordingly. She also aroused very little sympathy among the teachers. She had never been particularly talkative, and she had become known as a pupil who never raised her hand and often did not answer when a teacher asked her a direct question. No-one was sure whether this was because she did not know the answer or if there was some other reason" (*Dragon*, 251). In this passage, she is judged as "crazy" because she "had never been particularly talkative," and it is assumed that "she did not know" because she "did not answer." When she becomes an adult, her colleagues at work respond to her taciturn nature in a similar fashion: "She had a talent for irritating the other employees. She became known as 'the girl with two brain cells'—one for breathing and one for standing up. She never talked about herself. Colleagues who tried to talk to her seldom got a response and soon gave up" (*Dragon*, 42). Silence is read as a lack of intelligence (an obviously false equation). In fact, Lisbeth's famous dragon tattoo symbolizes her silence. When Jonasson asks her about the tattoo, Lisbeth does not respond. The narrator later reveals that Jonasson was trying to establish a social connection with Lisbeth: "He had asked about her dragon tattoo in the hope of finding a personal topic he could discuss with her. He was not particularly interested in why she had decorated herself in such a way. . . . He thought simply that it might be a way to start a conversation" (*Hornet's Nest*,

247). Lisbeth's dragon tattoo becomes a symbol of silence, of social disjointed-ness, of autism itself. The encounter with Jonasson highlights Lisbeth's social iso-lation—she is unable to establish a relationship or even to have a conversation with the kind physician. Again and again, Larsson generates sympathy for Lis-beth by showing that the other characters misinterpret her customary silence.

Larsson also uses Lisbeth's autistic silence as one element in his critique of the mental health care system. One of the primary problems the psychologists in the novels face is their inability to communicate effectively with Lisbeth: their struggle to "diagnose" her silence—while a caricature and exaggeration of how actual psychiatrists operate—allows Larsson to explore some of the inequities of modern psychiatry.[7] Lisbeth's customary silence is often read as a sign of devi-ance and resistance by the characters around her. Lisbeth, however, may in fact perceive her own silence as indifferent—it is not a sign, and it is not intended to convey any message at all. Indeed, it is remarkable how often Lisbeth's silence and indifference are interpreted as deviance and resistance. Lisbeth believes that "she minded her own business and did not interfere with what anyone around her did. Yet there was always someone who absolutely would not leave her in peace" (*Dragon*, 250). Lisbeth thinks of her social isolation as peaceful and poten-tially liberating:

> Normally seven minutes of another person's company was enough
> to give her a headache, so she set things up to live as a recluse. She
> was perfectly content as long as people left her in peace. Unfortu-
> nately society was not very smart or understanding; she had to pro-
> tect herself from social authorities, child welfare authorities, po-
> lice, curators, psychologists, psychiatrists, teachers. . . . There was
> a whole army of people who seemed not to have anything better to
> do than to try to disrupt her life, and, if there were the opportunity,
> to correct the way she had chosen to live it. (*Dragon*, 430)

She interprets the demand to speak as an intrusion on her peaceful stasis, while those around her read her silence as "disturbed behavior," a gap in the flow of social signs around her. Other characters automatically attribute social mean-ing to this perceived gap. As Teleborian explains it, "From a patient who sits and says nothing, you can learn only that this is a patient who is good at sitting and saying nothing. Even this is disturbed behavior" (*Hornet's Nest*, 722). Evert Gull-berg, a former senior administrative officer with the Security Police, interprets Lisbeth's silence as a sign of dangerous deviance: "He did not need a psychiatrist to tell him that she was not normal. . . . She did not say much. . . . She was a problem in the making" (*Hornet's Nest,* 103). The perceived gaps in Lisbeth's speech, the social lacunae that the neurotypical characters around her attempt to fill, are frequently interpreted as a resistance to authority. If it is in fact a resistance at all, it is a passive one that is carried out largely through lack—lack of speech, lack of eye contact: "All attempts by a teacher or any authority figure to initiate a conversation with the girl about her feelings, emotional life, or the state of her health were met, to their great frustration, with a sullen silence and a great deal of intense staring at the floor, ceiling, and walls. She would fold her arms and refuse to participate in any psychological tests" (*Dragon,* 173). However, Lisbeth reveals in the second novel that her silence in the presence of psychologists actually stems from a promise she made to herself: when she realized that no one was listening, that her speech was one-sided and communicatively incomplete, she gave up on speech as a means of communication altogether: "I don't talk to crazy-doctors because they never listen to what I have to say" (*Hornet's Nest,* 342). Thus, her "refusal" to communicate is actually a refusal to pretend to communicate, a refusal to engage in what she sees as the superficial social ritual of speech without purpose or meaning. Lisbeth is quite correct in perceiving deep miscommunication: the misunderstanding between the psychologists and Lisbeth is so profound that "the psychiatric evaluation that was done when Lisbeth was eighteen concludes that she is mentally retarded" (*Fire,* 412). Overall, Larsson's presentation of Lisbeth's perspective on silence serves as part of his critique of the larger social system and medical establishment, which constantly misunderstand and misinterpret her.

At least superficially, Larsson uses Lisbeth's status as "mentally disabled" to draw attention to the potential for inequity, discrimination, and abuse in the mental health care system: he emphasizes how Lisbeth's status as someone with a mental health record is disabling and disempowering. The authority figures Lisbeth encounters in the novels treat her with obvious inequity: "For her the police were a hostile force who over the years had put her under arrest or humiliated her." She is mistaken for a protestor because of her Gothic clothing and is assaulted by a police officer as she is walking home from work: "Without the slightest provocation on her part, he had struck her on the shoulders with his baton" (*Dragon,* 248). These kinds of misunderstandings between Lisbeth and authority figures abound throughout the trilogy—when the authorities are not deliberately cruel, they are often cruel through misunderstanding or oversight. Because she seems different and does not fit in, she is subject to all manner of official abuse. When Lisbeth defends herself against a man who attempts to assault her, "she was charged with assault and battery. Salander claimed that the man had groped her, and her testimony was supported by witnesses. The prosecutor dismissed the case. But her background was such that the district court ordered a psychiatric evaluation" (*Dragon*, 175). Because she was institutionalized in her teens, the authorities immediately regard Lisbeth with suspicion. The ultimate result is that she is again threatened with institutionalization, though she has committed no crime: "Since she refused, as was her custom, to answer any questions or to participate in the examinations, the doctors . . . handed down an opinion based on 'observations of the patient.' . . . The only determination made was that she must suffer from some kind of emotional disturbance, whose nature was of the sort that could not be left untreated. The medical/legal report recommended care in a closed psychiatric institution" (*Dragon*, 175). Someone without a mental health record would probably be released when the charges against her were dismissed: it is not likely that she would be held against her will for a mandatory psychiatric evaluation and then sent to an institution. When a similar scenario plays out later in her life, Lisbeth has a good lawyer to defend her from such injustice: "There is no reason whatsoever for my client to submit to a psychiatric evaluation. No-one else has to prove that they are not mentally ill if they are the victim of a crime," Giannini argues (*Hornet's Nest*, 745). Thus, Larsson depicts the authorities as discriminating against Lisbeth because of her perceived difference (different dress, different body language) and her mental health history.

Furthermore, Larsson portrays the treatment Lisbeth receives while under psychiatric care as a form of abuse. Lisbeth interprets the treatment she received while institutionalized as acts of torture: "The most common form of care in the secure ward . . . was to place 'unruly and unmanageable patients' in a room that was 'free of stimuli.' The room contained only a bed with a restraining belt. The textbook explanation was that unruly children could not receive any 'stimuli' that might trigger an outburst. When she grew older she discovered that there was another term for the same thing. *Sensory deprivation*. According to the Geneva Conventions, subjecting prisoners to sensory deprivation was classified as inhumane" (*Fire*, 450). From Lisbeth's perspective, the intent of the treatment is irrelevant: the overall effect is indistinguishable from torture. Again, Larsson depicts Lisbeth's time in the mental institution as incredibly cruel: "On the morning the court hearing was to take place, Lisbeth was brought from the psychiatric clinic for children where she had been confined. . . . [S]he felt like a prisoner from a concentration camp" (*Dragon*, 176). The comparison between the psychiatric institution and a concentration camp drives home Larsson's point about the cruel effect that the psychiatric intervention has on Lisbeth as a person.

The trilogy as a whole displays a general skepticism toward psychiatry, calling into question the subjective nature of diagnosis and highlighting mental disability as a purely social construct. For example, when Palmgren "cross-examined the physician . . . eventually it became clear that since the patient had refused to complete a single test, the basis for the doctor's conclusions was in fact nothing more than guesswork" (*Dragon*, 176). The narrator's conclusion that any diagnosis placed on Lisbeth is simply "guesswork" is part of the novels' larger commentary on psychology in general. Indeed, Giannini's cross-examination of Teleborian during the climactic courtroom scene calls attention to the subjective nature of mental disorders. When Teleborian interprets Lisbeth's piercings and tattoos as "a manifestation of self-hate" and claims that they are evidence that she is a danger to herself, Giannini objects: "So you believe that I am also dangerous to myself because I wear earrings and actually have a tattoo in a private place?" Her next question shows how ludicrous and illogical attempts to quantify human behavior can actually become: "At what percentage of tattooed body surface does it stop being fetishism and become a mental illness?" (*Hornet's Nest*, 708). Many of Lisbeth's choices (such as her decision to get piercings) are conceived as somehow dangerous or deviant, and when they are read through the lens of her mental disorder they become a sign of mental disorder. For example, because she is seen as mentally ill, her choice to sleep with older men is cast as deviant—her sexual behavior becomes a symptom. As Giannini points out, the assumption that Lisbeth has a mental disorder colors the social interpretation of everything she does: "When I read your so-called psychiatric assessment of Lisbeth Salander, I find point after point which, taken out of context, would apply to myself. Why am I healthy and sound while Lisbeth Salander is considered a dangerous sadist? . . . [I]n her case you pluck out details from her life and use them as the basis for saying that she is sick" (*Hornet's Nest*, 729). As Aryn Martin and Mary Simms argue, Larsson "illustrates the ways in which labels come to stand in for and eclipse the person. He shows that there is slippage among discrediting labels, so that we are more likely to believe, for example, that someone labeled mentally ill is also prone to violence, promiscuity, or substance abuse. Once someone enters the bureaucratic machinery of a psychiatric institution, behaviors that would go unnoticed in 'normals' are recorded as symptoms of illness."[8] While the fictional Giannini is able to rescue Lisbeth from such allegations, this kind of "slippage" is a dangerously real phenomenon: Larsson's fictional depiction of such slippage highlights the subjective and socially constructed nature of mental disorders.[9] In a further critique of the process of psychiatric diagnosis, Blomkvist suggests that the people who have attempted to diagnose Lisbeth behave in ways that could be classified as mentally disordered. Blomkvist attempts to explain the behavior of the Section for Special Analysis during an interview: "The only reasonable explanation I can give is that over the years the Section developed into a cult. . . . They write their own laws, within which concepts like right and wrong have ceased to be relevant. . . . And through these laws they imagine themselves isolated from normal society." "It sounds like some sort of mental illness, don't you think?" the interviewer asks. Blomkvist agrees that the authorities who diagnosed Lisbeth are themselves mentally disordered: "That wouldn't be an inaccurate description" (*Hornet's Nest*, 648). In short, Larsson's books take a skeptical approach to psychiatry and reveal "mental disorder" as a malleable, socially constructed, and subjective concept.

Yet Lisbeth's relationship with her abusive guardian, lawyer Nils Bjurman, offers the novels' most blatant attack against the mental health care system. Placed under Bjurman's authority, Lisbeth becomes the object of an endless stream of abuse. Nothing about her personal life is personal or private. In her first meeting with Bjurman, he "started in on a sort of interrogation: 'How much do you earn? I want a copy of your financial records. Who do you spend time with? Do you pay your rent on time? Do you drink? Did Palmgren approve of those rings you have on your face? Are you careful about hygiene?'" (*Dragon*, 179). Indeed, the novels point out the lack of privacy that is often accorded to those with mental disorders: when she is falsely accused of murder, Lisbeth "followed the commentary and speculation in the media with amazement, fascinated that confidential documents about her medical history seemed to be accessible to any newsroom that wanted to publish them" (*Fire*, 443). In addition to taking advantage of his legal right to her personal information, Bjurman uses his position of authority to sexually assault Lisbeth. Bjurman tells Lisbeth that her social disability is the reason for the abuse, using it as a justification for his crime. When he initially molests her in his office, Bjurman tells Lisbeth that "you need to learn to be more sociable and get along with people" (*Dragon*, 242). Couched in the language of "therapy," his encouragement for her to improve her social skills is actually a sinister coercion, clearly implying that if she refuses to have sex ("to be more sociable"), he will not give her access to the funds stored in her account. The implication of Bjurman's statements seems to be that because of Lisbeth's poor social skills, she is a social outcast, and this has given Bjurman social power

The Autistic Label

over her. Unfortunately, Bjurman is right that Lisbeth's mental health record makes her socially vulnerable. After forcing her to perform oral sex, Bjurman threatens Lisbeth with institutionalization if she tells anyone about the abuse: "If you make trouble, I can put you away in an institution for the rest of your life. Would you like that?" Because her ethos and credibility have been undermined by her mental health record, Bjurman may be right that no one in authority would believe Lisbeth if she reported the abuse: "Think about it—who would believe you? There are documents stating that you're non compos mentis. It would be your word against mine. Whose word do you think would carry more weight?" (*Dragon*, 243). Even if the authorities would believe her, Lisbeth's previous interactions with the police leave her unlikely to report the rape. The narrator explains that there is rarely any abuse in Sweden's guardianship system—or at least abuse is rarely reported: the fact that such situations "are relatively rare may be the result of two things: the authorities are carrying out their jobs in a satisfactory manner, or the clients have no opportunity to complain and in a credible way make themselves heard by the media or the authorities" (*Dragon*, 246). Bjurman's abuse of Lisbeth certainly suggests the latter. Overall, Lisbeth's relationship with her guardian shows how disempowered she is as a result of her mental health diagnosis.

When Bjurman later rapes Lisbeth, the rape becomes symbolic of the violation she suffers at the hands of the social order—it is a symbol of the larger systematic discrimination, violence, and cruelty she experiences as a result of her interactions with the mental health care system. Although Lisbeth never engaged in prostitution, her mental health record includes conjecture from a social worker that she might work as a prostitute. Ironically, the very system that was put in place to "protect" Lisbeth actually forces her to sell her body. Bjurman assumes that Lisbeth will perform sexual favors in exchange for access to the money stored in her account: "This is better than a whore. She gets paid with her own money" (*Dragon*, 244). Lisbeth understands that her mental health record has put her in a disempowered position that makes her vulnerable to Bjurman (and people like him): "The sadist's best victim was the one who voluntarily went to him because she did not think she had any choice. The sadist specialized in people who were in a position of dependence. Advokat Bjurman had chosen her as a victim. That told her something about the way she was viewed by other people" (*Dragon*, 277). There is a clear parallel between the rape scene, in which Bjurman ties Lisbeth to the bed and tortures her, and the scene that opens the second book, in which the psychiatrist Teleborian straps Lisbeth to the bed in the children's hospital. Later, the third book reveals that Teleborian is a pedophile. The narrator describes the psychiatrist as "the most loathsome and disgusting sadist that Lisbeth had ever met in her life. . . . Teleborian . . . was shielded behind a curtain of documents, assessments, academic honors, and psychiatric mumbo-jumbo. Not a single one of his actions could ever be reported or criticized. He had a state-endorsed mandate to tie down disobedient little girls with leather straps" (*Fire*, 451). While Lisbeth's documented history of mental disorder has damaged her ethos and made her less credible to the authorities, Teleborian has all the documentation and authority he needs to give him power over Lisbeth. The novels' villainization of Lisbeth's abusive psychiatrist creates a memorable critique of the unequal power dynamic between psychiatric health care provider and psychiatric health care consumer. In short, Larsson depicts the mental health care system as metaphorically and literally raping Lisbeth.

Undiagnosing Lisbeth:
Silencing Autism in the Millennium Trilogy

While Larsson overtly presents a critique of the mental health care system, there are many covert ways in which the trilogy reinforces stigmas against people with mental disorders: the narrator's neurotypical interpretation of Lisbeth's behavior and the stereotypical metaphors Larsson employs subtly encourage readers to judge Lisbeth in negative and dehumanizing ways. While Larsson presents Lisbeth as an autistic character, the characters around her (and the neurotypical narrative voice of the novels) actually filter most of the information the reader receives about Lisbeth through a normative perspective: these narrative tactics invite readers to judge Lisbeth's behavior as abnormal, implicitly feeding into a medical understanding of difference as deficient. The narrative voice continually reminds the reader of how "abnormal" Lisbeth is by stating it point-blank: for example, a statement such as "Lisbeth was not like any normal person" clearly invites readers to view Lisbeth's mental difference as "abnormality" (*Dragon*, 248). She is defined throughout the books by other people's ability (or inability) to deal with her or relate to her—both measures that tell us more about her external presentation and how people perceive her than about what she is actually thinking. The narrator explains that Lisbeth's unwillingness (or inability?) to answer questions "had consequently become associated with the great difficulty of even diagnosing her mental deficiencies. In short, Lisbeth Salander was anything but easy to handle" (*Dragon*, 173). According to the (presumably objective) narrative voice of the novels, Lisbeth is mentally "deficient." Readers are also frequently privy to other characters' interpretations of Lisbeth's behavior (although very rarely privy to Lisbeth's actual thoughts or feelings). For example, "Giannini . . . had no idea what Lisbeth was up to. Sometimes she thought that there was nothing going on in there at all" (*Hornet's Nest*, 241). Armansky interprets her awkward social skills as a sign that she does not care about other people. "I don't know why I didn't say goodbye," Lisbeth says apologetically. Armansky's response invites readers to view Lisbeth's behavior unsympathetically: "I'll tell you why: because you don't give a shit about other people. . . . You've got an attitude problem and you treat other people like dirt when they're trying to be your friends. It's that simple" (*Fire*, 161). Overall, the novels view and explain Lisbeth from an outsider's perspective, often adopting a judgmental and negative interpretation of her behavior and rarely offering a glimpse of events from Lisbeth's autistic point of view.

Overall, the Millennium Trilogy builds on many negative autism stereotypes in its characterization of Lisbeth: for example, Lisbeth is depicted as being incapable of strong emotion. Jonasson describes her as "a person who stubbornly kept her distance from those around her and showed no emotion at all" (*Hornet's Nest*, 250). Armansky refers to Lisbeth's "astonishing lack of emotional involvement" as something that "upset" him (*Dragon*, 40). In fact, Armansky sees this emotional disengagement in terms of the popular trope that imagines autism as a protective "shell" closing out the rest of the world; often, this shell is imagined as a barrier that only a neurotypical relationship can "break down." Armansky sees himself as the person who must break through this imaginary barrier and rescue Lisbeth: "Armansky felt so provoked by her lack of emotional response that sometimes he wanted to grab hold of her and shake her. To force his way into her shell and win her friendship, or at least her respect" (*Dragon*, 47). Dr. Jonasson responds to her in the same way, feeling that her "aloof" demeanor is a cry for help, a sign that someone must "break through" the barriers that render her a prisoner inside of herself: "He could not work out this strange girl. . . . She was locked up inside her shell and kept her distance from those around her" (*Hornet's Nest*, 246). The novels' most disturbing engagement with this stereotype is the scene in which Lisbeth is raped. After Bjurman brutally assaults her, the narrator describes Lisbeth's response: "An ordinary person might have felt that her lack of reaction had shifted the blame to her—it might have been another sign that she was so abnormal that even rape could evoke no adequate emotional response" (*Dragon*, 249). The description of Lisbeth as "abnormal" becomes a covert way of justifying the rape—a "lack of reaction" obviously does not "shift the blame" for rape. Bjurman is the rapist: Lisbeth is the victim of a crime. Furthermore, there is no "adequate emotional response" to rape. Individuals respond to sexual assault (and to other trauma) with diverse reactions. Finally, the idea that being raped would evoke no emotional response in an autistic person is a terrible misconception, perpetuating the stereotype that people on the spectrum are incapable of feeling and, therefore, are not people (we become cast as victims who cannot really be hurt and, therefore, cannot really be victims). The narrator suggests that the violence against Lisbeth may not emotionally harm her, thus representing violence against autistic people as violence without consequences, violence without pain, violence without victims. Overall, the dehumanizing and damaging stereotype of those on the spectrum as incapable of emotion is strongly present in Larsson's characterization of Lisbeth.

Throughout the books, Larsson also plays on other stereotypes that depict autistic people as nonhuman: Lisbeth is represented as a supernatural creature, an alien, a machine, and a puzzle. Armansky definitely indulges in autism as fascination and exotic source of wonder: "But the attraction, Armansky thought, was that Lisbeth was a foreign creature to him. He might as well have fallen in love with a painting or a nymph or a Greek amphora. Lisbeth represented a life that was not real for him, that fascinated him though he could not share it—and in any case she forbade him from sharing it" (*Dragon*, 46).[10] But while Armansky imagines her as a "nymph," a strange "creature" as inaccessible as a painting, she is more often depicted as otherworldly in a decidedly less flattering way. She is an ephemeral outsider, hovering on the edges of social life: "She came into his office as silently as a ghost, and he became aware that she was standing in the shadows inside the doorway, watching him" (*Dragon*, 47–48). Lisbeth's brother imagines her autistic facial expressions as nonhuman: "He met Lisbeth's expressionless eyes and was amazed. She had defeated him. *She's supernatural. . . . She's a monster*" (*Hornet's Nest*, 810). Alexander Zalachenko, Lisbeth's father, also imagines Lisbeth as "a monster" when she escapes from him, and her brother, in a state of hallucination, literally mistakes Lisbeth for a supernatural being and actually runs away from her: "The creature on the floor was no girl" (*Fire*, 713). The books even employ the classic metaphors that are traditionally used to dehumanize people on the spectrum, presenting Lisbeth as both alien and machine. Lisbeth uses her clothing to consistently cast herself as "Other": "Lisbeth was dressed for the day in a black T-shirt with a picture on it of E.T. with fangs, and the words I AM ALSO AN ALIEN" (*Dragon*, 51). The climactic section of the third book, in which Lisbeth wins her court case, is entitled "Rebooting System," using a computer metaphor that builds on her work as a hacker and equates her life with a computer system. The novels also repeatedly use the classic trope of the autistic character as a puzzle for the neurotypical characters to solve. For example, Blomkvist explains that "Salander became more and more of an enigma" (*Dragon,* 428), and Criminal Inspector Jan Bublanski admits that "the more I hear about Lisbeth Salander, the more puzzled I become" (*Fire,* 412). Thus, the novels depict Lisbeth as shrouded in mystery, inhuman, and enigmatic, all stereotypical (and potentially damaging) metaphors used to describe people on the spectrum.

When autistic adults appear in fictional works, they are often imagined as children, and this is certainly the case with Lisbeth. Perhaps the common impulse to infantilize autistic adults is a conceptual misunderstanding about the nature of disability: based on cultural attitudes toward interdependency, adults who rely on social coaching or support from others may be imagined as childlike. The titles of the English translations of the trilogy refer to Lisbeth as "the girl," even though she is twenty-four years old at the start of the first book. Indeed, her diminutive stature (four foot nine) and delicate frame (she weighs ninety pounds) make her look like an adolescent, further feeding characters' (and readers') fantasies of her as a perpetual child. She is frequently infantilized because of her poor social skills, particularly by Armansky. Armansky feels "protective" toward Lisbeth and "He sometimes caught himself comparing Lisbeth to his daughters" (47, 60). Blomkvist thinks of Lisbeth as "an information junkie with a delinquent child's take on morals and ethics" (420). Like many autistic adults, Lisbeth finds that she must constantly object to being treated like a child. She tells Armansky: "I appreciate that you actually showed yourself to be greater than your prejudices and have given me a chance here . . . and you're not my father" (49). "I'm not a child anymore," Lisbeth tells Bjurman angrily (181). In fact, Armansky believes that what he perceives as Lisbeth's childlike nature may make her vulnerable to abuse: "he had always imagined her as a victim . . ." and "He thought about how she had laughed with Blomkvist in her office and wondered if she was finally growing up . . . He also felt a strange uneasiness. He had never been able to shake off the feeling that Lisbeth Salander was a perfect victim" (*Fire,* 289, 447). Armansky imagines Lisbeth as a child because of her poor social skills: when he sees her laughing with Blomkvist he imagines her as "growing up." Specifically, it is her autism that makes her seem like a child and a victim to Armansky and to the other characters—their perception reflects common stereotypes regarding adults on the autism spectrum, as interdependency and social difference are frequently interpreted as signs of immaturity and vulnerability.

In addition, Lisbeth also fits the stereotype of the autistic savant: the novels set up a false binary in which Lisbeth's savant skills are imagined to compensate for her social disability as well as consistently connecting her savant skills with the supernatural (read: inhuman). Specifically, Blomkvist imagines Asperger's primarily in terms of ability rather than disability, viewing autism as a form of extra perception. When he learns about her eidetic memory, Blomkvist thinks that Salander must have "Asperger's syndrome . . . or something like that. A talent for seeing patterns and understanding abstract reasoning where other people perceive only white noise" (*Dragon*, 551). Responding to her many savant skills, Blomkvist describes her Asperger's as an enviable "talent": "Most people would give an eye tooth to have such a gift" (*Dragon*, 551). The other characters in the novel also interpret Lisbeth's savant skills as a "compensation cure" for her autism.[11] After reading her highly detailed reports, Armansky too "was convinced that she possessed a unique gift," and he later describes her "unbelievable talents" (*Dragon*, 38; *Fire*, 291). Her skills are also consistently imagined as supernatural and otherworldly.[12] Armansky perceives her special interest in computers as mysterious in origin: "How she did it, he had never understood. Sometimes he thought that her ability to gather information was sheer magic. . . . [S]omehow she had always had this gift" (*Dragon*, 38–39). Her colleagues also find her savant computer skills to be mysterious in origin: "No-one knew how she had come by her skills" (*Hornet's Nest*, 576). Lisbeth's knowledge of technology is presented as magical and innate: "The fact that Lisbeth was a wizard at computers was widely known at Milton Security" (*Hornet's Nest*, 576). Thus, the novels play into the idea of savant skills as a "compensation" for disability and subtly refer to Lisbeth's unusual abilities in ways that further dehumanize her.

Throughout the Millennium Trilogy, Lisbeth's character becomes a conglomeration of savant stereotypes, as she demonstrates an unrealistic plethora of skills that add to the novels' sensational appeal: because Larsson depicts her as having virtuoso skills in multiple areas (this is virtually unheard of in actual savants), Lisbeth's skill set is extremely unrealistic and contributes to the cultural stereotype claiming that all people with AS are geniuses. Palmgren discovers that she is not only a computer savant but also a chess savant: "She had no real interest in the game, but after she learned the rules, she never lost a match" (*Dragon*, 180). Demonstrating that she is also a science savant, Lisbeth can beat the intelligent Palmgren at chess while reading a book "on the frequency calibration of radio telescopes in a weightless state" (*Fire*, 185). Considering her lack of formal education, Dr. Jonasson is amazed that Lisbeth reads scientific journals "with obvious interest" (*Hornet's Nest*, 254): "She asked if I had any scientific journals that dealt with genetics and brain research" (*Hornet's Nest*, 253). Blomkvist discovers that she is hyperlexic: "She seemed to be skimming, spending no more than ten or fifteen seconds on each page. She turned the pages mechanically, and Blomkvist was amazed at her lack of concentration" (*Dragon*, 425). Indeed, she reads so quickly that Blomkvist initially assumes that she must not be reading at all. Building on another common savant stereotype, Larsson depicts her mind as a machine: "There was a flood of news. Click. Click. Click. Her brain was working at high speed as she focused and absorbed the information from the yellowing pages" (*Dragon*, 472). Because the first novel presents a mystery that is solved through photography, this autistic detective uses her "photographic" mind to help close the case. Even her unusual abilities as a boxer are compared to a savant skill and connected to the image of her mind as a computer or camera. In the climactic fight with Ronald Niedermann, Larsson shows that her brain is processing information quickly with the same camera sound effect: "Her brain was working at high speed. Click, click, click" (*Hornet's Nest*, 805). The precision and speed with which her brain processes information is unrealistically presented as a superpower that aids in her fighting abilities.[13] In crime fiction, the savant detective often serves as a human deus ex machina, resolving plot problems with his ability to interpret any esoteric clue. Lisbeth, on the other hand, does not need all of her savant abilities to solve the mystery: many of her savant skills are used only to create shock and wonder, gratuitously adding to the sensational nature of the novels.[14]

Lisbeth's eidetic memory, however, is a savant skill that actually serves to advance the narrative. Not only does she use it to help solve the mystery in *The Girl with the Dragon Tattoo*, but Larsson also uses it to develop her character: a conversation with Blomkvist about her memory skills reveals that Lisbeth struggles with internalized oppression and thinks of her cognitive difference as a source of shame. When Blomkvist starts asking questions about Lisbeth's eidetic memory, she responds in an unexpected way: "Her reaction was almost explosive. She fixed her eyes on Blomkvist with such fury that he was astounded. Then her expression changed to despair, and she turned on her heel and ran for the gate" (*Dragon*, 462). In Lisbeth's mind, her memory skills are a symbol of her cognitive difference and therefore a symbol of the rejection she has suffered as a social outcast and the abuse she has suffered in her interactions with the mental health care system. As Blomkvist tries to comfort her, she says, "There's nothing to talk about. . . . I'm just a freak, that's all" (*Dragon*, 462). Lisbeth thinks of her savant skills as a symbol of difference and persecution. Blomkvist is completely unable to relate to this perspective: "I'd be overjoyed if my memory was what yours is" (*Dragon*, 462). Lisbeth presents her own mind as a mystery that she herself cannot understand: "That's just how it is. I know computers. I've never had a problem with reading a text and absorbing what it said. . . . I just have no idea how it works. It's not only computers and telephone networks, but the motor in my bike and TV sets and vacuum cleaners and chemical processes and formulae in astrophysics. I'm a nut case, I admit it: a freak" (*Dragon*, 551). Lisbeth understands her savant skills as a sign that she deserves to be labeled and judged. Indeed, she displays this kind of internalized oppression elsewhere in the trilogy, as she seems to loathe her own mind. Lisbeth thinks to herself that "her brain was being eaten up by worms and that she deserved to be flogged" (*Dragon*, 432). Even her courage, one of her best attributes as a character, becomes a trait that Lisbeth chalks up to her autism and therefore interprets negatively: "Lisbeth was afraid of no-one and nothing. She realized that she lacked the necessary imagination—and that was evidence enough that there was something wrong with her brain" (*Hornet's Nest*, 812).[15] She interprets her fearless attitude in terms of an autism stereotype (the idea that people with autism have less imagination than their neurotypical peers) and understands it as "something wrong," a flaw in her cognitive faculty. Overall, Lisbeth's attitude toward her savant skills (especially her eidetic memory) reveals that Lisbeth herself believes in a medical model of mental disability, viewing her cognitive difference as a painful flaw.

Larsson also uses Lisbeth's skills as a mathematical savant to further develop her character, showing that Lisbeth uses equations to calm herself when she is under extreme stress: this depiction, however, forms part of a larger autism stereotype that views special interests as a means of compensating for the autistic person's imagined lack of control and perception. Lisbeth solves Fermat's Last Theorem while creeping up to Zalachenko's house in the night—to her the complex riddle seems like a joke: "And all of a sudden she understood. The answer was so disarmingly simple. A game with numbers that lined up and then fell into place in a simple formula. . . . Then she giggled. . . . She wished she could have known Fermat. He was a cocky devil" (*Fire*, 682). Solving Fermat's theorem during a moment of extreme stress suggests that (like the child savant of *The Curious Incident of the Dog in the Night-Time*) Lisbeth uses her intense interest in numbers to create a sense of calm in a dangerous situation. While she is incarcerated and waiting for a psychiatric evaluation, "Lisbeth . . . spent the next hour solving equations in her head" (*Hornet's Nest*, 605). When Teleborian enters, "he smiled at her, and she froze. The components of the equation she had constructed in the air before her came tumbling to the ground. She could hear the numbers and mathematical symbols bouncing and clattering as if they had physical form" (*Hornet's Nest*, 605). Clearly, Lisbeth is a visual thinker, and she takes comfort in order and logic. Her strong emotional reaction to Teleborian is represented symbolically in the disruption of her equations. She can only regain control over the situation and establish a sense of order when "again she fixed her eyes on the spot on the wall, and gathered up the scattered numbers and symbols and began to reassemble the equation" (*Hornet's Nest*, 606). In this way, the novel contributes to the common perception of special interests as a means for autistics to create order in a neurotypical world that may appear disordered from an autistic perspective.[16] Such theories cast deep interests in a negative and restrictive light, suggesting that autistic people use their deep interests to retreat from a "real world" that is supposedly beyond their grasp.

While subtle metaphors and the use of stereotypes could be seen as undermining the novels' critical approach to mental health care, the conspiracy plotline and final courtroom scene damage Larsson's critique in more overt ways. The trilogy of novels first undermines psychiatric bureaucracy by pointing out that Lisbeth has been abused and mistreated, only to later reaffirm the reader's faith in the system. In the third book, Lisbeth's trial reveals that she was committed to an institution as part of a criminal conspiracy. Lisbeth's mistreatment and suffering are caused not by a broken mental health care system but by the flagrant abuse of that system by corrupt officials. In the second book, we find out that even the rapist Bjurman is a part of the conspiracy against Lisbeth, thus taking the symbolic responsibility for her abuse away from the health care system and placing it on the criminal underworld working against the heroine. The distrust of authority remains, but the novels seem to suggest that those with cognitive differences only face injustice or abuse when a deliberately cruel and criminal element manipulates the system. The implausibility of the conspiracy plot that keeps Lisbeth labeled, institutionalized, and silenced thus strips Larsson's potential critique of its political power—the implausibility of the conspiracy leads us to believe that what has happened to Lisbeth does not happen to real consumers of the mental health care system. Of course, people on the autism spectrum who are institutionalized against their will are not usually the victims of a criminal conspiracy. In the fictional world of the novels, the corrupt Section works to remove the blame placed on the system for Lisbeth's mistreatment and to place it on individual criminals.

Furthermore, the third book officially "undiagnoses" Lisbeth: she is only allowed to triumph over her enemies by being transformed into a neurotypical. The court ultimately concludes that Lisbeth is not in need of any psychiatric care or evaluation and that she never had any kind of mental disorder in the first place. Giannini sets out to prove that Lisbeth is "just as sane and intelligent as anyone in this room," and she seems to be successful in doing so (*Hornet's Nest*, 484). After spending the better part of three long novels piling a plethora of diagnoses on Lisbeth and emphasizing how eccentric and different her mind really is, the final novel uses its climactic scene to erase Lisbeth's labels. As Martin and Simms argue, "It seems that Lisbeth is victimized and later vindicated only because she was *wrongly* labeled. . . . This reading ignores countless people—the so-called *rightly* labeled—whose stigma appears justified."[17] The mental health care system as Larsson depicts it could be seen as abusive—but only if you do not have a mental disorder. While many elements of the books are sensational, the treatment Lisbeth receives while she is institutionalized (restraint, force-feeding, and unwanted medication) is a reality for some people in psychiatric institutions.[18] It is telling that the villain Zalachenko imagines a mental disorder diagnosis as the perfect way to "get rid" of Lisbeth: "She has to disappear. Her testimony has to be declared invalid. She has to be committed to a mental institution for life" (*Hornet's Nest*, 75). Zalachenko's line of reasoning equates mental disorder with "invalid" and silenced and "committed" with "disappeared" and invisible. In other words, Lisbeth's mental health diagnosis is depicted as lowering her social status to the point that she will effectively be erased as a person—Zalachenko believes that a mental disorder label is the ultimate way to silence and disempower someone. The novels seem to affirm his logic, since the only way for Lisbeth to find a happy ending at the end of the trilogy, the only way for her to find a voice and a listening and understanding audience, is for her to become "unlabeled" and "undiagnosed," for her to be declared officially and legally neurotypical.[19]

While Larsson's novels superficially champion the cause of neurodiversity, this cause is eventually subsumed by narrative tactics that depict mental disability using dehumanizing and belittling stereotypes and by an overarching plot that finally eliminates and silences the presence of a disability narrative altogether. In the end, Lisbeth Salander is an intriguing character primarily because she is herself a kind of cultural lacuna—she is imagined by the neurotypical characters around her as a curious absence, a void to be filled, a gap in the flow of social information that demands interpretation and explanation. Indeed, for neurotypical readers she may become a blank space for cultural projection: the reader is asked to diagnose the novels' silences—to fill in the gaps in the depiction of mental disorder. The books give Lisbeth a presence only to render her an absence, they force her to speak only to make her be silent—they tell a story of oppression only to erase the story told. When the final courtroom scene denies Lisbeth's mental disability, the books' plotline seems to reiterate the attitude of the narrator in interpreting Lisbeth's reaction to rape: in order for the court to recognize injustice as injustice, it must see a neurotypical victim, not a disabled one. The trilogy's conclusion subtly suggests that our society can only understand (and humanize and sympathize with) the neurotypical Lisbeth, thus suggesting that while readers can be expected to accept a heroine who is sexually, physically, religiously, politically, and legally other, our culture may still not be ready to embrace a fully neurodiverse heroine.

Afterword

> "The speed of light," Lou said. "They have a value for the speed of light in a vacuum . . . but the speed of dark . . ."
>
> "Dark doesn't have a speed," Lucia said. "It's just what's there when light isn't—it's just a word for absence."
>
> —Elizabeth Moon, *The Speed of Dark*

"We are unable to work with the diagnosis that you have been given." "Our program is not the best fit for your family at this time." "Would you be likely to harm a child or be a danger to society?" "We need as much information as possible about . . . the stage of the disease, the undertaken treatment." "I spoke to the National Adoption Center regarding your situation. . . . [I]t looks like it isn't going to work out." I had already warned my husband that my autism diagnosis was likely to prevent us from adopting, but this did nothing to mitigate the fresh pain of each new rejection. A few days before my son was born, I found out that I would not be able to have any more children. A year later, I was becoming accustomed to attaching my medical records to emails and sending them out to strangers all over the country: "I have Asperger's syndrome. Can my husband and I adopt a second child?" My friend Lisa said that accounts of discrimination always sound exaggerated and unbelievable. Discrimination acts completely outside of reason and logic. It is something visceral and incomprehensible. It never feels real until it happens to someone you love.

In this book, I have explored some of the theoretical concerns (and common misconceptions) that underpin our society's depictions of autistic people, trying to unpack some of the stereotypes that contribute to misunderstanding and discrimination. Literature both reflects the society that creates it, bearing the indelible mark of its historical place and time, and reinforces and re-creates the social understandings and ways of being that created that literature. In other words, our literature reflects our collective beliefs and attitudes at the same time that it continues to shape them. The classic classroom texts depicting autistic characters that I have examined here (Conan Doyle's Sherlock Holmes stories, *Pygmalion, Of Mice and Men, Flowers for Algernon, To Kill a Mockingbird, The Glass Menagerie,* and *The Sound and the Fury*) are works of literature that teach new generations of students—whether teachers and students recognize that process or not—about autistic ways of being, initiating students in subtle (and not-so-subtle) ways into cultural definitions of what it means to have a mental disability. Contemporary best sellers (*Extremely Loud and Incredibly Close, The Curious Incident of the Dog in the Night-Time,* and *The Girl with the Dragon Tattoo*) show readers how attitudes toward autistic characters have continued to evolve in more recent years, reflecting our culture's simultaneous obsession with and yet prejudice against autism spectrum disorder.

There is a sense of historical continuity in the literary representation of these characters, whether the authors recognize them as autistic or not. Thus, these very diverse works of literature show a lineage of evolving cultural attitudes toward autistic characteristics. Moving from the fin de siècle to today, the connections among these works reveal an interweaving cluster of major themes. In spite of their origins in different times and places, these literary figures are connected: they all deal with feelings of social alienation, explore failures of verbal communication, struggle under neurotypical systems of judgment, and face the denial of autistic subjectivity. Looking at these works as a group, one can trace the evolution of stereotypes about cognitive disability through the literature of the past century. Some stereotypes remain entrenched in the popular imagination (the figure of the autistic detective is still giving us disabled but detail-oriented sleuths—figures such as Lisbeth Salander, Oskar Schell, and Christopher Boone are clearly descended from Sherlock Holmes), while other stereotypes about cognitive difference are slowly changing (the fear of excessive sexuality in Lennie Small and Benjy Compson has given way to asexual savants such as Spencer Reid). The Gothic mystery surrounding characters like "Boo" Radley and Benjy Compson is now a more subtle and nuanced affair, underlying the narrative rather than dominating it, as readers witness Lisbeth Salander's grotesque and Gothic methods of revenge. Even when they appear in works published before the diagnostic label was established, these characters are clearly connected. Whether their respective tales present them as eccentric detective, childlike innocent, Gothic monster, or genius savant, they share many of the same basic traits (sensory sensitivities, social struggles, deep interests) and face many of the same problems (social rejection, familial violence, damaging labels).

However, the list of autistic texts examined in this book is not exhaustive, and some texts have been omitted that could have been included. This book focuses on works that are a well-established part of the literary canon or that have gained recent acclaim and popularity. While this mixture of classroom classics with contemporary best sellers represents a diverse range of genres, approaches, and historical eras, it does not include every literary character who has been described as (or who could be considered) autistic. Although I have tried to present literary characters who represent the full diversity of the autism spectrum (both "low" and "high functioning," both nonverbal and verbal, both classic autism and Asperger's syndrome, both those with and those without intellectual disability), this is a nearly impossible task. As the popular saying goes, "If you know one person with autism, you know one person with autism." Autistic people are a remarkably diverse group, and no one book could hope to adequately address that diversity. Some readers will no doubt notice that nonverbal autistic people are underrepresented in the literary works examined here. It is true that most recent works about autistic characters (those written since the 1950s) tend to focus on "high-functioning" (and verbal) individuals. In the 1990s and early 2000s, our culture has developed a particular obsession with the autistic savant. In other words, the predominance of "high-functioning" characters represented here is partially a reflection of literary interest—in recent years, more authors have chosen to create characters who fit these stereotypes. Finally, my perception of which characters qualify as "autistic" must, of necessity, be somewhat swayed by my own personal experience both as an autistic person and as a professor of literature.

There are plenty of areas left for critical inquiry at the intersection between cognitive difference and disability studies. In terms of autism and fiction, more work needs to be done on film, television, and theater performances that represent life on the spectrum. (When is someone going to write a critical analysis of *The Big Bang Theory*?) More work needs to be done on the intersection between autism and race. (Why does the cultural imagination believe that all autistic people are white?) Gender and sexuality also intersect with representations of autism in important ways (gender issues play only a tangential role in this book). This book focuses on literary works from 1887 forward, but assuming that a certain percentage of the population has always been autistic, there is room to reread early modern characters labeled as "mad" but who display autistic traits. I have limited myself to fictional works in this book (and have also stayed aligned with the traditional literary canon in the early chapters), so I have not included any analysis of texts *by* autistic people. There have been many scholarly articles published on autistic autobiography, but it would add a new dimension to such studies to place autistic autobiography in dialogue with fictional representations of life on the spectrum. Overall, there needs to be more work in the field of disability studies on mental disabilities in general—a critical trend that is only now gathering speed. Finally, there needs to be more work done on mental disabilities by and for people with mental disabilities.

Of course, some people might say that a lack of theory of mind prevents autistic people from really understanding autism.[1] Such claims are yet another way that our culture denies autistic subjectivity. Autism is so often defined in terms of deficit, lack, and absence that such claims are all too often given unquestioning credence.[2] Refusing to adhere to the stereotype of the autistic person as ultimately disengaged, closed off by metaphorical barriers, and severed from human connections by silence, Elizabeth Moon's 2003 science fiction novel *The Speed of Dark* presents autism as presence rather than absence, as a central reality rather than a minority experience. The book is narrated by Lou Arrendale, an autistic with a deep interest in astronomy. Lou's interest in exploring the "speed of dark" becomes a metaphor with multiple meanings—chief among them the presence of autism as a source of positive identity. Although the neurotypical characters repeatedly tell him that "dark doesn't have a speed . . . it's just what's there when light isn't—it's just a word for absence," Lou argues that darkness has its own presence.[3] His friend Lucia is particularly insistent on this point: "Light is real. Darkness is the absence of light" (86). Lou sees the term "real," however, as synonymous with the term "neurotypical." Recognizing that neurotypical judgments define reality for autistics, Lou frequently refers to neurotypical people as "real" and to autistic people as "not completely real": "Her face has that look. I don't know what most people would call it, but I call it the I AM REAL look. It means she is real and she has answers and I am someone less, not completely real" (3). As a person who is imagined by his society as "not completely real," Lou has a reason to think carefully about the speed of dark, to explore the possibility of dark as something other than deficient, as a force with presence, identity, and agency outside of conceptions of absence and lack. When Lucia says, "Light is real. Darkness is the absence of light," Lou may in fact hear, "Neurotypical people are real. Autism is the absence of neurotypicality."[4] This book has endeavored to turn such assumptions upside down, to treat autism as a presence, an identity, a source of agency, to read autistic characters as "real" in Lou's sense of having validation, authority, and voice—not to view literary representations of autism as vacancy or absence but to explore fictional depictions of the spectrum as signs of disabled presence. This book is merely a starting point in rereading the cultural lineage of perceived dark, of assumed absence, of supposed silence—the critical history of imagining autism.

NOTES

Introduction

1. For a more detailed discussion of the stereotype that associates mental disabilities with violent behavior, see Margaret Price, *Mad at School: Rhetorics of Mental Disability and Academic Life* (Ann Arbor: University of Michigan Press, 2011), Kindle edition, locators 2939–3589. In this book, I have chosen to use electronic editions wherever possible: this is simply a matter of accessibility. Although some may be surprised by this use of electronic editions, digital texts, in keeping with the spirit of disability studies, offer myriad accessibility options. For statistical data showing that autistic people commit violent crimes less often than their neurotypical counterparts, see Marianne Mordre et al., "Is Long-Term Prognosis for Pervasive Developmental Disorder Not Otherwise Specified Different from Prognosis for Autistic Disorder? Findings from a 30-Year Follow-Up Study," *Journal of Autism and Developmental Disorders* 42, no. 6 (2011): 920–928.

2. The other two books currently available on autism and the humanities are Mark Osteen's *Autism and Representation* (New York: Routledge, 2008) and Stuart Murray's *Representing Autism: Culture, Narrative, Fascination* (Liverpool: Liverpool University Press, 2008). Murray's book focuses mostly on popular culture and the media, while the edited collection by Osteen focuses on autism and the humanities more generally. The only other book on autism and literature to date is Phyllis Ferguson Bottomer's *So Odd a Mixture: Along the Autistic Spectrum in "Pride and Prejudice"* (London: Jessica Kingsley Publishers, 2007). The book deals only with characters in *Pride and Prejudice*. It was not well received: the National Association for the Teaching of English described the book as "wonderfully absurd" (quoted in Graeme Paton, "Why Mr. Darcy Was the Strong but Silent Type," *Telegraph*, 7 April 2007, http://www.telegraph.co.uk/news/uknews/1547881/Why-Mr-Darcy-was-the-strong-but-silent-type.html, accessed 4 January 2015).

3. See Osteen, *Autism and Representation,* 3; and Murray, *Representing Autism,* 8.

4. David T. Mitchell and Sharon L. Snyder, *Narrative Prosthesis: Disability and the Dependencies of Discourse* (Ann Arbor: University of Michigan Press, 2000), 3. In addition, participation in academic discourse depends on privileges, opportunities, and abilities that some autistic people may not have—the mediums of scholarly discourse and the structures that surround scholarly discourse can function as a form of exclusion.

5. For a practical explanation of the *Diagnostic and Statistical Manual of Mental Disorders* (*DSM*) criteria, see Tony Atwood, *The Complete Guide to Asperger's Syndrome* (London: Jessica Kingsley Publishers, 2007). Although the *DSM-5* does not include "Asperger's syndrome" as a distinct diagnosis, many people still have this term on their medical records and consider the label a part of identity. I decided to keep the term in this book (which I began writing before the *DSM* change) as a way of designating a certain subset of the autistic population in terms of stereotypes and the popular imagination.

6. Some people on the spectrum prefer the term "deep interest" (thus avoiding the condescending potential of "special"). I use the terms "special interest" and "deep interest" interchangeably throughout this book.

7. Osteen, *Autism and Representation*, 10.

8. Murray, *Representing Autism*, xvii.

9. Erica Goode, "Lifting the Veils of Autism, One by One by One," *New York Times*, 24 February 2004, http://www.nytimes.com/2004/02/24/science/lifting-the-veils-of-autism-one-by-one-by-one.html, accessed 22 September 2012; Claudia Wallis, "A Powerful Identity, a Vanishing Diagnosis," *New York Times*, 2 November 2009, http://www.nytimes.com/2009/11/03/health/03asperger.html, accessed 22 September 2012.

10. Murray, *Representing Autism*, xvii.

11. Stuart Murray, "Autism and the Contemporary Sentimental: Fiction and the Narrative Fascination of the Present," *Literature and Medicine* 25, no. 1 (2006): 24–25.

12. Osteen, *Autism and Representation*, 36.

13. See Murray, *Representing Autism*, 5. According to Murray, "Autism is in some ways a condition that has acquired a particular and specific emphasis, and indeed popularity, in the very contemporary period. It is, we might say, the condition of fascination of the moment, occupying a number of cultural locations that reflect a spectrum of wonder and nervousness—the allure of potentially unquantifiable human difference and the nightmare of not somehow being 'fully' human" (ibid., 5).

14. Price, *Mad at School*, locator 331. It is not clear if this is due to an actual increase in cases or to changing diagnostic criteria and increasing awareness among educators and medical professionals.

15. See Murray, *Representing Autism*, 97.

16. See Nick Walker, "Liberating Ourselves from the Pathology Paradigm," in *Loud Hands: Autistic People, Speaking*, ed. Julia Bascom (Washington, D.C.: Autistic Press, 2012), Kindle edition, locator 154. My points here summarize the ones Walker makes in this essay.

17. See ibid., 155.

18. See Sharon L. Snyder and David T. Mitchell, *Cultural Locations of Disability* (Chicago: University of Chicago Press, 2006), 6.

19. Murray, *Representing Autism*, 12.

20. Snyder and Mitchell, *Cultural Locations*, 6.

21. Osteen, *Autism and Representation*, 2.

22. For more information regarding the terminology debate, see Murray, *Representing Autism*, 23–24. As Douglas Biklen points out, "Even saying the person 'is autistic' could be problematic if the person does not chose the label and if the labeling implies that autism is a tangible reality." Biklen suggests yet another possibility, recommending terms such as "classified autistic" and "diagnosed as being on the autistic spectrum" to remind speakers and listeners that "autism is a concept developed and applied, not discovered" (*Autism and the Myth of the Person Alone* [New York: New York University Press, 2005], Kindle edition, locators 296, 304).

23. The general consensus of the scientific community is that autism has a genetic component. Autistic behaviors have sometimes been observed in infants as young as six months old.

24. Patrick McDonagh, "Literature and the Notion of Intellectual Disability," *Disability Studies Quarterly* 17, no. 4 (1997): 268.

25. On Asperger's and autism, see Atwood, *The Complete Guide*.

26. Walker, "Liberating Ourselves," 157–158.

27. Ibid., 158.

28. PhebeAnn M. Wolframe, "The Madwoman in the Academy, or, Revealing the Invisible Straightjacket: Theorizing and Teaching Saneism and Sane Privilege," *Disability Studies Quarterly* 33, no. 1 (2013), http://dsq-sds.org/article/view/3425.

29. See the discussion in ibid.

30. Snyder and Mitchell, *Cultural Locations*, 10.

31. Walker, "Liberating Ourselves," 161.

32. For a discussion of "passing" in the disabled community at large, see Simi Linton, *Claiming Disability: Knowledge and Identity* (New York: New York University Press, 1998), 19–21.

33. Snyder and Mitchell, *Cultural Locations*, 18.

34. Price, *Mad at School*, locator 378.

35. Melanie Yergeau, "Clinically Significant Disturbance: On Theorists Who Theorize Theory of Mind," *Disability Studies Quarterly* 33, no. 4 (2013), http://dsq-sds.org/article/view/3876.

36. Ibid.

37. For further information on Bettelheim's theories regarding autism, see Bruno Bettelheim, *The Empty Fortress* (New York: Free Press, 1967). On Baron-Cohen's ideas regarding ToM, see Simon Baron-Cohen, *Mindblindness: An Essay on Autism and Theory of Mind* (Cambridge, Mass.: MIT Press / A Bradford Book, 1995).

38. Ian Hacking, "Autistic Autobiography," *Philosophical Transactions of the Royal Society B* 364 (2009): 1467–1473.

39. Ibid., 1471.

40. Ibid., 1468.

41. On the subjective and objectifying nature of medical discourse, see Snyder and Mitchell, *Cultural Locations*, 21.

42. On the language of "deficit and loss" in medical discourse, see Linton, *Claiming Disability*, 5.

43. Bill Rocque, "Science Fictions: Figuring Autism as Threat and Mystery in Medico-therapeutic Literature," *Disability Studies Quarterly* 30, no. 1 (2010), http://dsq-sds .org/article/view/1064.

44. For example, see Julia Bascom, "Quiet Hands," in Bascom, *Loud Hands*, 120.

45. I use the terms "modern" and "postmodern" to refer to literary movements and to the characteristics traditionally associated with works of those movements (e.g., the fragmentation of modernist narratives such as *The Sound and the Fury* or the repetition and pastiche of postmodern works such as *Extremely Loud and Incredibly Close*) but also more loosely to denote a certain span of time: this book examines works of literature ranging from 1887 (the publication of *A Study in Scarlet*) through 2007 (the English-language publication of *The Girl Who Kicked the Hornet's Nest*).

46. Murray, *Representing Autism*, 49.

47. See the discussion in ibid., 49–50.

48. Christopher Krentz, "A 'Vacant Receptacle'? Blind Tom, Cognitive Difference, and Pedagogy," *PMLA* 120 (2005): 553.

49. See Bennett Kravitz, *Representations of Illness in Literature and Film* (Newcastle upon Tyne, England: Cambridge Scholars Publishing, 2010), 40.

50. Ian Hacking, "Making Up People," *London Review of Books* 28, no. 16 (2006), http://www.lrb.co.uk/v28/n16/ian-hacking/making-up-people, accessed 9 February 2015.

51. Ibid.

52. Ibid. The work of literary critic and theorist Judith Butler provides a helpful analogue: when Butler argues that gender is performative (women enact the culturally imposed role of femininity), she is not suggesting that women do not exist or arguing that men and women do not have different biological organs; instead, she is pointing out the ways in which the cultural definition of being a woman affects one's perception of oneself as (and therefore one's behavior as) a woman. See Judith Butler, *Gender Trouble* (New York: Routledge, 1990).

53. Hacking, "Making Up People."

54. Ian Hacking, *Mad Travelers: Reflections on the Reality of Transient Mental Illness* (Cambridge, Mass.: Harvard University Press, 2002).

55. Hacking, "Making Up People." "High-functioning autism" is Hacking's term, not mine. Functioning labels are potentially offensive and a source of conflict within the autism community (see my discussion in this chapter).

56. Price, *Mad at School*, locator 361.

57. Rocque, "Science Fictions."

58. Rosemarie Garland-Thomson, "Roosevelt's Sister: Why We Need Disability Studies in the Humanities," *Disability Studies Quarterly* 30, nos. 3/4 (2010), http://dsq -sds.org/article/view/1278/1311.

59. Snyder and Mitchell, *Cultural Locations,* 19.

60. Murray, *Representing Autism,* 4.

61. Meg Evans, "And Straight On till Morning," in Bascom, *Loud Hands,* 111.

62. Susan Sontag, *Illness as Metaphor and AIDS and Its Metaphors* (New York: Farrar, Straus and Giroux, 1977), 58.

63. Mitchell and Synder, *Narrative Prosthesis,* 10.

64. Zoe Gross, "Metaphor Stole My Autism: The Social Construction of Autism as Separable from Personhood, and Its Effect on Policy, Funding, and Perception," in Bascom, *Loud Hands,* 179.

65. See Gross's discussion in "Metaphor Stole My Autism," 179–182.

66. Ibid., 180.

67. Ibid., 185.

68. Rosemarie Garland-Thomson, "From Wonder to Error—a Genealogy of Freak Discourse in Modernity," in *Freakery: Cultural Spectacles of the Extraordinary Body,* ed. Rosemarie Garland-Thomson (New York: New York University Press, 1996), 2.

69. Murray, *Representing Autism,* 9, 28. As Murray explains, "The label 'autistic' today is not necessarily always a description of an individual with a clear neurological difference. It is, in many ways . . . a word that is increasingly used to describe both people, and indeed situations, as generically 'odd' or even dangerous" (ibid., 9).

70. Price, *Mad at School,* locator 697.

71. See Murray, *Representing Autism,* 68. Murray notes "the increasingly common idea that autism can be understood through comparisons with technology, and particularly with computing" (ibid., 68). As Osteen points out, "Today's autism culture . . . represents autism through postmodern tropes such as the cyborg or computer" (*Autism and Representation,* 11).

72. This misconception could be caused by charity organizations that focus on children as a source of donor sympathy. Additionally, speaking autistics are often not recognized as "autistic" by the general public, and most autistic children speak by the time they reach adulthood: this could be another reason why the public imagines autism as a condition affecting only children. There are reports of "recovered" autistics, and some adults report that their autistic traits fade as they reach adulthood, but the general consensus of the psychiatric community is that autism is a lifelong condition.

73. Oliver Sacks, quoted in Osteen, *Autism and Representation,* 31.

74. Ibid., 13.

75. Murray, *Representing Autism,* 209, 66.

76. Osteen, *Autism and Representation,* 30.

77. Murray, *Representing Autism*, 93.

78. Osteen, *Autism and Representation*, 8–9.

79. Ibid., 16.

80. Ibid., 33.

81. Mitchell and Snyder, *Narrative Prosthesis*, 1–2.

82. As Snyder and Mitchell note in *Cultural Locations*, "People with autism may resist or internalize the designation (or, perhaps more usually, some combination of these two options)" (11).

1. The Autistic Detective

1. One could make a case for Christopher Boone of *The Curious Incident of the Dog in the Night-Time* as the literary character most commonly associated with autism for this generation, but for a classic literary character one must look to Sherlock Holmes.

2. See James Berger, "Alterity and Autism: Mark Haddon's *Curious Incident* in the Neurological Spectrum," in Osteen, *Autism and Representation*, 271–288. See also Uta Frith, *Autism: Explaining the Enigma* (Malden, Mass.: Blackwell Publishing, 2003). Both Frith and Berger note that the detective is "a generic role strongly marked by autistic qualities" (Berger, "Alterity and Autism," 280). In many important ways, Sherlock Holmes is the starting point in this tradition.

3. Lisa Sanders, "Hidden Clues," *New York Times*, 4 December 2009, http://www.nytimes.com/2009/12/06/magazine/06diagnosis-t.html?pagewanted=all&_r=0, accessed 17 March 2013.

4. For a discussion of the damaging and discriminatory use of the term "mind-blind," see Yergeau, "Clinically Significant Disturbance."

5. Christopher Badcock, "The Genius of Detective Fiction," *Psychology Today*, 21 January 2010, http://www.psychologytoday.com/blog/the-imprinted-brain/201001/the-genius-detective-fiction, accessed 17 March 2013.

6. Karl Albrecht, "Did Sherlock Holmes Have Asperger Syndrome?," *Psychology Today*, 13 October 2011, http://www.psychologytoday.com/blog/brainsnacks /201110 /did-sherlock-holmes-have-asperger-syndrome-0, accessed 17 March 2013.

7. Frith, *Autism*, 23–24.

8. Eric Altschuler, "Asperger's in the Holmes Family," *Journal of Autism and Developmental Disorders* 43, no. 9 (2013): 2238–2239.

9. Mitchell and Snyder, *Narrative Prosthesis*.

10. See the various discussions of autistic identity in Bascom, *Loud Hands*.

11. See Irene Rose, "Autistic Autobiography: Introducing the Field," *Proceedings of the Autism and Representation: Writing, Cognition, Disability Conference*, 2005, http://www.cwru.edu/affil/sce/Representing%20Autism.html, accessed 12 December 2013. Julia Miele Rodas summarizes some of the common themes of autistic autobiography: "As this genre grows and offers increasing clarity regarding the diversity of autistic per-

sonality and experience, readers can also begin to recognize certain shared themes and ideas within the literature. These frequently include: a feeling of misunderstanding and being misunderstood by others in everyday interactions; a powerful and elaborate sense of connection in some special arena or skill area (e.g., numbers, color, animals, drawing/painting, languages); the experience of being excluded, especially in childhood when rigid social structures prevail; and a sense of peace and satisfaction that comes with order and ordering, both in material and in logical terms" ("'On the Spectrum': Rereading Contact and Affect in *Jane Eyre*," *Nineteenth Century Gender Studies* 4, no. 2 [2008], http://www.ncgsjournal.com/issue42/rodas.htm).

12. For example, see Temple Grandin, *Emergence: Labeled Autistic* (Novato, Calif.: Arena Press, 1986); Donna Williams, *Nobody Nowhere: The Extraordinary Autobiography of an Autistic* (New York: Avon, 1992); Dawn Prince-Hughes, *Songs of the Gorilla Nation* (New York: Harmony Books, 2004); Liane Holliday Willey, *Pretending to Be Normal* (London: Jessica Kingsley Publishers, 1999); John Elder Robison, *Look Me in the Eye* (New York: Crown Publishers, 2007).

13. I'm inspired here by PhebeAnn Marjory Wolframe's thinking. See her "The Madwoman in the Academy."

14. Murray, *Representing Autism*, 9.

15. On the subjective and objectifying nature of medical discourse, see Snyder and Mitchell, *Cultural Locations*, 21.

16. Albrecht ("Did Sherlock Holmes") also notes Holmes's intense interests and poor people skills. As Sanders describes Holmes's autistic traits, "He appears oblivious to the rhythms and courtesies of normal social intercourse—he doesn't converse so much as lecture. His interests and knowledge are deep but narrow. He is strangely 'coldblooded,' and perhaps as a consequence, he is also alone in the world. He has no friends other than the extremely tolerant Watson; a brother, even stranger and more isolated than he, is his only family" ("Hidden Clues").

17. Arthur Conan Doyle, *A Study in Scarlet* (New York: Oxford University Press, 1993), 14. Hereafter cited parenthetically in the text as *Study*.

18. Arthur Conan Doyle, *The Sign of the Four* (New York: Oxford University Press, 1993), 6. Hereafter cited parenthetically in the text as *Sign*. Both Frith (*Autism*) and Sanders ("Hidden Clues") note that this unusual research topic is a potential sign that Holmes has autism.

19. Arthur Conan Doyle, *The Hound of the Baskervilles* (New York: Oxford University Press, 1993), 143. Hereafter cited parenthetically in the text as *Hound*.

20. Arthur Conan Doyle, *The Adventures of Sherlock Holmes* (New York: Oxford University Press, 1993), 29. Hereafter cited parenthetically in the text as *Adventures*.

21. Gross, "Metaphor Stole My Autism," 179.

22. *Sherlock Holmes*, directed by Guy Ritchie, performed by Robert Downey Jr. and Jude Law (Warner Bros., 2009).

23. *Sherlock Holmes: A Game of Shadows,* directed by Guy Ritchie, performed by Robert Downey Jr. and Jude Law (Warner Bros., 2011).

24. See Murray on the "wonder and awe" evoked by savant figures (*Representing Autism,* 99).

25. "A Study in Pink," *Sherlock,* season 1, episode 1, performed by Benedict Cumberbatch and Martin Freeman, BBC, aired 25 July 2010.

26. The misconception may be due in part to the stereotype of those with autism as lacking in empathy. See Christine Hughes, "BBC's Sherlock, Asperger's Syndrome, and Sociopathy," *Global Comment,* 20 June 2012, http://globalcomment.com/bbcs-sherlock -asperger%E2%80%99s-syndrome-and-sociopathy/, accessed 12 December 2012.

27. "The Hounds of Baskerville," *Sherlock,* season 2, episode 2, performed by Benedict Cumberbatch and Martin Freeman, BBC, aired 8 January 2012.

28. The detective as the doppelgänger for the criminal is a common motif in crime fiction. See Lee Horsley, "From Sherlock Holmes to the Present," in *A Companion to Crime Fiction,* ed. Charles J. Rzepka (Chichester: Wiley-Blackwell, 2010), 28–42; and Christiana Gregoriou, "The Poetics of Deviance and the Curious Incident of the Dog in the Night-Time," in *The Millennial Detective: Essays on Trends in Crime Fiction, Film and Television, 1990–2010,* ed. Malcah Effron (Jefferson, N.C.: McFarland, 2011), 97–111. As Horsley points out, "Detective fiction is haunted by all it purports to contain. There are, for example, ambiguities present in the doubling of the detective and the murderer" ("From Sherlock Holmes," 29). Gregoriou notes that "the literary figure of the detective continues to be a marginal figure who frequently bears a closer likeness to the criminal he pursues than to the police officers with whom he supposedly collaborates. . . . [D]etectives are often as socially estranged as criminals are" ("The Poetics of Deviance," 99).

29. For a further discussion of this myth, see Price, *Mad at School.*

30. Peter Beresford quoted in ibid., locator 3001.

31. Ibid., locator 3017.

32. Ibid., locator 2992.

33. Ruth Allen and Raymond G. Nairn, "Media Depictions of Mental Illness: An Analysis of the Use of Dangerousness," *Australian and New Zealand Journal of Psychiatry* 31 (1997): 375–381. See Price's discussion as well (*Mad at School,* locator 3009).

34. Price, *Mad at School,* locator 3009.

35. As Margaret Price has argued, "Prevailing myths about mental disability and violence shore up an ongoing structural violence in American society" (ibid., locator 2964).

36. Altschuler, "Asperger's in the Holmes Family," 2238–2239.

37. "A Study in Pink."

38. See http://www.bbc.co.uk/programmes/b018ttws/characters/sherlock-holmes.

39. "A Scandal in Belgravia," *Sherlock,* season 2, episode 1, performed by Benedict Cumberbatch and Martin Freeman, BBC, 1 January 2012.

40. See Rodas's discussion of this stereotype.

41. Arthur Conan Doyle, *The Casebook of Sherlock Holmes* (New York: Oxford University Press, 2009), 7. Hereafter cited parenthetically in the text as *Casebook.*

42. See Yergeau's discussion in "Clinically Significant Disturbance."

43. Sanders also cites some of these characters as imitating Holmes's autistic tendencies: "Clearly Holmes's peculiarities have a persistent appeal. Just look at Temperance Brennan of 'Bones,' Adrian Monk of 'Monk,' and, of course, Gregory House of 'House,' who exhibit at least a few Asperger-like symptoms and owe much to Sherlock Holmes" ("Hidden Clues"). See also Ana E. La Paz, "Making the Transition: The Modern Adaptation and Recreation of the Scientist Detective Hero," in *Sherlock Holmes for the 21st Century: Essays on New Adaptations,* ed. Lynnette Porter (Jefferson, N.C.: McFarland, 2012), 81–92; and J. Madison Davis, "Mr. Monk & the Pleasing Paradigm," *World Literature Today* 83, no. 3 (2009): 11–13. La Paz notes that Temperance Brennan of *Bones* resembles Holmes in her reliance on logic over emotion: "Other detective series usually have at least one character who is highly intelligent and less emotional than the others" ("Making the Transition," 85–86). Davis points out that "Monk was deliberately conceived as a mirror of Holmes" ("Mr. Monk," 11).

44. "Broken Mirror," *Criminal Minds,* season 1, episode 5, performed by Matthew Gray Gubler and Mandy Patinkin, CBS, aired 19 October 2005.

45. "Through the Looking Glass," *Criminal Minds,* season 8, episode 3, performed by Matthew Gray Gubler and Jeanne Tripplehorn, CBS, aired 16 October 2012.

46. "Corazon," *Criminal Minds,* season 6, episode 12, performed by Matthew Gray Gubler, CBS, aired 19 January 2011.

47. Sharon Lee Watson and Harry Bring, "Full Transcript—Live Chat with Writer, Sharon Lee Watson and Line Producer, Harry Bring," CM Set Report: Behind the Scenes of *Criminal Minds,* 18 October 2012, http://cmsetreport.tumblr.com/post /34127594413/full-transcript-live-chat-with-writer-sharon-lee, accessed 12 December 2013.

48. "Zugzwang," *Criminal Minds,* season 8, episode 12, performed by Matthew Gray Gubler, CBS, aired 15 January 2013.

49. Indeed, schizophrenia and autism do not frequently appear in the same families.

50. Rachel Thomas, "An Interview with Matthew Gray Gubler," About.com: TV Dramas, http://tvdramas.about.com/od/criminalminds/a/matgraygubint.htm, accessed 16 December 2013.

51. "Sex, Birth, Death," *Criminal Minds,* season 2, episode 11, performed by Matthew Gray Gubler, CBS, aired 29 November 2006.

52. For a further discussion of Bones's relationship to Holmes, see La Paz, "Making the Transition," 81–92.

53. In the show's pilot episode, a montage in which Brennan examines bones over-night features Howie Day's "Collide" in the background sound track: "The dawn is breaking / A light shining through / You're barely waking / And I'm tangled up in you." "Pilot," *Bones,* season 1, episode 1, performed by Emily Deschanel, Fox, aired 13 September 2005.

54. "The Man in the Morgue," *Bones,* season 1, episode 19, performed by Emily Deschanel and Eric Millegan, Fox, aired 26 April 2006.

55. "Pilot."

56. "The Man in the SUV," *Bones,* season 1, episode 2, performed by Emily Deschanel, Fox, aired 20 September 2005.

57. "The Girl in the Fridge," *Bones,* season 1, episode 8, performed by Emily Deschanel, Fox, aired 29 November 2005.

58. "A Boy in a Tree," *Bones,* season 1, episode 3, performed by Emily Deschanel and David Boreanaz, Fox, aired 27 September 2005.

59. "Pilot."

60. Alan Sepinwall, "How TV Shows Try (or Choose Not) to Depict Asperger's Syndrome: Sepinwall on TV," *Star-Ledger,* 28 February 2010, http://www.nj.com/entertainment/tv/index.ssf/2010/02/how_tv_shows_try_or_choose_not.html, accessed 12 December 2013.

61. Hart Hanson, quoted in ibid.

62. Ellen Gray, "Boreanaz Says *Bones* Is Not Procedural," *Philadelphia Daily News,* 31 January 2007, http://www.philly.com/philly/columnists/ellen_gray/20070131_Ellen_Gray_Boreanaz_says_Bones_is_not_procedural.html, accessed 12 December 2013.

63. Deschanel quoted in ibid.

64. "Pilot."

65. "The Pathos in the Pathogens," *Bones,* season 8, episode 23, performed by Emily Deschanel, Fox, aired 22 April 2013.

66. "Pilot."

67. "The Man in the SUV."

68. "Pilot."

69. Ibid.

70. "A Boy in a Tree."

71. "The Girl in the Fridge."

72. Ibid.

73. "Pilot."

74. This stereotype involves a gross (but common) misinterpretation of Baron-Cohen's work. For an explanation of the actual theory, see Simon Baron-Cohen, "The Extreme Male Brain Theory of Autism," *TRENDS in Cognitive Sciences* 6, no. 6 (2002): 248–254.

75. "The Girl in the Fridge."

76. "Pilot."

2. The Autistic Savant

1. For example, lists of historical figures suspected to have autism or other neuro-logical differences appear on websites such as http://www.2-b-well.org/famous autistics.html; http://www.autism-world.com/index.php/2007/09/13/famous-people -with-autism-traits/; http://www.disabled-world.com/artman/publish/article_2086 .shtml; http://www.managing-autism-one2one.com/famous-people-with-autism.html; http://www.in-spite-of.org/disney/; and http://www.sunderland4autism.com /diversity-works-event.html. Such lists are usually dominated by scientists and inven-tors. All of these lists include Shaw, and some include other literary figures such as Mark Twain, Emily Dickinson, Jane Austen, and Virginia Woolf. However, Shaw gen-erally appears on such lists with more consistency than these other writers. The T-shirt using Shaw's image to promote neurodiversity can be found at www.cafepress.com.

2. Autism was not a distinct diagnosis until the 1950s, but a certain percentage of the population has always been autistic. See Osteen, *Autism and Representation,* 12. Es-sentially, the autism community is writing a history where there is no written history (or perhaps attempting to rewrite a history of marginalization and discrimination). The problems of "diagnosing the dead" are manifold, and many would argue that the post-humous diagnosis of any person as "autistic" is simply impossible (ibid., 12). Although the diagnosis of the dead is scientifically unsound, the decision of which historical fig-ures get such a "diagnosis" (and why) tells us something important both about current stereotypes regarding autism and about the public reception of those figures embraced by the autism community.

3. The misconception that one must have autistic traits to understand autistic char-acters seems to be widespread. While one might point to Shaw's early years in London as a sign of potential awkwardness or outsider status, his youthful shyness hardly seems evidence of autism. I do not believe that Bernard Shaw was autistic: what inter-ests me here are the reasons for (and implications of) this erroneous diagnosis.

4. Depending on how he is played onstage, the brilliant Andrew Undershaft of *Major Barbara* could be seen as an Asperger's character: defined by his rejection of so-cial rules, he is socially awkward, oddly eccentric, and a self-taught genius—he man-ages much better in his chosen field (inventing weapons and running an arms business) than he does in social situations. More importantly, he is an outsider whose defiance of social norms is a defining attribute of his character. While social awkwardness is not a defining characteristic for the protagonist of Shaw's *Caesar and Cleopatra,* eccentricity certainly is. Like Undershaft, Caesar's defiance of the norm sets him apart from more conventional characters. The eccentric Audrey of *Too True to Be Good* may not have au-

tism, but he is definitely socially odd. Even this short list suggests why Shaw's characters, so often depicted as outsiders who reject social norms, might appeal to readers on the spectrum.

5. Reading only a few discussion threads on "Wrong Planet" will reveal this trend (www.wrongplanet.net).

6. Sylvan Barnet, "Bernard Shaw on Tragedy," *PMLA* 71, no. 5 (1956): 892.

7. George Bernard Shaw, *Saint Joan,* ed. Dan H. Laurence (London: Penguin Books, 2003), 23. Hereafter cited parenthetically in the text.

8. As Mark Osteen notes, popular conceptions of people on the spectrum mistakenly depict autistic people as "either geniuses or freaks; what they are not is regular people" (*Autism and Representation,* 33).

9. Christopher Innes, "'Nothing but Talk, Talk, Talk—Shaw Talk': Discussion Plays and the Making of Modern Drama," in *The Cambridge Companion to George Bernard Shaw,* ed. Christopher Innes (Cambridge: Cambridge University Press, 1998), 162.

10. For the only scholarly discussion of Higgins as having Asperger's, see Rodelle Weintraub, "Bernard Shaw's Henry Higgins: A Classic Aspergen," *Literature in Transition 1880–1920* 49, no. 4 (2006): 388–397. Weintraub discusses many of the same episodes and characteristics I note here: Higgins's awkward social skills, his self-stimulating habits, his struggle with empathy, and his general clumsiness.

11. See Weintraub's discussion (ibid., 390–395).

12. George Bernard Shaw, *Pygmalion,* ed. Dan H. Laurence (London: Penguin Books, 2000), 13. Hereafter cited parenthetically in the text. See also Weintraub's discussion of this scene ("Bernard Shaw's Henry Higgins," 391).

13. See Weintraub's discussion ("Bernard Shaw's Henry Higgins," 392).

14. Ibid.

15. Ibid.

16. See ibid., 393, on Mrs. Pearce and Mrs. Higgins and their "social coaching."

17. This is clearly an example of social coaching (ibid.).

18. Ibid.

19. See Weintraub's discussion of the at-home (ibid., 394).

20. Ibid., 395.

21. Ibid., 389.

22. Ibid.

23. See Murray, *Representing Autism,* 97.

24. Osteen, *Autism and Representation,* 8–9.

25. MudandStars, "Being 'Unreasonable,'" 7 October 2011, www.wrongplanet.net, accessed 22 September 2012.

26. Janissy, "Being 'Unreasonable,'" 7 October 2011, www.wrongplanet.net, accessed 22 September 2012.

27. On the subjective and objectifying nature of medical discourse, see Snyder and Mitchell, *Cultural Locations*, 21.

28. On the language of "deficit and loss" in medical discourse, see Simi Linton, *Claiming Disability: Knowledge and Identity* (New York: New York University Press, 1998), 5.

29. Snyder and Mitchell, *Cultural Locations*, 4.

30. Innes, "'Nothing but Talk,'" 163.

3. The Autistic Victim

1. Thanks to Kerima Cevick, whose insightful blog post inspired my choice of epigraph. See Kerima Cevick, "Invisible Autistic Filicide Victims," *INterSected*, 19 December 2013, http://intersecteddisability.blogspot.com/2013/12/autisms-invisible -filicide-victims.html, accessed 25 July 2014. See studies such as Mark T. Palermo, "Preventing Filicide in Families with Autistic Children," *Offender Therapy and Comparative Criminology* 47, no. 1 (2003): 47–57: "Autism . . . has been associated with an increased risk of social victimization, and a recent rise in number of acts of filicide of developmentally disabled children has included several cases of autism" (ibid., 47); and Rohini Coorg and Anne Tournay, "Filicide-Suicide Involving Children with Disabilities," *Journal of Child Neurology* 28, no. 6 (2013): 745–751. Although official record keeping is difficult, Coorg and Tournay found that 54 percent of disabled filicide victims were autistic: "Children with autism may be at risk for filicide-suicide, but accurate record keeping is needed to determine the incidence and risk factors" (ibid., 745). Many disability rights activists have noted the prevalence of autistic filicides. For example, see Cevick, "Invisible Autistic Filicide Victims."

2. Throughout this introduction, I'm indebted to Stuart Murray's excellent discussion of autistic filicide in *Representing Autism*, 167–171.

3. Ibid., 168. Cevick comments that "murder apologists continue to respond in posted comments about the difficulties in parenting autistic children rather than reacting to the horrific nature of this pattern of filicide-suicide. . . . Children and disabled adult victims are treated as collateral damage for exhausted parents" ("Invisible Autistic Filicide Victims").

4. Murray, *Representing Autism*, 168.

5. Ibid., 168–169. This is part of what Michelle Jarman describes as "media inattention to disability oppression" ("Dismembering the Lynch Mob: Intersecting Narratives of Disability, Race, and Sexual Menace," in *Sex and Disability*, ed. Robert McRuer and Anna Mollow [Durham, NC: Duke University Press, 2012], 89–107, quote at 91).

6. ABC news story quoted in Murray, *Representing Autism*, 169.

7. Ibid.

8. On the "cure or kill" trope in literary works, see Rosemarie Garland-Thomson, "Seeing the Disabled: Visual Rhetorics of Disability in Popular Photography," in *New*

Disability History, ed. Longmore K. Longmore and Lauri Umansky (New York: New York University Press, 2001), 355.

9. Ed Pilkington, "Texas Set to Execute Death Row Inmate Diagnosed as 'Mentally Retarded,'" *Guardian,* 5 August 2012, http://www.theguardian.com/world/2012/aug/05/texas-death-row-mentally-retarded, accessed 24 July 2014.

10. Ibid.

11. Ibid.

12. Ibid.

13. Quoted in ibid.

14. See Pilkington's discussion in ibid.

15. Rania Khalek, "Steinbecks: Leave Lennie Alone," *Salon,* 8 August 2012, http://www.salon.com/2012/08/08/steinbecks_leave_lennie_alone/, accessed 24 July 2014.

16. See Edward E. Waldron, "Using Literature to Teach Ethical Principles in Medicine: *Of Mice and Men* and the Concept of Duty," *Literature and Medicine* 7 (1988): 170–176.

17. Sally Chivers, "Disability Studies and the Vancouver Opera's *Of Mice and Men,*" *Disability Studies Quarterly* 23, no. 1 (2003), http://dsq-sds.org/article/view/402/551; Mitchell and Snyder include both *Of Mice and Men* and *Flowers for Algernon* on their list of novels about disability that have shaped U.S. education (*Narrative Prosthesis,* 167).

18. Patrick McDonagh, "Literature and the Notion of Intellectual Disability," *Disability Studies Quarterly* 17, no. 4 (1997): 272.

19. Licia Carlson, *The Faces of Intellectual Disability* (Bloomington: Indiana University Press, 2010), 3.

20. See Stephanie Jensen-Moulton, "Intellectual Disability in Carlisle Floyd's *Of Mice and Men,*" *American Music* 30, no. 2 (2012): 129–156. Jensen-Moulton comes closest by comparing Lennie to Kanner's early description: "Steinbeck's understanding of intellectual disability was grounded not only in his own experience working alongside the man on whom he later based Lennie's character, but would also have found its basis in contemporary thought. Psychiatrist Leo Kanner had already established himself as a prominent teacher and scholar by the early 1930s, specializing in the intellectual disability he would later call autism. As Kanner writes—albeit with dated terminology—'mental defectives were viewed as a menace to civilization, incorrigible at home, burdens to the school, sexually promiscuous, breeders of feebleminded offspring, victims and spreaders of poverty, degeneracy, crime and disease.' Clearly, Steinbeck's Lennie—whose seemingly innocent desire to touch soft things results in such a tragic outcome—falls somewhere within the categories outlined above by Kanner, thereby reinforcing negative stereotypes about cognitive differences" (ibid., 146–147).

21. Elaine Liner, "Theatre Arlington Stages a Solid and Serious *Of Mice and Men,*" *Dallas Observer,* 31 October 2013, http://www.dallasobserver.com/2013-10-31/culture/theatre-arlington-stages-a-solid-and-serious-of-mice-and-men/full/, accessed 25 July 2014.

22. John Steinbeck, *Of Mice and Men* (New York: Penguin Books, 1994), Kindle edition, page 11. Hereafter cited parenthetically in the text.

23. See Martin Halliwell, *Images of Idiocy: The Idiot Figure in Modern Fiction and Film* (Aldershot, England: Ashgate, 2004). As Halliwell explains, "Retelling the story of the farm is a ritual to comfort Lennie when he feels vulnerable or tired" (ibid., 147).

24. As Jensen-Moulton notes, "Lennie's need for sensory stimulation would, in the end, be the downfall of their dream" ("Intellectual Disability," 131).

25. Marianne Mordre et al., "Is Long-Term Prognosis for Pervasive Developmental Disorder Not Otherwise Specified Different from Prognosis for Autistic Disorder? Findings from a 30-Year Follow-Up Study," *Journal of Autism and Developmental Disorders* 42, no. 6 (2011): 920–928.

26. See Susan Baglieri and Arthur Shapiru, *Disability Studies and the Inclusive Classroom* (New York: Routledge, 2012), 226. Lennie is a classic example of at least two established tropes for disabled characters: "the victim of violence" and "the Holy innocent or the eternal child" (ibid.).

27. See Chivers, "Disability Studies," for further discussion of Lennie's size.

28. Janice Brockley quoted in ibid.

29. I have a friend who teaches in a classroom in which all of the children are autistic. When people find out where she works, they often ask with concern, "Are your students big?" This odd question seems to be inspired by a fear for my friend's physical safety (she is a very petite woman). Although there is no scientific basis for the belief that autistic people will be larger than neurotypical people, my friend and I have often wondered if this perception may be based on cultural fears that all autistic people are uncontrollable and need to be physically restrained.

30. William Faulkner, *The Sound and the Fury* (New York: Vintage International, 1990), 4.

31. Halliwell, *Images of Idiocy,* 144. In this chapter, some of my sources refer to medical terminology used to describe mental disabilities in previous eras (such as "feebleminded," "moron," "idiot," and "retarded"). These terms are outdated and offensive and are not my terms.

32. Carlson quoted in Jensen-Moulton, "Intellectual Disability," 140. See also Anupama Iyer, "Portrayal of Intellectual Disability in Fiction," in *Mindreadings: Literature and Psychiatry,* ed. Femi Oyebode (London: RCPsych Publications, 2009), Kindle edition. Iyer notes that "resemblance to and kinship with animals is often called forth to emphasize the difference of people with intellectual disabilities and signal that they are not quite human" (locator 2665).

33. As Jensen-Moulton notes, Steinbeck "perpetuates the stereotype of the intellectually disabled as animalistic or subhuman in behavior as well as level of communication and predictability" ("Intellectual Disability," 140).

34. Licia Carlson and Eva Feder Kittay quoted in ibid., 145. As Jensen-Moulton argues, "Steinbeck's novel unsubtly reflects the link between intellectual disability and animal rights through the litany of small animals left dead in Lennie's wake and his motivic use of animals in the novel. While Steinbeck himself was no animal rights activist, the animals in the novel represent both the fragility of life and the connection between these innocent creatures' deaths and Lennie's euthanasia" (ibid., 146).

35. Carlson, *The Faces of Intellectual Disability,* 2.

36. "Men, Mice, and Mr. Steinbeck: New York Times/1937," in *Conversations with John Steinbeck,* ed. Thomas Fensch (Jackson: University Press of Mississippi, 1988), 8–10.

37. Jensen-Moulton, "Intellectual Disability," 131. Jarman also explores "the presumed sexual threat of cognitively disabled men" during Steinbeck's lifetime ("Dismembering the Lynch Mob," 91).

38. Jarman, "Dismembering the Lynch Mob," 100.

39. Jensen-Moulton, "Intellectual Disability," 149.

40. Leo Gurko, "The War between Good and Evil," *Readings on "Of Mice and Men"* (San Diego, Calif.: Greenhaven, 1998), 62.

41. Baglieri and Shapiru, *Disability Studies,* 227.

42. Halliwell, *Images of Idiocy,* 148.

43. Anecdotal evidence on "Wrong Planet" seems to suggest that autistics who are hypersensitive to touch may be less likely to engage in sexual activity, although I'm not aware of any studies on this subject.

44. Disabled people are often portrayed as "sexual predators" or "sexual innocents" (Heather Garrison, "Adolescents' Perceptions of the Sociocultural Construct of Disability When Responding to Literature: *Of Mice and Men,*" 44, *ETD Collection for Fordham University,* http://fordham.bepress.com/dissertations/AAI3302114, accessed 7 August 2014).

45. See Jarman's discussion in "Dismembering the Lynch Mob." For an approach to eugenics specific to *Of Mice and Men,* see Baglieri and Shapiru: "The character, Lennie, exemplifies a view of intellectually disabled persons as social menaces contributing to the genetic decline and social disorganization that proliferated during the era of eugenics" (*Disability Studies,* 227).

46. Jarman, "Dismembering the Lynch Mob," 89–90.

47. Ibid., 93.

48. Ibid.

49. Waldron, "Using Literature," 172. Chivers ("Disability Studies") and Halliwell (*Images of Idiocy*) also make the same point.

50. Jensen-Moulton, "Intellectual Disability," 152.

51. Waldron, "Using Literature," 176.

52. Ibid.

53. Many critics have viewed *Of Mice and Men* as a novella about euthanasia (e.g., see Waldron, "Using Literature"; Chivers, "Disability Studies"; and Jensen-Moulton, "Intellectual Disability").

54. Waldron, "Using Literature," 175.

55. I am not arguing that racism and ableism are parallel cultural phenomena (these two forms of discrimination are distinct entities that function in different ways; see Jarman's discussion in "Dismembering the Lynch Mob," 103). It is important to note both the ways that discourses of race and disability overlap and inform each other and the key ways in which they differ. I'm merely using this imaginary exercise in an attempt to highlight the ways in which the disability rights movement has lagged far behind the civil rights movement.

56. Jarman, "Dismembering the Lynch Mob," 90.

57. See Jarman's discussion of private versus public in lynching and castration (ibid., 104).

58. Halliwell, *Images of Idiocy,* 138.

59. Many autistic self-advocates have critiqued media rhetoric that seems to "blame" autistic filicide on a lack of appropriate support for caregivers. Such rhetoric seems to imply that autistic filicide could be prevented if only caregivers received more social and financial support. Arguing that a caregiver who becomes a killer simply needed more resources evokes sympathy for the killer and draws attention away from the autistic victim. By saying that better care, education, and therapy might improve the fictional Lennie's prospects, I am not espousing that kind of rhetoric. Do autistics and their families need better services and support? Of course they do. Is a lack of services and support an extenuating circumstance that justifies homicide? Of course it isn't. In this chapter, I am arguing that cultural attitudes that devalue and deny autistic subjectivity and personhood contribute to autistic filicide, not that a lack of services encourages filicide.

60. See Jarman's discussion of disability, family, and violence ("Dismembering the Lynch Mob," 104).

61. Garland-Thomson, "Seeing the Disabled," 355. See Jensen-Moulton's discussion in "Intellectual Disability."

62. See Jensen-Moulton, "Intellectual Disability," for further discussion.

63. The work appeared (under the same title) in both short story (1959) and novel (1966) forms. My discussion in this chapter addresses the novel.

64. In the novel, Professor Nemur explains that "we don't know exactly what causes the type of phenylketonuria that Charlie was suffering from as a child" (147). In the world of the novel, a diagnosis of phenylketonuria creates a completely unrealistic situation. PKU is a genetic disorder that prevents the body from breaking down specific amino acids: this buildup in the body can cause intellectual disability and other complications. But if Charlie has PKU, why wasn't it detected when he was an infant and prop-

erly treated? More importantly, why don't Professor Nemur and his colleagues (and the now genius Charlie, for that matter) realize that if Charlie's PKU is left untreated, he may develop intellectual disability again even after the brain surgery that increased his IQ? This is bad science on the part of the novel, but in the world of science fiction some bad science may be allowable (after all, the procedure that increases Charlie's IQ is completely imaginary).

65. Some people with autism dispute the idea that autism is a spectrum, arguing that conceptions of autism as a spectrum disorder encourage divisions among autistic people (such as functioning labels). I use the term "spectrum" throughout this book because I feel that it is the term that most accurately conveys my meaning in interpreting a text such as *Flowers for Algernon*. This choice of terminology is not intended to be an endorsement of functioning labels: because functioning labels are a part of how our culture constructs autism stereotypes, I use them here as a way of engaging discussion of those stereotypes.

66. Again, I am not presenting racism and ableism as parallel cultural phenomena. I am using race as a metaphor here to explain the potentially offensive nature of Keyes's assumed narrative persona.

67. Daniel Keyes, *Flowers for Algernon* (New York: Harcourt, 1987), Kindle edition, page 67. Hereafter cited parenthetically in the text.

68. Brent Walter Cline, "'You're Not the Same Kind of Human Being': The Evolution of Pity to Horror in Daniel Keyes's *Flowers for Algernon*," *Disability Studies Quarterly* 32, no. 4 (2012), http://dsq-sds.org/article/view/1760.

69. As Cline notes, "Rather than simply becoming hyper-intelligent, he also becomes cruel and selfish. This is pointed out to Charlie by nearly all those around him: the doctors involved in the experiment, Burt the graduate student, Charlie's love Alice, and Charlie's casual partner Faye" (ibid.).

70. On the "compensation cure," see Murray, *Representing Autism,* 66.

71. Cline argues compellingly that "Keyes recognizes that Charlie's regression, despite the fact that he merely returns to his original state, is a source of tragedy. This tragedy is read as pity at the beginning of the novel because Charlie's disability causes him to be powerless and unaware. By the end of the novel, however, disability causes the book's clear protagonist, the intelligent Charlie, to no longer exist. All that which makes the post-operative Charlie a distinct character—purpose, love, imagination, sexuality—fades away. Therefore, it is as though the intelligent Charlie is dying" ("'You're Not the Same'").

72. See Cline's discussion in ibid.

73. Quoted in ibid.

74. Ibid.

75. See the introduction to Mark Osteen's *Autism and Representation* for further discussion of these controversial issues.

76. See Mitchell and Snyder's discussion of people with physical disabilities' efforts to separate themselves from people with cognitive disabilities in the introduction to *Narrative Prosthesis*.

4. The Autistic Gothic

1. Many disability studies scholars have noted that disabled characters often reflect most directly on the concerns of nondisabled characters. As Sara Hosey puts it, "Disabled individuals' experiences" are "only literary or significant when they are deployed in order to explore non-physical conditions or a non-disabled character's experiences" ("Resisting the S(crip)t: Disability Studies Perspectives in the Undergraduate Classroom," *Teaching American Literature: A Journal of Theory and Practice* 6, no. 1 [2013]: 23–44, quote at 23).

2. The only other disability studies readings of the novel that I am aware of are the brief look in Mitchell and Snyder, *Narrative Prosthesis*, and two chapters in a recent collection. See also Lisa Detweiler Miller, "'Enable Us to Look Back': Performance and Disability in *To Kill a Mockingbird*," in *Harper Lee's "To Kill a Mockingbird": New Essays*, ed. Michael J. Meyer (Lanham, Md.: Scarecrow Press, 2010), 193–210; and Hugh McElaney, "'Just One Kind of Folks': The Normalizing Power of Disability in *To Kill a Mockingbird*," in Meyer, *Harper Lee's "To Kill a Mockingbird*," 211–231.

3. Snyder and Mitchell make the same point (*Narrative Prosthesis*, 173). See also McElaney, "'Just One Kind,'" 226; and Miller, "'Enable Us,'" 194.

4. Harper Lee, *To Kill a Mockingbird* (New York: Harper Collins, 1993), 3. Hereafter cited parenthetically in the text.

5. McElaney, "'Just One Kind,'" 226.

6. Since the novel is set in the 1930s and was published in 1960, an overt autism diagnosis for Arthur Radley would have been impossible at the time. On "autistic presence" see Stuart Murray's discussion in *Representing Autism*.

7. For examples, see Sarah Adams, "A Curious Phenomenon," *Guardian*, 6 December 2005, http://www.theguardian.com/society/2005/dec/07/socialcare.guardiansocietysupplement, accessed 6 July 2014, and lists of fictional characters on the spectrum compiled by parents and advocacy groups such as http://www.child-autism-parent-cafe.com/famous-people-with-autism.html. In passing, Gordon Bates describes Boo Radley as one of those autistic characters who are presented as "guileless faux naifs whose role in the narrative is to act as a mirror to the social mores or the inequities of the world around them" ("Autism in Fiction and Autobiography," in Oyebode, *Mindreadings*, locator 2835).

8. Matt Hargrave, "Side Effects: An Analysis of Mind the Gap's *Boo* and the Reception of Theatre Involving Learning Disabled Actors," *Research in Drama Education* 15, no. 4 (2010): 497–511.

9. See the discussion in ibid.

10. Some people on the spectrum have a hard time modulating the volume of their voice.

11. See chapter 5 for a discussion of Oskar's use of objects to communicate.

12. Claudia Durst Johnson argues that "TKM is essentially a social novel, but social in a peculiarly Gothic way, in that it presents a microcosm that focuses the reader on social taboos and social boundaries and emphasizes the tribal nature of the community" (*"To Kill a Mockingbird": Threatening Boundaries* [New York: Twayne Publishers, 1994], 58).

13. See Durst Johnson for an extensive analysis of the novel's participation in the Gothic tradition.

14. As Durst Johnson points out, "Boo's activities are very like those generally attributed to a community of witches" (*Threatening Boundaries*, 41).

15. Ibid.

16. Bradley Shaw views Radley in a similar light, arguing that in the novel's climactic scene, "Boo is a Frankenstein-like monster carrying away a child's limp body" ("Baptizing Boo: Religion in the Cinematic Southern Gothic," *Mississippi Quarterly: The Journal of Southern Cultures* 63, nos. 3–4 [2010]: 454).

17. See Ruth Bienstock Anolik, "Diagnosing Demons: Creating and Disabling the Discourse of Difference in the Gothic Text," in *Demons of the Body and Mind: Essays on Disability in Gothic Literature,* ed. Ruth Bienstock Anolik (Jefferson, N.C.: McFarland, 2010), Kindle edition, locator 73.

18. Quoted in Durst Johnson, *Threatening Boundaries*, 69.

19. Ibid., 51.

20. Murray, *Representing Autism*, 15.

21. Shaw, "Baptizing Boo," 453.

22. Durst Johnson, *Threatening Boundaries*, 40.

23. Ibid., 43.

24. Ibid, 57.

25. David Punter quoted in ibid., 63.

26. Mitchell and Snyder, *Narrative Prosthesis*, 2.

27. Punter quoted in Durst Johnson, *Threatening Boundaries*, 40.

28. Bienstock Anolik, "Diagnosing Demons," locator 45.

29. The novel makes this connection blatant. When Atticus says to Scout, "Mr. Ewell fell on his knife. Can you possibly understand?" she responds, "I understand. . . . It'd be sort of like shootin' a mockingbird, wouldn't it?" (321).

30. As Mitchell and Snyder argue, "Disability studies will find that *Mockingbird* bears much the same weight for disability issues as it does for race relations" (*Narrative Prosthesis,* 172).

31. Ibid., 173.

32. Shaw, "Baptizing Boo," 470.

33. Jennifer Murray, "More Than One Way to (Mis)Read a Mockingbird," *Southern Literary Journal* 43, no. 1 (2010): 86.

34. On the novel's prioritizing of white characters and their perspectives, see Gerald Early, "The Madness in the American Haunted House: The New Southern Gothic, and the Young Adult Novel of the 1960s: A Personal Reflection," in *Harper Lee: Essays and Reflections,* ed. Alice Hall Petry (Knoxville: University of Tennessee Press, 2007), 100; and Isaac Saney, "The Case against *To Kill a Mockingbird*," *Race & Class: A Journal for Black and Third World Liberation* 45, no. 1 (2003): 102.

35. Saney, "The Case," 102.

36. Michael Kreyling quoted in Rachel Watson, "The View from the Porch: Race and the Limits of Empathy in the Film *To Kill a Mockingbird*," *Mississippi Quarterly: The Journal of Southern Cultures* 63, nos. 3–4 (2010): 419–443, quote at 420–421. See also Early, who notes that "readers are never really permitted to walk in the shoes of Tom Robinson, his family, Calpurnia, or any of the other black characters" ("The Madness," 100).

37. Mitchell and Snyder also note that the novel "merge[s] racial violence and disability identity" (*Narrative Prosthesis*, 174).

38. Bienstock Anolik, "Diagnosing Demons," locator 121. Ato Quayson notes that "the colonial encounter and the series of migrations that it triggered in its wake served to displace the discourse of disability onto the discourse of otherness that was correlated to racial difference" (*Aesthetic Nervousness: Disability and the Crisis of Representation* [New York: Columbia University Press, 2007], Kindle edition, locator 353).

39. Mitchell and Snyder note that *To Kill a Mockingbird* "represents a powerful reflection of dangerous beliefs back to the dominant culture. Both its African American and disabled characters present us with noble victims" (*Narrative Prosthesis*, 172).

40. Jennifer Murray agrees: "One might add that the plight of Arthur Radley is not much improved by the compassionate but ineffective symbolic attribution of mockingbird status. Is no better life imaginable for him than to return to his gothic shadows?" (*More than One Way*, 88). Mitchell and Snyder argue that the novel "must enshrine respectful distance as a form of charitable cohabitation—safely returning him [Boo] to his isolated status in the neighborhood" (*Narrative Prosthesis*, 173).

41. Clay Morton has written the only other critical analysis of Laura as autistic and offers a detailed overview of her autistic traits. See "Not like All the Other Horses: Neurodiversity and the Case of Rose Williams," *Tennessee Williams Annual Review* 13 (2012): 3–18, http://www.tennesseewilliamsstudies.org/journal/work.php?ID=113.

42. I draw here on Morton's excellent discussion in ibid.

43. Quoted in ibid.

44. Tennessee Williams, *The Glass Menagerie* (New York: New Directions, 1970), 31. Hereafter cited parenthetically in the text.

45. Morton, "Not like All the Other Horses."

46. Almost every critical article on *The Glass Menagerie* addresses this facet of Laura's characterization. Robert J. Cardullo describes her as "a fragile, almost unearthly ego" ("Liebestod, Romanticism, and Poetry in *The Glass Menagerie*," *ANQ: A Quarterly Journal of Short Articles, Notes, and Reviews* 23, no. 2 [2010]: 76). Morton is the only critic to connect this depiction to autism stereotypes: "*The Glass Menagerie* depicts its neurodivergent heroine as a fragile victim" ("Not like All the Other Horses").

47. Cardullo, "Liebestod," 78.

48. Hosey offers a disability studies reading of the play that emphasizes this same point: "Amanda resolves to find 'somebody to take care of' Laura" ("Resisting the S[crip]t," 27).

49. As Morton explains it, "Lower-functioning people, the play tells us, must rely on higher-functioning people to take care of them, and it is shameful for higher-functioning people to neglect this responsibility" ("Not like All the Other Horses").

50. Quoted in Hosey, "Resisting the S(crip)t," 23.

51. Morton, "Not like All the Other Horses."

52. See the discussion of special interests in chapter 6.

53. That Laura's physical disability represents her emotional state is a critical commonplace. As Hosey notes, scholarly readings of *The Glass Menagerie* have generally "focused on physical impairment as reflecting larger social ills and/or characters' internal failings" ("Resisting the S[crip]t," 23). Although the disability community has reclaimed the term "crippled," I'm surprised by how often Laura is described as "emotionally crippled" in critical discourse about *The Glass Menagerie*. When applied to autistic people, this term is not only potentially offensive but also inaccurate. (Autistic people experience strong emotions; they may simply have trouble recognizing and expressing those emotions.) Morton views Laura's physical disability as both a symbol of and an augmentation to her mental disability: "Like other psychological realities presented in the play, Rose's social and emotional crippling is given a physical manifestation. . . . But this outward and visible sign augments rather than replaces social, communicative, and cognitive impairments" ("Not like All the Other Horses"). Elmo Howell describes Laura as "crippled, physically and emotionally" ("The Function of Gentleman Callers," in *Tennessee Williams's "The Glass Menagerie,"* ed. Harold Bloom [New York: Chelsea House Publishers, 1988], 43–46, quote at 45). John Strother Clayton argues that Laura's physical disability works "to represent and to account for the flawed nature of her character. It is an outward and visible sign of an inward and spiritual flaw" ("The Sister Figure in the Plays of Tennessee Williams," in *Twentieth Century Interpretations of "The Glass Menagerie,"* ed. R. B. Parker [Upper Saddle River, N.J.: Prentice Hall, 1983], 109–119, quote at 113).

54. Mitchell and Snyder, *Narrative Prosthesis*, 18.

55. Tom Shakespeare offers a nuanced and fair-minded discussion of the issues involved in *Disability Rights and Wrongs Revisited*, 2nd ed. (London: Routledge, 2014), Kindle edition, locator 1788.

56. Snyder and Mitchell, *Cultural Locations*, 6.

57. Quoted in Morton, "Not like All the Other Horses."

58. Quoted in Morton, "Not like All the Other Horses."

59. The term "crazy" is clearly discriminatory and offensive: I use it here only to parallel the social and linguistic effect of describing oneself as "crippled."

60. Bernadette Clemens comments on the play's nostalgic tone: "*The Glass Menagerie*'s Amanda Wingfield is trapped within an existence built only on memory of her past—unable to participate in the present, and jeopardizing Laura's ability to do so. Moreover, the opening monologue, spoken by autobiographical narrator Tom, literally tells the audience that the play is memory. Overt nostalgia is dominant in Williams" ("Desire and Decay: Female Survivorship in Faulkner and Williams," *Tennessee Williams Annual Review* 10 [2009]: 73–80, quote at 78).

61. I'm excluding here Mark Haddon's Christopher Boone, for whom any other diagnosis, given his obviously autistic traits, is extremely unlikely.

62. For an excellent discussion of the ableist language and assumptions underpinning the critical history of *The Sound and the Fury*, see Maria Truchan-Tataryn, "Textual Abuse: Faulkner's Benjy," *Journal of Medical Humanities* 26 (2005): 159–172. As Truchan-Tataryn notes, "The demonstration of a sustained insistence on a naturalized correlation between subhuman existence and intellectual disability in critical work on *The Sound and the Fury* from its publication in 1929 until the end of the 20th century foregrounds the need for a disability studies reading of literature generally and Faulkner specifically" (ibid., 164). She goes on to argue that "whereas feminist and cultural theories have exposed the socio-political currency of fictional portrayals of race and gender, images of disability still remain largely unexamined. . . . Despite the growth of a global disability rights movement and the development of the discipline of disability studies in the humanities, the figure of Benjy's mindless, voiceless subhumanity continues to resonate through Faulknerian scholarship as a believable portrait of disability" (ibid., 160).

63. Sara McLaughlin, "Faulkner's Faux Pas: Referring to Benjamin Compson as an Idiot," *Literature and Psychology* 33, no. 2 (1987): 34–40; Mark Decker, "I Was Trying to Say: Listening to the Fragmented Human Center of William Faulkner's *The Sound and the Fury*," *Kaleidoscope: Exploring the Experience of Disability through Literature and the Fine Arts* 47 (2003): 6–9; Ineke Bockting, *Character and Personality in the Novels of William Faulkner* (Lanham, Md.: University Press of America, 1995); Patrick Samway and Gentry Silver, "In *The Sound and the Fury*, Benjy Compson Likely Suffers from Autism,"

Faulkner Journal of Japan 12 (2010), http://www.faulknerjapan.com/journal/no12/pdf /EJNo12_Samway_Silver.pdf, accessed 8 August 2014; Jesse Bering, "Eugene Hoskins Is His Name: The Long-Forgotten Story of a Black Autistic Man in Oxford, Miss., Who Crossed Paths with William Faulkner," *Slate*, 15 February 2012, http://www.slate.com /articles/health_and_science/science/2012/02/eugene_hoskins_the_black_autistic _man_who_crossed_paths_with_william_faulkner.html, accessed 8 August 2014.

64. Michael Bérubé, *Life as We Know It: A Father, a Family, and an Exceptional Child* (New York: Vintage, 1998), xv; Mitchell and Snyder, *Narrative Prosthesis*, 167.

65. See Bering, "Eugene Hoskins Is His Name."

66. McLaughlin notes Benjy's sensory issues, especially his powerful sense of smell ("Faulkner's Faux Pas"). Samway and Silver address Benjy's issues with eye contact: his mother frequently holds his face in her hands and turns his head so that he will look at her ("Benjy Compson Likely Suffers," 12). See Decker's discussion of Benjy's autistic traits: "He also evidences other telltale behaviors: Benjy's hands flap uncontrollably, he becomes very upset when exact routines are not followed, he indicates his distress by bellowing loudly, and he cannot bear to be touched by most people" ("I Was Trying to Say," 6).

67. Decker, "I Was Trying to Say," 6. Numerous critics cite the meltdown in the carriage (when Luster turns left around the monument) as a sign that Benjy is autistic (see McLaughlin, "Faulkner's Faux Pas," 38).

68. Decker discusses Benjy's literal use of language ("I Was Trying to Say," 6). Bockting notes the special interest in nature and the outdoors: "The lexical sets that can be identified in Benjy's text show how fond he is of nature. The pasture, the trees, the flowers, the bright grass, the farm animals, the smooth shapes of the fire and the branch sustain him and bring him peace" (*Character and Personality*, 50–51). See Bockting's discussion of Benjy's echolalia: "Much of Benjy's text consists of quotations from others. . . . Benjy, it seems, understands the words only on the level of sounds. His quoting is therefore better called 'echoing' or 'echolalia'" (ibid., 50).

69. For further information on Edwin Chandler, see Arthur F. Kinney, "Faulkner's Families," in *A Companion to William Faulkner*, ed. Richard C. Moreland (Malden, Mass.: Blackwell Publishing, 2007), 190.

70. Samway and Silver, "Benjy Compson Likely Suffers," 4.

71. R. N. Froehike and Robin Zaborek, *When Down Syndrome and Autism Intersect* (Bethesda, Md.: Woodbine House, 2013).

72. Faulkner's ableism is clear: "The only emotion I can have for Benjy is grief and pity for all mankind. You can't feel anything for Benjy because he doesn't feel anything. The only thing I can feel about him personally is concern as to whether he is believable as I created him. . . . Benjy is incapable of good and evil because he had no knowledge of good and evil. . . . Benjy wasn't rational enough even to be selfish. He was an animal.

He recognized tenderness and love though he could not have named them" (quoted in Samway and Silver, "Benjy Compson Likely Suffers," 2). Winthrop Tilley suggests that the resulting disability depiction is amorphous: "All things considered, Benjy seems to turn out a fabricated literary idiot whose correspondence to any idiot, living or dead, would be not only coincidental, but miraculous" (quoted in McLaughlin, "Faulkner's Faux Pas," 34).

73. This interpretation of Benjy is a critical commonplace. According to Decker, "Benjy's autism outwardly makes him appear as the confused harbinger of the Compson family's eventual decline" ("I Was Trying to Say," 8). Martin Halliwell agrees: "The alcoholism an[d] invalidity of the Compson parents are signs of such decay that manifests itself in the three brothers as idiocy (Benjy), insanity (Quentin) and brutal sadism (Jason). Each brother represents the end of the dynastic line. . . . [A]lthough the novel treats Benjy more sympathetically than the other brothers . . . his idiocy is a symptom of the decline of his family and culture" (*Images of Idiocy*, 19). As Truchan-Tataryn notes, "Although Benjy serves as the conventional literary trope for corruption, critical discussions affirm the relevancy of this correlation between disability and decay" ("Textual Abuse," 168).

74. William Faulkner, *The Sound and the Fury: The Corrected Text*, ed. Noel Polk (New York: Vintage International, 1984), Kindle edition, page 5. Hereafter cited parenthetically in the text. Decker makes the same point: "His mother changed his name from Maurice, her brother's name, to Benjamin, a biblical allusion designed to reflect her conviction that Benjy's autism is 'a judgment on' her" ("I Was Trying to Say," 8).

75. Samway and Silver also interpret the name change as a loss of familial identity: "Benjy is robbed of his identity as a member of the larger Compson-Bascomb family and relegated to the last of the tribes of Israel" ("Benjy Compson Likely Suffers," 21).

76. Frank Whigham, "Incest and Ideology: *The Duchess of Malfi*," in *Staging the Renaissance*, ed. David Scott Kastan and Peter Stallybrass (New York: Routledge, 1991), 268.

77. Ibid. See also my discussion of literary incest in *Shakespeare's Surrogates: Rewriting Renaissance Drama* (New York: Palgrave Macmillan, 2013), 50–59.

78. Whigham, "Incest and Ideology," 268.

5. The Autistic Child Narrator

1. James Berger regards the communication problems in *The Curious Incident of the Dog in the Night-Time* in a slightly different light: "What readers discover through Christopher's investigation—is that the social order is itself on the autistic spectrum. That is, his society is characterized by its members' isolation and inability to communicate with each other" ("Alterity and Autism: Mark Haddon's *Curious Incident* in the Neurological Spectrum," in *Autism and Representation*, ed. Mark Osteen [New York: Routledge, 2008], 279). He goes on to argue that Haddon offers an "apparent critique of a

specifically post-Thatcher social fragmentation" (ibid., 280). Bennett Kravitz's discussion of Haddon's novel makes a similar point: "We have come to understand our state of affairs as autistic, a metaphor for the lack of communication among states and individuals in the late capitalist reality of the postmodern world" (*Representations of Illness in Literature and Film* [Newcastle upon Tyne, England: Cambridge Scholars Publishing, 2010], 40).

2. Although most articles on *Extremely Loud and Incredibly Close* focus on trauma, some of these articles also deal with the themes of incomplete communication and ineffable tragedy. Elaine Safer argues that Foer's novels "move toward the ineffable" ("Illuminating the Ineffable: Jonathan Safran Foer's Novels," *Studies in American Jewish Literature* 25 [2006]: 112–132, quote at 114). Kristiaan Versluys notes that "the disruptions in the texture of the text, the strangeness of its tone, and the pyrotechnic visual devices serve to underscore the incommunicability of experiences of extremity. . . . [T]he novel is full of ploys and devices that hamper the meaning-making process" (*Out of the Blue: September 11 and the Novel* [New York: Columbia University Press, 2009], 81). See also S. Todd Atchison, "'Why I Am Writing from Where You Are Not': Absence and Presence in Jonathan Safran Foer's *Extremely Loud & Incredibly Close*," *Journal of Postcolonial Writing* 46, nos. 3–4 (2010): 359–368.

3. See Todd Gilchrist, "Stephen Daldry Talks Asperger's, Depicting 9/11 in *Extremely Loud and Incredibly Close,* and the Oscars," *Indiewire,* 20 December 2011, http:// blogs.indiewire.com/theplaylist/stephen-daldry-talks-aspergers-depicting-9-11-in -extremely-loud-and-incredibly-close-and-the-oscars, accessed 15 March 2014; Joseph P. Kahn, "Autism Gaining Greater Visibility in Films, TV," *Boston Globe,* 25 January 2012, http://www.bostonglobe.com/arts/2012/01/25/autism-gaining-greater-visibility-films /aZQraDAfBEHXL4yfeIF6bJ/story.html, accessed 15 March 2014. Although Jonathan Safran Foer claimed in an interview that he did not intend for Oskar to be autistic, the author's response on the subject was decidedly ambiguous: "Which is not to say he isn't—it's really up for readers to decide" (Kahn, "Autism Gaining").

4. On these themes, see the introductory chapter to Murray, *Representing Autism.*

5. Jonathan Safran Foer, *Extremely Loud and Incredibly Close* (Boston: Houghton Mifflin, 2005), 6. Hereafter cited parenthetically in the text.

6. For a discussion of Oskar's autistic traits as they appear in Daldry's film, see Beth Arky, "Extremely Loud and Incredibly Familiar: Autism Advocates Embrace the Movie, Slam Critics Who Disparage the Hero," *Child Mind Institute,* http://www .childmind.org/en/posts/articles/2012-2-7-extremely-loud-incredibly-close-autism, accessed 16 March 2014. Specifically, Arky notes Oskar's social struggles, his focus on numbers, his sensory integration issues, and his stimming.

7. Quoted in Ralph Savarase, "River of Words: Raft of Our Conjoined Neurologies," *Fourth Genre* 14, no. 1 (2012): 48. Some people on the spectrum struggle to inter-

pret physical feedback from their bodies: stimming can be both a source of identity and a way to feel physically engaged with one's body.

8. For a discussion of the autism community's reaction to the film, see Arky, "Extremely Loud and Incredibly Familiar."

9. Gilchrist, "Stephen Daldry Talks Asperger's."

10. All quotations from the film are taken from *Extremely Loud and Incredibly Close*, directed by Stephen Daldry, performed by Thomas Horn and Tom Hanks (Warner Bros., Scott Rudin Productions, Paramount Pictures, 2011).

11. See Arky, "Extremely Loud and Incredibly Familiar."

12. See ibid.

13. Technically, sensory issues and other characteristics associated with AS are not phobias, but this seems to be the film's interpretation.

14. I only know of one autistic person who was once verbal and later became nonverbal in adulthood. This is unusual but not impossible.

15. I recognize that the choice of the term "incomplete communication" prioritizes neurotypical social norms and that the notion of incomplete acts of communication is necessarily based on the idea that communication is intended to be reciprocal. Not all communication is intended to be reciprocal, although our society presumes a role for both speaker and listener and often views nonreciprocal acts of communication as "incomplete."

16. I am not arguing against nonreciprocal communication as a form of communication. Indeed, I probably communicate in nonreciprocal ways most of the time. Although it is possible to communicate and to connect with other people using nonreciprocal means, reciprocal communication is probably the most effective way to achieve mutual understanding in both speaker and listener.

17. Versluys notes that Foer "charges language to the limits of expressiveness only to point out the limits of language" (*Out of the Blue*, 97).

18. Versluys explains the irony of this phone call: "But he cannot be heard. His moment of utter forthrightness is also the moment of total incomprehension" (ibid., 90).

19. Atchison interprets these letters as a symbol of "the inability of language to fully represent the chaos of life experience" ("'Why I Am Writing,'" 363). Versluys also notes that the letters are an important symbol of incomplete communication: "These letters, elaborate but undelivered . . . never mature into a dialogue" (*Out of the Blue*, 90). She further goes on to note that "Grandpa's tale, in a way, is a non-tale: it fails to complete itself in the presence of an interlocutor. . . . [T]hough full of affect, it is without effect" (ibid., 95).

20. As Atchison points out, Foer shows "the futility in expressing experience to another, even a loving husband and wife. Such breakdowns exemplify the outsider status always occupied by another person" ("'Why I Am Writing,'" 364). Versluys notes

that there are subjects Oskar's grandfather "finds incommunicable even to his closest relative. . . . [H]e speaks his secrets, but in such a way that nobody can hear" (*Out of the Blue*, 91).

21. Atchison notes that Foer's "meta-textual representations" symbolize "speaking the unspeakable" ("'Why I Am Writing,'" 364). Versluys argues that "this dark page is the completion of Grandpa's blank voice: muteness and semiotic overload share the condition of incomprehensibility, and for Grandpa, losing his words has the same effect as this overabundance of words. Both result in the erasure of communicability. The darkened page is a visible illustration of the writing of disaster as an impossibility. . . . [A]fter the writing becomes illegible, Grandpa goes on scribbling for a full three pages. . . . [H]is perseverance underscores what has been obvious all along: he writes only for himself" (*Out of the Blue*, 95–96).

22. Certainly, the answering machine message is one example of "nonreciprocal communication." Atchison compares the answering machine message to the censored letter that Oskar's grandmother receives earlier in the novel: "The conveyed concept that we receive is the need to communicate, a need to be heard. Like most representations throughout the novel, this correspondence remains one-sided and unanswered (even though Grandmother eventually writes a reply). The letter mirrors the phone messages left by Oskar's father on 9/11 that Oskar keeps hidden in his closet" ("'Why I Am Writing,'" 364).

23. Atchison notes that this is a novel in which "discourse becomes tangible artifact" ("'Why I Am Writing,'" 362). He explains this as a symbol of language's expressive failure: "Ultimately all we have is the representation of life experience captured through discourse; thus discursive acts become materialized artifacts" (ibid., 364). The artifact, frozen in time, can never be the thing it struggles to express.

24. Atchison argues that the theme of incommunicability in the novel emphasizes "how no two people can share the same position" (ibid., 364).

25. See Gyasi Burks-Abbott, "Mark Haddon's Popularity and Other Curious Incidents in My Life as an Autistic," in Osteen, *Autism and Representation*, 279. As Burks-Abbott notes, "Certainly, the increased public awareness of and interest in the autism spectrum can account for much of the attention *The Curious Incident of the Dog in the Night-Time* has received" (ibid., 289).

26. Both Burks-Abbott (ibid., 290) and Vivienne Muller ("Constituting Christopher: Disability Theory and Mark Haddon's *The Curious Incident of the Dog in the Night-Time*," *Explorations into Children's Literature* 16, no. 2 [2006]: 119) address this point.

27. As Christiana Gregoriou explains, "The portrayal of Chris's autistic mind may be characterized as 'believable' rather than good; it is not accurate, but the depiction of autism correlates closely with the way people *understand* autism" ("The Poetics of Deviance and *The Curious Incident of the Dog in the Night-Time*," in Effron, *The Millennial De-*

tective, 97–111, quote at 101). Burks-Abbott agrees: "Haddon has invoked an archetypal image of autism" ("Mark Haddon's Popularity," 291). Murray describes Haddon's depiction of autism as "a genuine, though highly stylized, attempt to present the workings of the autistic mind" (*Representing Autism,* 161).

28. As Kravitz notes, "This sophisticated yet simplistic narrative style captivates the reader precisely because of the dichotomy between these stylistic perspectives" (*Representations of Illness,* 47). The term "splinter skills" basically refers to uneven skill development: for example, Christopher has unusually elevated math skills for a fifteen-year-old, while his writing skills are typical of a much younger child.

29. Gregoriou also comments on Christopher's "unnecessary self-reflection" ("The Poetics of Deviance," 103).

30. Mark Haddon, *The Curious Incident of the Dog in the Night-Time* (New York: Vintage Books, 2008), Kindle edition, page 91. Hereafter cited parenthetically in the text.

31. Nicola Allen, "'The Perfect Hero for His Age': Christopher Boone and the Role of Logic in the Boy Detective Narrative," in *The Boy Detectives: Essays on the Hardy Boys and Others,* ed. Michael G. Cornelius (Jefferson, N.C.: McFarland, 2010), 170.

32. Muller, "Constituting Christopher," 120.

33. Ibid.

34. See Simon Baron-Cohen, "The Extreme Male Brain Theory of Autism," *TRENDS in Cognitive Sciences* 6, no. 6 (2002): 248–254.

35. Allen points out that for Christopher, "Holmes works as a buffer against emotional trauma in such situations" ("'The Perfect Hero,'" 169).

36. This narrative technique has received a great deal of critical attention. See Burks-Abbott, "Mark Haddon's Popularity," 291; Gregoriou, "The Poetics of Deviance," 102; Stephan Freißmann, "A Tale of Autistic Experience: Knowing, Living, Telling in Mark Haddon's *The Curious Incident of the Dog in the Night-Time,*" *Partial Answers: Journal of Literature and the History of Ideas* 6, no. 2 (2008): 414; and Bettina Kümmerling-Meibauer, "Emotional Connection: Representation of Emotions in Young Adult Literature in Mary Hilton and Maria Nikolajeva," in *Contemporary Adolescent Literature and Culture: The Emergent Adult* (Farnham, England: Ashgate, 2012), 135.

37. Berger also notes Christopher's intense vulnerability ("Alterity and Autism," 283).

38. It seems clear that the problems in the Boone marriage are caused by a complex web of interrelated stressors and issues (infidelity, the father's temper, etc.).

6. The Autistic Label

1. For a discussion of Lisbeth as revenge hero, see Emma L. E. Rees, "The Principled Pleasure: Lisbeth's Aristotelian Revenge," in *"The Girl with the Dragon Tattoo" and Philosophy: Everything Is Fire,* ed. Eric Bronson (Hoboken, N.J.: John Wiley & Sons, 2012), Kindle edition, locator 3741.

2. The Internet is rife with supposition on this subject.

3. Stieg Larsson, *The Girl Who Played with Fire*, trans. Reg Keeland (New York: Alfred A. Knopf, 2009), Kindle edition, page 637. Hereafter cited parenthetically in the text as *Fire*.

4. Stieg Larsson, *The Girl Who Kicked the Hornet's Nest*, trans. Reg Keeland (New York: Alfred A. Knopf, 2010), Kindle edition, page 250. Hereafter cited parenthetically in the text as *Hornet's Nest*.

5. For an argument that Lisbeth is not autistic but that she has posttraumatic stress disorder, see Hans Steiner, "If Lisbeth Salander Were Real," in *The Psychology of "The Girl with the Dragon Tattoo*," ed. Robin S. Rosenberg and Shannon O'Neill (Dallas: Benbella, 2011), Kindle edition, locator 2286. The very fact that one would need to argue against an Asperger's diagnosis in order to offer an alternative confirms that many readers of Larsson's novels view Lisbeth as autistic.

6. Stieg Larsson, *The Girl with the Dragon Tattoo*, trans. Reg Keeland (New York: Alfred A. Knopf, 2008), Kindle edition, page 250. Hereafter cited parenthetically in the text as *Dragon*.

7. For an actual psychologist's take on Lisbeth's silence, see David Anderegg, "What to Say When the Patient Doesn't Talk: Lisbeth Salander and the Problem of Silence," and Marisa Mauro, "Confidential: Forensic Psychological Report—Lisbeth Salander," in Rosenberg and O'Neill, *Psychology*.

8. Aryn Martin and Mary Simms, "Labeling Lisbeth: Sti(e)gma and Spoiled Identity," in Bronson, *Everything Is Fire*, locator 395.

9. See ibid.; Martin and Simms offer some examples from real-life court cases.

10. See Murray *Representing Autism*, on the "fascination" and "exoticism" of autism.

11. On the "compensation cure," see ibid., 209.

12. Robin S. Rosenberg, "Salander as Superhero," in Rosenberg and O'Neill, *Psychology*, also discusses Salander's savant abilities as "magical." It is interesting to note that many of the "superpowers" Rosenberg discusses (such as what she calls "superperseverance") could be seen as overlapping with Lisbeth's autistic traits. The cultural perception of AS traits as "superhuman" is certainly at play in Lisbeth's character.

13. See the discussion of Sherlock Holmes films in chapter 1 for a similar treatment of savant skills as a combat "superpower."

14. On the shock and wonder created by the savant, see Murray, *Representing Autism*, 93; and Osteen, *Autism and Representation*, 8–9.

15. People with autism are commonly believed to lack imagination—this stereotype may stem from the disinterest in "pretend play" that many autistic children show in their interactions with other children. For further information, see Bruce Mills, "Autism and the Imagination," in Osteen, *Autism and Representation*, 117–132.

16. Personally, I think this perception is a massive oversimplification of the complex phenomenon of deep interests, eliding the passion, joy, and sense of vocation they can bring.

17. Martin and Simms, "Labeling Lisbeth," locator 395.

18. For two different perspectives on Lisbeth's experiences at St. Stefan's, see ibid.; and Steiner, "If Lisbeth Salander Were Real." Martin and Simms argue that Lisbeth's "experiences in the institution—many of which can be understood as typical—forged the lonely, resilient, distrustful, and angry person she would become" ("Labeling Lisbeth," locator 458). Steiner, himself a psychiatrist, argues that the depiction is unrealistic: "Teleborian is a one-dimensional, despicable evildoer. . . . The use of physical restraints in health care settings is very carefully regulated and supervised by state agencies. . . . Restraints are administered by nursing staff and floor staff. It is highly unlikely that they would have passively stood by and watched such flagrant abuse for over two years. There also must have been other doctors in the system who would cover for Teleborian at the hospital during his absences, and such temporary coverage often results in shedding light on abusive practices. . . . [I]n all my work in juvenile justice settings over several decades, I have not encountered such predatory malice. I have encountered ineptitude, disinterest, uninvolvement, and passivity, and ultimately this story could have been told in such a context, with the advantage of added realism and plausibility" ("If Lisbeth Salander Were Real," locator 2497).

19. There has even been some critical effort to "undiagnose" Lisbeth. For example, Mauro concludes that "there is no evidence" showing that Lisbeth "suffer[s] from a clinical disorder" ("Confidential," locator 2781).

Afterword

1. For further discussion of dehumanizing theories about theory of mind, see Yergeau, "Clinically Significant Disturbance."

2. See Murray's discussion of "autistic presence" in *Representing Autism*.

3. Elizabeth Moon, *The Speed of Dark* (New York: Random House, 2003), Kindle edition, page 85. Hereafter cited parenthetically in the text.

4. This symbolic alignment of autism with dark (a traditional symbol of mystery, death, and villainy) and neurotypicality with light (a traditional symbol of knowledge, life, and heroism) creates its own set of representational problems.

INDEX

ableism. *See* discrimination

abuse, mental health system and, 137–138, 140–141, 148–149

adoption, 151

"Adventure of the Mazarin Stone, The" (Conan Doyle), 23, 37

Adventures of Sherlock Holmes, The (Conan Doyle), 29

aliens, autistics depicted as, 4, 17, 45, 143

Allen, Nicola, 126

Altschuler, Eric, 25

animals, comparisons with, 65–66, 68–69, 72, 90, 171n32, 172n34

Applied Behavior Analysis (ABA), 11

asexuality, 36–37, 41, 67, 75, 152

Asperger, Hans, 49

Asperger's syndrome vs autism, 7

Autism: Explaining the Enigma (Frith), 24

Autism Research Institute, 1

autism spectrum disorder (ASD): characteristics of, 3–4; diagnosis of, 4; diversity of, 153; as lifelong condition, 161n72; public fascination with, 4, 15, 129, 153, 158n13; as source of positive identity, 125–127, 154; terminology and, 6–7, 8–9, 159n22, 161n69, 171n31, 174n65

autistic community, 4–5; functioning levels in, 77; identity in, 22, 49, 58, 125; narratives of, 11, 26, 154, 162n11; terminology in, 6, 8–9

Autistic Self Advocacy Network, 61

autistic subjectivity, denial of: cultural, 20, 154; in *Flowers for Algernon*, 71–73, 77; in *Of Mice and Men*, 62–64, 66, 68–69, 70–71, 77–78; in Sherlock Holmes stories, 25

autobiographies, autistic, 26, 154, 162n11

Barnet, Sylvan, 50

Baron-Cohen, Simon, 10

Bascom, Julia, 1, 61

Beresford, Peter, 31

Bering, Jesse, 101

Bettelheim, Bruno, 10

Bienstock Anolik, Ruth, 89

Bockting, Ineke, 101, 180n68

body language: in *Bones*, 45; in *Extremely Loud and Incredibly Close*, 114–115; in *Glass Menagerie*, 94; in Millennium Trilogy, 133; neurotypical privilege and, 8; Sherlock Holmes's, 28–29; in *To Kill a Mockingbird*, 81–82

Bones (TV show), 42–47

Boo (Kenny), 81

Boone, Christopher (fictional character), 108, 124–129

Brennan, Temperance "Bones" (fictional character), 42–47

Briseño factors, 62

Cardullo, Robert, 95

Carlson, Licia, 63–64, 65–66

children: as narrators, 21, 108, 125–126, 127–129. *See also* families, autism compared to tragedy in; infantilization of autistic adults

Chivers, Sally, 63

Cline, Brent Walter, 72, 77, 174n69, 174n71

cognitive difference, terminology of, 6–7

cognitive disability, terminology of, 7

communication: impairments to, 5–6; nonreciprocal, 117–118, 118–122, 133–134, 183n15, 183n16; nonverbal, 81, 105–106, 153; written, 116, 118, 119–120

communication disorders: in *Extremely Loud and Incredibly Close*, 109, 116–122;

eugenics movement, 67, 68, 172n45
"Eulogy for the Martyred Children"
    (King), 61
euthanasia, 63, 68–69, 70–71, 172n34
Evans, Meg, 15
exoticism, 4, 16, 17, 27, 38, 39, 132, 143
Extremely Loud and Incredibly Close (Foer),
    108, 109–124; communication in, 116–
    124; compared with *Curious Incident*,
    128, 129; film adaptation of, 114–116;
    Oskar's autistic traits in, 109–114

Falk, Signi, 96
families, autism compared to tragedy in:
    child narrators and, 128–129; in *Glass
    Menagerie*, 91–92, 94, 95, 98–99, 100; in
    Sound and the Fury, 101–102, 103–104,
    105, 106–107; stereotype of, 17; in *To Kill
    a Mockingbird*, 89
Faulkner, William, 101, 180n72; *The Sound
    and the Fury*, 65, 101–106, 107
filicide, autistic: autistic subjectivity and,
    20, 61, 173n59; in *Flowers for Algernon*,
    73; in *Of Mice and Men*, 68–69, 70–71, 77;
    prevalence of, 169n1
"Final Problem, The" (Conan Doyle), 32, 35
Flowers for Algernon (Keyes), 71–77, 78
Foer, Jonathan Safran, 108, 109, 182n3. See
    also *Extremely Loud and Incredibly Close*
    (Foer)
Frith, Uta, 24
functioning labels, 9, 13–14, 71, 76–77, 153

Garland-Thomson, Rosemarie, 15, 16,
    70–71
Gay Science, The (Nietzsche), 130
gender, 46, 68, 160n52
genius: in detective stories, 23, 33, 39, 41,
    43; in Millennium Trilogy, 145–146; in
    Shaw's plays, 50, 51–52, 52–53, 54, 55,
    58–59; stereotypes of, 17–18, 41, 52–53.
    See also savantism
"Genius May Be an Abnormality: Edu-
    cating Students with Asperger's Syn-
    drome, or High Functioning Autism"
    (Grandin), 49

Girl Who Kicked the Hornet's Nest, The
    (Larsson). *See* Millennium Trilogy
    (Larsson)
Girl Who Played with Fire, The (Larsson).
    See Millennium Trilogy (Larsson)
Girl with the Dragon Tattoo, The (Larsson).
    See Millennium Trilogy (Larsson)
Glass Menagerie, The (Williams), 91–100;
    family decay in, 91–92; Gothic themes
    in, 107; Laura's autistic traits in, 92–96;
    Laura's physical disability in, 96–100
Gordon, Charlie (fictional character), 71–
    77, 78
Gothic tradition, 87–90, 102, 105–106, 106–
    107, 152
Grandin, Temple, 49
Grinker, Roy Richard, 92
Gross, Zoe, 16
Gubler, Matthew Gray, 41
Gurko, Leo, 67

Hacking, Ian, 10, 13
Haddon, Mark, 108, 124–129
Halliwell, Martin, 65, 67, 181n73
Hanson, Hart, 43
Higgins, Henry (fictional character), 55–58
Holmes, Sherlock (fictional character), 23,
    24–38; autistic traits of, 26–29, 163n16;
    contemporary adaptations of, 29–30,
    35–36; dehumanizing stereotypes and,
    19, 23–24; diagnosis of, 24–30; linked
    with criminality, 30–36; references to in
    Criminal Minds, 40; references to in *Cu-
    rious Incident*, 125–126, 127, 128
Horn, Thomas, 114
Hoskins, Eugene, 101
Hound of the Baskervilles, The (Conan
    Doyle), 27, 33–34, 35, 125
humanity of autistic people, 12; in *Bones*,
    47; communication and, 17; in *Ex-
    tremely Loud and Incredibly Close*, 113,
    117; Gothic mode and, 88; in Millen-
    nium Trilogy, 143–144, 145; Sherlock
    Holmes and, 23, 37–38; in *Sound and the
    Fury*, 105–106
hyperfocus, 126, 129. *See also* special in-
    terests

Ibsen, Henrik, 54, 57
Ide, Jonathan, 81
impairment vs disability, 5
incest, 103, 104–105
infantilization of autistic adults: in *Flowers for Algernon*, 72, 75; in *Glass Menagerie*, 95, 96; in *Millennium Trilogy*, 144; in *Of Mice and Men*, 65, 70; in *Sound and the Fury*, 102; in *To Kill a Mockingbird*, 86
Innes, Christopher, 54
institutionalization: in *Flowers for Algernon*, 77; in *Millennium Trilogy*, 137–138, 148, 149, 187n18; in *Sound and the Fury*, 105
intellectual disability: death penalty and, 62–63; in *Flowers for Algernon*, 71–72, 77; in *Of Mice and Men*, 64, 65; terminology of, 7
interests. *See* special interests
interiority: in *Extremely Loud and Incredibly Close*, 113, 124; in *Glass Menagerie*, 107; Gothic themes and, 20, 79; in *Millennium Trilogy*, 135, 142; in Sherlock Holmes stories, 28; in *Sound and the Fury*, 102, 103, 104–106, 107; *Speed of Dark* and, 154; in *To Kill a Mockingbird*, 86–87, 88, 107
IQ, 7

Jarman, Michelle, 68, 69
Jensen-Moulton, Stephanie, 68, 170n20, 171n33, 172n34
Joan, Saint (fictional character), 51–54
Johnson, Claudia Durst, 87, 176n12
Journal of Autism and Developmental Disorders, 25

Kenny, Mike, 81
Keyes, Daniel: *Flowers for Algernon*, 71–77, 78
King, Martin Luther Jr., 61

Larsson, Stieg. *See* Millennium Trilogy (Larsson)
Lee, Harper. *See To Kill a Mockingbird* (Lee)
"Letter to John Moffat" (Einstein), 108
lobotomies, 92, 100

logic: juxtaposed with emotion, 36–37, 46, 47, 75–76, 112–113; pride in, 127; prioritization of, 49, 50, 52, 53, 54
looping effect. *See* "Making Up People" (Hacking)
Loud Hands: Autistic People, Speaking (Bascom), 1, 61
love. *See* relationships, romantic/sexual

machines, autistics depicted as: in *Bones*, 44; in *Extremely Loud and Incredibly Close*, 113; in *Millennium Trilogy*, 143–144, 146; in Sherlock Holmes stories, 36–37; stereotype of, 4, 17, 161n71
Mad at School: Rhetorics of Mental Disability and Academic Life (Price), 9
magical/mystical/supernatural, autism depicted as, 17; in *Bones*, 44; in *Glass Menagerie*, 94–95; in *Millennium Trilogy*, 143, 145, 186n12; in *Sound and the Fury*, 102–104; in *To Kill a Mockingbird*, 86, 87
"Making Up People" (Hacking), 13–14
Man and Superman (Shaw), 59
Martin, Aryn, 138, 149
Maxwell, Jackie, 57
McDonagh, Patrick, 63
McLaughlin, Sara, 101
media: coverage of autistic filicide by, 20, 61; public fascination with autism in, 4; stereotype of violence in, 1–2
medical discourse about autism, 4–5, 6, 7, 10–11, 59
medical ethics, 63
memory skills, 29, 39, 73, 125, 145, 146–147
mental disorder: crime stereotypically linked with, 31; genius stereotypically linked with, 20, 41, 52–54; morality stereotypically linked with, 76; silencing of, 96–98, 100; subjectivity of people with, 138–139
mental health care system, 70, 135, 136–141, 148–149. *See also* institutionalization
mental illness, terminology of, 6
mercy killings, 61, 68–71
metaphor, autism as, 12–13, 15–16, 19, 109, 117–118, 181n1

Millennium Trilogy (Larsson), 130–150;
autistic traits of Salander in, 132–136,
145–148; cultural stigmas reinforced in,
141–150; diagnosis of Salander in, 131–
132, 138–139; mental health care system
critiqued in, 135, 136–141
Mitchell, David, 3, 8, 15, 59, 89, 90, 101
modernism, 11–12, 160n45
Moon, Elizabeth, 151, 154–155
Morton, Clay, 94, 96
Mukhopadhyay, Tito, 112
Muller, Vivienne, 126, 127
Murray, Jennifer, 90, 177n40
Murray, Stuart, 4, 5, 12, 16, 17–18, 61,
158n13, 161n69, 161n71
mystery/puzzle, autism depicted as,
17; child narrators and, 128; detective figures and, 23–24; in Millennium Trilogy, 132, 143, 144; in Sherlock
Holmes stories, 19, 27, 38; in To Kill a
Mockingbird, 86
mystical, autism depicted as. See magical/
mystical/supernatural, autism depicted as

neurodiversity paradigm, 5; in Curious Incident, 125–126, 126–127; in Millennium
Trilogy, 149–150; Shaw and, 20, 49, 50,
53, 54, 58–59; terminology and, 6
neurodiversity.com, 61
neurotypical, terminology of, 8
neurotypical as norm: in Millennium
Trilogy, 141–142, 149–150; Sherlock
Holmes and, 24, 25, 28–29; in Speed of
Dark, 154
neurotypical privilege, 8, 157n4
neurotypical traits as disabling, 126–127
New York Times, 4, 24, 77
Newton, Isaac, 53
Nietzsche, Friedrich, 130

Of Mice and Men (Steinbeck), 62–71; disability studies perspective on, 63–66; effect of on public policy, 62–63; Lennie's
death in, 68–71; real-life basis for, 66;
sexuality in, 66–68
online community, 8, 49, 58–59, 134

Osteen, Mark, 6, 18, 161n71, 168n8
overcoming disability trope, 18; in Extremely Loud and Incredibly Close, 114,
115–116; in Flowers for Algernon, 72; in
Glass Menagerie, 98–100; in To Kill a
Mockingbird, 83, 84

passing (for able-bodied), 80
passing (for neurotypical), 9, 11
pathology paradigm, 4–5, 6, 9, 10–11, 59,
147. See also neurodiversity paradigm
phenylketonuria (PKU), 71, 173n64
pleasure of repetition, 12
postmodernism, 11, 12, 160n45
Price, Margaret, 9, 14, 17, 31, 164n35
"Problems of Infantile Autism" (Asperger), 49
psychiatry. See mental health care system
Psychology Today, 24
puzzle, autism depicted as. See mystery/
puzzle, autism depicted as
Pygmalion (Shaw), 55–58

race, 67–68, 69, 90–91, 107, 153, 173n55
Radley, Arthur "Boo" (fictional character),
80–83, 85–88, 90, 91
rape, 67–68, 139–140, 142–143
Reid, Spencer (fictional character), 39–42
relationships, romantic/sexual: in Bones,
46; in Criminal Minds, 41; in Flowers for
Algernon, 73, 74–75, 75–76; in Glass Menagerie, 94, 95; in Millennium Trilogy,
138, 139–140; in Of Mice and Men, 67;
in Sherlock Holmes stories, 36–37; in
Sound and the Fury, 103–105
repetition, 12, 28, 111–112, 120, 121; echolalia, 12, 92, 101, 180n68. See also self-
stimulating behaviors
Robinson, Tom (fictional character), 80,
90, 91
robots, autistics depicted as, 17, 45
Rocque, Bill, 11, 14

Saint Joan (Shaw), 51–54
Salander, Lisbeth (fictional character),
130–150; autistic traits of, 132–134; critique of mental health care system

through, 135–141; diagnosis of, 131–132, 138–139, 149–150; savant skills of, 145–148; silence of, 133–136; stereotypes applied to, 142–146

Samway, Patrick, 101, 181n75

Sandy Hook school shooting, 1–2

Saney, Isaac, 91

sanity, as cultural construct, 53–54. *See also* neurotypical as norm

savantism: cultural interest in, 153; detective figures and, 29–30, 33, 39, 44; in *Flowers for Algernon*, 71, 73–74, 75–76; in *Millennium Trilogy*, 145–147; in Shaw's plays, 20, 49–50, 51–52, 58; stereotypes of, 17–18. *See also* genius

"Scandal in Bohemia, A" (Conan Doyle), 27, 36

Schell, Oskar (fictional character), 108, 109–124; autistic traits of, 109–114; communication and, 117, 121, 122–124; compared with Christopher Boone, 128, 129; in film adaptation, 114–116; grandfather and, 116–117, 120

schizophrenia, 41, 92

self-care, difficulty with: of detective figures, 30, 40, 43; in *Glass Menagerie*, 95; in *Of Mice and Men*, 64

self-stimulating behaviors: as autism characteristic, 3; in *Extremely Loud and Incredibly Close*, 111–112; in *Of Mice and Men*, 64; in *Pygmalion*, 56; of Sherlock Holmes, 28, 29

sensory integration issues, 3; in *Criminal Minds*, 40; in *Curious Incident*, 127; disrupting idea of shared reality, 12; in *Extremely Loud and Incredibly Close*, 111–112, 114–115; in *Glass Menagerie*, 92–93; in *Millennium Trilogy*, 133; in *Of Mice and Men*, 64, 66, 67; in *Pygmalion*, 55; sexuality and, 67, 172n43; in Sherlock Holmes films, 29–30; in *To Kill a Mockingbird*, 81, 82

September 11, 2001, 109, 112, 117, 120

sexuality: asexuality, 36–37, 41, 67, 75, 152; diagnosis of mental disability and, 138; equated with disability, 103–104; fears of disabled sexuality, 66–68, 73, 100, 105, 152; gender roles and, 46

Shaw, Bernard, 49–60; claimed as autistic by neurodiversity movement, 18, 20, 49, 50, 58–59, 167n1, 167n3; as eccentric genius, 58–59; *Man and Superman*, 59; *Pygmalion*, 55–58; *Saint Joan*, 51–54; on social change, 54

Shaw, Bradley, 89

Sherlock (TV show), 30, 35–36

Sherlock Holmes (film), 29–30, 35

Sign of the Four, The (Conan Doyle), 27–28, 40

silence, 16–17, 28, 117, 133–136. *See also* interiority

Silver, Gentry, 101, 181n75

Simms, Mary, 138, 149

Small, Lennie (fictional character), 62–71; autistic traits of, 64; death of, 67–70; physical characteristics of, 65; real-life basis for, 66; use of in Texas legal system, 62–63

Snyder, Sharon, 3, 8, 15, 59, 89, 90, 101

social change, 54, 58–59

social injustice against those with cognitive differences, 8, 130–131, 148–150

social outsiders: Gothic themes and, 107; Lisbeth Salander as, 130, 135–136, 139–140, 146–147; Shaw's characters as, 20, 50–51, 53–54, 58–59; in *To Kill a Mockingbird*, 83–84, 91

social skills, difficulty with: in *Bones*, 42–43; in *Criminal Minds*, 40–41; in *Extremely Loud and Incredibly Close*, 109–110; in *Flowers for Algernon*, 73–74; in *Glass Menagerie*, 93–94, 97, 98, 99; in *To Kill a Mockingbird*, 82–83; in *Millennium Trilogy*, 132, 142; in *Pygmalion*, 55–56, 57–58; in *Saint Joan*, 51; in Sherlock Holmes stories, 27

sociopaths, 30, 44–45, 131

Socrates, 52

Sontag, Susan, 15

Sound and the Fury, The (Faulkner), 65, 101–106, 107

special interests, 3; in *Bones*, 42, 43–44; in *Curious Incident*, 126; in *Extremely Loud*